P9-DTF-398

Praise for The Legacy of the Gold Banded Box series

BOOK 1: *Folayan's Promise*

Phyllis Jane Brown

Winner of the Outstanding Fiction Award,
Southern California Writers' Conference

"Beautifully written and poignantly executed this heart gripping series captivates the reader. Through rich portrayals and details, Folayan's life unfolds, capture threatens, and she refuses to relinquish dignity."

—Victoria Pitts Caine, best-selling author of
*Alvarado Gold, Cairo, The Tempering Agent, Cotton*

*Folayan's Promise* and Phyllis Brown are a debut novel and author to treasure.

—Sheri Humphreys, author of
*A Hero to Hold*

Phyllis Brown has crafted an extraordinary five book series in *The Legacy of the Gold Banded Box,* a saga about faithfulness when there is no reason for faith, grace when all seems lost, God's sovereignty when we don't understand what is happening, and love in the unexpected. From village, to castles, to plantation, to inner city, Brown's attention to historical detail, along with compelling characters, and lyrical prose will keep you riveted to the last word and teardrop.

—Carrie Padgett, Golden Heart Finalist-Inspirational Romance,
and author of *Brook Runs Away*

*Folayan's Promise* brings a new type of saga to the reader. Rich with author Phyllis Brown's expressive storytelling, the reader is pulled into Africa's Gold Coast delivering an eye-opening window to the slave trading threatening every village. Our heroine Folayan is beautiful, talented and very different from other girls in the village. She's smart and feisty and in Book I, her core is revealed that strengthens as each page is turned. Loved it ... I look forward to Book II.

—Judith Briles, author of
*When God Says NO*

# Folayan's Promise

LASAN PRESS | CARMICHAEL, CALIFORNIA

# Folayan's Promise

BOOK ONE

**The Legacy of the Gold Banded Box**

PHYLLIS JANE BROWN

Lasan Press
3644 Mission Avenue
Carmichael, CA 95608
www.LasanPress.com
LasanPress@gmail.com
559-601-0434

Copyright © 2021
Phyllis Jane Brown

All rights reserved.
No part of this book may be reproduced, distributed, or transmitted in any written,
electronic, recording, or photocopying form without written permission of the publisher.
The exception would be in the case of brief quotations embodied in critical articles or reviews
and pages where permission is specifically granted by the publisher.

This is a work of fiction.
Names, characters, places, and incidents are a product of the author's imagination.
Locales and public names are sometimes used for atmospheric purposes.
Any resemblance to actual people, living or dead, or to businesses, companies, events,
institutions, or locales is completely coincidental.

Speaking Notice:
Phyllis Jane Brown can speak at your live or virtual event.
For more information. or to schedule an event contact Lasan Press
at 3644 Mission Ave., Carmichael, CA 95608, or visit
www.TheGoldBandedBox.com.

Books may be purchased by contacting the publisher directly:
Lasan Press, 3644 Mission Avenue, Carmichael, CA 95608,
by calling 1-559-601-0434, or email LasanPress@gmail.com

Cover and Interior design: Rebecca Finkel, F + P Graphic Design
Cover design contributor: Tony Carranza
Cover Illustrator: Peter Valdez | Interior Illustrator: Neill Brengettsey
Author photos: Ashlee Bratton, Ashography | Photographer: Andrew Kerekes
Book Consultant: Judith Briles, The Book Shepherd

CIP data:
The Legacy of the Gold-Banded Box: Folayan's Promise/Phyllis Jane Brown. — 2nd ed.

Library of Congress Number: 2020911175

Hardcover: 978-1-948550-00-0
Softcover: 978-1-948550-01-7
eBook: 978-1-948550-02-4
Audiobook: 978-1-948550-03-1

African History Studies  |  Cultural Heritage  |  Historical Fiction

To William Robert Brown

My patient, encouraging, supportive husband,

God's gift to me.

You kept your promise from our youth.

Thank you, my Kofi,... my love.


To Elnora King

A few words for years of gratitude to my writing teacher:

*Thank you*

for your beautiful heart, your inspiration and life mentoring,

your love, encouragement and relentless determination

to make sure these books are sent out into the world.

*A Note from the Author*

The Legacy of the Gold Banded Box book series was inspired by two poems and a concert: "Yet Do I Marvel" by Countee Cullen, "O Black and Unknown Bards" by James Weldon Johnson, and the Oakwood College Aeolian Choir's thrilling Negro spirituals from their album, "O Freedom!" I wanted to explore these latter times in world history with the saga of a girl who comes of age in Ghana in 1796, endures perils, and how her descendants cope in the 21st century.

Years of pouring over slave narratives, histories, cultural traditions, and travels in three continents, including fourteen African countries, provide catalysts for scenes portrayed. A few are inspired by events I discovered in the legacy of my own genealogy. So, although the characters never lived, experiences and secrets similar to theirs have repeated too many times throughout the sojourn from Africa to the Americas. They reverberate in these days of multi-cultural adjustments, learning to understand, keeping watch in this current precarious age, and struggling to achieve the ultimate cessation of the residuals of slavery. May these five books assist pilgrims of today, as we journey beyond "if onlys" with determined dignity and hope onward together to a future truly free.

# Contents

# Cast of Characters

Pronunciation: Every letter sounds, the short vowels are "a" (ah), "e" (eh), the long vowels are "i" (ee), "o" (oh); "u" (oo)

| Name | Pronunciation | Relationship to Folayan |
|------|---------------|-------------------------|
| Folayan | Foh-lah-yahn | Protagonist |
| Akosua (Maame) | Ah-koh-shoo-ah (Mah-ah-meh) | Folayan's mother |
| Kwabena (Papa) | Kwah-beh-nah | Folayan's father |
| Kwesi broni | Kweh-see broh-nee | Pale skin Sunday man/the fort's preacher |
| Serwaa | Seh-wah-ah | Folayan's aunt/father's sister |
| Kwamina | Kwah-mee-nah | Folayan's eldest brother |
| Emissah | Eh-mee-sah | Folayan's brother #2 |
| Kwesi | Kweh-see | Folayan's brother #3 |
| EkowAta Panin | Eh-koh At-ah Pah-neen | Folayan's brother #4 (twin) |
| Ata Kumaa | At-ah Koo-mah-ah | Folayan's brother #5 (deceased twin) |
| Akonor Kwodwo | Ah-koh-nor Kwo-joe | Folayan's brother #6 |
| Esi | Eh-see | Folayan's age mate |
| Adwoa | Ahd-joo-wah | Folayan's age mate/best friend |
| Abena | Ah-beh-nah | Folayan's age mate |
| Ekua | Eh-kwee-ah | Folayan's age mate |
| Yaa | Yah-ah | Folayan's age mate |
| Afua | Ah-fwee-ah | Folayan's age mate/chieftain's daughter |
| Amba | Ahm-bah | Folayan's age mate |
| Fatima | Fah-tee-mah | Folayan's age mate |
| Kofi | Koh-fee | Adowa's brother/Folayan's friend |
| Abeeku | Ah-beh-ee-koo | Folayan's male friend |
| Jojo | Joe-joe | Folayan's male friend |
| Nanabesia | Nah-nah-beh-see-ah | Folayan's Rite of Passage Examiner |

# If Only

If only their song I could hear
        a legacy of ritual, redress, and redemption
        floating far across the sea.
In my vessels—my cells, my chromosomes, my genes,
The memories they keep
        of place and plague and pride and promise,
        my father's smile, my eyes, my face.
If only I
Could trace
        the furrow
        in his brow.
Whose? O whose hands like mine
        wrested with betrayal's distress,
        or clutched baby to breast?
If only I could know secrets my DNA holds.

# *Fantiland*

o the western side of the giant continent Africa, by camel
caravan and white-winged ships, from 750-1900 AD, Muslim,
Christian, and atheist strangers came, changing names, changing times,
changing laws, changing peace.

Toward the end of the sixteeth century, they found a land abundant
in gold, for which they traded colorful cloth, fine flour, unusual tools, and
trinkets. Much of Europe's wealth was established when, in three month
tides, men became rich from exploits in this land they called the Gold
Coast. Kingdoms of Akyem, Akuapem, Akwamu, Kwahu, Anyi, Asante,
Attie, Baule, Brong, and Fante Africans called it the Land of the Akan
people.

Merchants embarked on a simpler business. Compared to the
hard-to-get ivory and gold, the new trade of flesh brought them far
greater wealth. Each garrison had dungeon holding cells filled with
captives who waited, often for months, until slaver ships took aboard
human cargo. Thus, from their cannon-guarded strongholds, European
nations clashed in many ruthless battles among themselves, each
striving to gain control and treasure.

Africans resisted.

In Fantiland and throughout the continent--captives fought, and
died by starvation, suicide, dehydration, the strangers' diseases, murders
by hanging, stabbing, shooting, dismemberment, or broken-hearted
despair for one thousand, one hundred, and fifty years. Some say, 12.5
million were kidnapped to the Americas, yet millions more began and
endured the forced journey out of Africa to Arabia, Asia, and Europe.

The treasure taken—over 100 million Africans.

# CHAPTER 1

# The Pebble

When my people come here and take
out the gold, you must understand
that we mean no good to you.

**Late November 1780, Village of Kormantse, Fantiland**

*On Saturday, the early morning beach recuperated from the weekly throng*
*of diligent Fanti fishermen. Waves rose on the roaring Atlantic Ocean*
*tossing white caps to the sky. Breezes whispered promises of freedom to tall*
*palm trees standing sentry over El Mina, the first of forty-two fortresses*
*built by European traders along the three-hundred-mile coast of Ghana.*

COMFORT ELUDED HER. Sleep mocked her. Peace escaped her.
Belly heavy and huge, body exhausted, Akosua rolled off the
floor pallet, crawled to the four-foot-long carved mahogany chest,
and propped her elbows on it.

In the dim *hwaani hwaani* "who is that" light of morning, she
turned to see *Kwabena*, her slumbering husband, shift onto his side
into her warm space, oblivious to the anxiety eddying in her over the
last several days. Content with knowing she had but to wake him and

speak only a few words, he would do his best to provide anything she requested. He was the one she desired, and as yet, shared with no other wife. This knowledge gave her strength, and she did not wake him, nor want him to come with her, or to persuade her against her will. She had to do this now. Alone.

Lifting the chest lid, she let her hands be her eyes. Besides Akosua and Kwabena's things, seventeen—other gifts hid in the chest.

Kwabena had carried the *Kwantunyi* chest home from one of his yearly merchant travels. As he always brought gifts for family members, he also put one gift each year into the chest waiting for the unborn girl child, this family's desperate need. Akosua felt a twinge tighten for a moment, then subside; she massaged her taut belly and prayed that this one stirring now would claim these treasures.

However, she was not searching for his gifts. She felt down inside the front right corner for a tiny ball of cloth containing a present that did not come from her husband. Three days ago, she placed it there after returning from the market. The black-robed preacher with hair like the guinea hen, speckled black and gray, had given it to her.

She shivered and shut the lid. Something inside her stirred wrong, and she could not calm her worry. Was the old *kwesi broni* preacher evil, or his words evil, or was the stone evil?

With the knotted cloth nestled in her fist, she left the house and headed toward the spot overlooking the ocean, where she and her husband sometimes went to talk and think.

Nearing the last house before the path to the hill's edge, she felt the eyes before she heard the rustling. Vultures up in a tree, perched on one branch, six of them pressed together, barely visible in the shadows. Though their heads appeared rigid, they watched.

She quickened her pace.

At her destination, she longed to sit down; this morning, though, she hesitated. Fearing that she would not be able to get herself back up with no wall to prop against, she stood on the hilltop, surveying the beach below. The sea roaring, coaxed by the wind, rushed foamy fingers up to grab borders of the deserted marketplace between her hill and the fort.

Her fingers worked inside the cloth and smoothed the yellow pebble. As the water retreated, she looked across to the right, at the other prominent hill, where she beheld Fort Kormantin, pygmy though it was compared to the giants in the nearly visible distance at Cape Coast and at El Mina, near her birthplace. Like them, Fort Kormantin stood gray stone imposing against the sky, watching her watch it. Named first after her husband's village, Kormantse, the stubborn fortress, survived in spite of its one hundred and twenty year trespass.

The *kwesi broni* came from a place called Europe, outside of Africa. These intruders, most of them Dutch soldiers and the preacher, lived inside Fort Kormantin, which they renamed Fort Amsterdam. Long ago, the English built the fort. Her people called them kwesi broni, "fair-skinned Sunday men" because of their pale color and the day on which they worshipped. Since Market Day, most of the footprints in the sand leading to the stronghold had washed away.

If only the old preacher's words could wash to nothing.

She rubbed the stone in her hand with her thumb, recalling the conversation of three days past, at the mid week market day. Her family's place was at the end of the row, nearest to the fort side.

The preacher always walked past her first, eyed the items she had for sale, then went shopping down the line, returning to linger at her mat last to chat. That day he had asked, "And soon you shall have another—a girl child?"

She caressed her swollen middle. "I pray daily for a girl."

"Yes." He spoke thoughtfully, and then pointed to shucks of corn, garden eggs, and cassava. "I'll have more of those."

The racket of a fire-spitter jolted them. They turned to watch the distant commotion of a link of slaves dashing into the sea dragging one a few feet until surrounded by their captors. When the dead man was dislodged from the chains, the coffle proceeded toward the marketplace.

Frightened, bewildered, Akosua stood still for a moment collecting her thoughts, then remembered the sack in her hand. She started putting in the requested items, but confusion swelled in her head. She kept swallowing to moisten her dry mouth. Her hand began to twitch and she dropped the sack. All her produce toppled and spilled across her mat out onto the sand.

The preacher and other women came to her aid.

Like a rebellious *djembe* drum, Akosua's head pounded out of sync with her heart. She told herself to calm.

*A man dead, why?* Confusion roiled inside her. Why was he dead? Finally, she dropped the last shiny, purple garden egg into the preacher's soft straw sack.

He reached into a fistsized, black cloth bag that hung at his waist. He pulled out cowry shells, paused, looked at her again, and held his hand toward her to pick up the correct amount. Though she always waited, he never bargained. Ignoring the custom of haggling to a place of satisfaction on both sides, first price with him was the last. She picked up all but three cowrys and the pebble, which in size and shape favored a yellow, unshelled peanut.

"You take this, too." He proffered the pebble.

She shook her head. "No. This is enough."

"I insist. If you do not want it, give it to your girl child as a bauble. Use it to teach your children. It is more valuable than they know. Your people do not realize the value of this gold. It is so plentiful here. See how soft it is, different from gold in other places. When my people come here and take out the gold, you must understand that we mean no good to you."

She looked into his eyes, searching for motive.

His pale hand put the gold stone into her palm and pressed her fingers around it. Unnerved by the strange man's touch, she drew her hand back, the stone cold in the heart of it.

The preacher asked, "Why do you think those people came to be in that coffle?"

"Debtors? Criminals? Defeated warriors?" As in conversations with family or friends about slaves, she always assumed, but today she wasn't sure. Nothing was sure. Trouble shivered again, making pinpricks on her arms.

"My people perish for lack of knowledge," he muttered, shaking his head.

She looked into his eyes, and swallowed. "What do you mean?"

"Akosua, I mean no harm," his voice dropped lower, "but the mountain can be moved. Somebody has to start pushing to bring an end to this slave trading. There are men and women in England who are doing their parts. You do your part. I will do mine. Perhaps, together, we can make a small difference here. Then others will join us. This is the third day of August. This is the day you and I pledge to do what we must."

She stared at her closed hand, then back at the man. He spoke carefully, trying to make it plain, saying much of plots and unknown places that jumbled in her head. She heard his words, and with his gestures, understood much more.

He spoke of the murdering of whole villages to gain thirty captives, and of the plunder from wars incited by those intruders who took immense treasure from East, North, and West Africa. Took them from capture, to death march, to dungeons, across the Sahara and seas through the Middle Passage, to Arabia, India, China, Europe, the Americas.

He asked, "Why do you see so many cannons? Every fifteen kilometers a castle, fort, or lines of cannons with stacks of balls on the towers, on the ground—here, there, poised—ready to kill and capture."

His hands and voice trembled, trying to convince her. Still she did not know if she could trust him. She promised herself that she would take time another day to ponder what these things meant. But most of it her soul knew was true.

Customers had come, purchased, and left, and still the preacher remained, standing aside until he could continue speaking to her. She sensed questions darting her way from other market women.

He'd been at her space too long. She stared up at the fortress. A catch of warning bobbled inside her. She blurted, "Why have you chosen me?"

Just as he opened his mouth to answer, the crunching of feet on the dry palm branches drew Akosua's attention to the stand of trees not fifty feet from the market space. Prodded on by five slave traders, eight men, and three women with wrists and necks linked by chains and iron collars, entered the path leading to the fort.

From behind her mat of neatly lined fresh cassava, eggplants, boiled corn, and fried fish, Akosua glanced back at the captives trailing up the hill. Then she turned to the edge of the sea, where the one they left still lay.

Already vultures circled in the sky.

She asked, "Are you not fearful to tell me these secrets?"

"I have lived long enough" he said, "to learn that I must keep my opinions to myself and I am selective about speaking what is on my heart. I have watched you. Your eyes speak, when your mouth does not. Your few words bring comfort, not hurt. You are a leader, but in a quiet way." He paused and sucked in air. "Your walk reveals your strength. The women respect and listen to you.

"As for me, few people regard my opinions, neither here nor ... I think I shall not return to Holland. I have no more family there. I am not well. Twenty-six years of suffering with malaria and the effluvium seeping from the dungeons. Reaping the whirlwind of my own lust and bad judgment has worn me too weak, even to make the journey home. I came to serve the soldiers I ... ."

He looked up toward the fort. A flash of revulsion twisted his face, sending a stab of fear through Akosua. Then he turned back, his expression sad. "I lost my way."

She followed his glance down the row of businesses, from mat to mat, each full of merchandise, then back into her eyes. He finished his thought, "When I found it again, I stayed to bring Christ to the people born here.

"Yet, I have learned that you already know Him, by a different name. You practice many of the teachings and rituals that are in His Book. When I tell priests and preachers who came to serve in the other castles here on the Gold Coast, they laugh at me, and then they become angry. I am an old fool, they say.

She dared to look at his sad, tired eyes.

"Anymore, I do not attempt to enlighten them. They disregard their vows. Like the soldiers and traders, they are mesmerized by greed and gluttony, drink and wantonness ... like me ... in times past. They have lied to themselves and send lies back home, saying you are animals who need to be civilized.

"As they brutalize your people, they do not perceive the irony of their words. They do not see what I now see. They are blinded to the gold in you."

# CHAPTER 2

# Water of Life

*At that moment, she knew she had not lived the truth,*
*had seen and not seen, watched, but not wondered.*
*She had ignored the fearful faces and discounted the reality.*

**Late November 1780, Village of Kormantse**

Akosua had come out to this place on the hilltop this morning to throw the stone as far from herself as she could. For three nights, since the preacher had put it in her hand, she had not slept well. His words troubled her more each day.

He spoke of riches she had never imagined; riches shipped out from castles and forts by different European crowns. Intruding nations believed themselves entitled to the wealth each had discovered in the wilderness of this new domain.

She surveyed the murky outline of the coastline as far as she could see in the dim light. Her mind's eye filled in obscure places where she knew the ocean shore wound from the El Mina castle down past Fort Amsterdam which brooded on a jutting hill across from her Fanti village, Kormantse.

It was as the preacher said: "Every half day's journey protrudes a post to lay claim to this new sovereign territory, and now in 1780, Africans from far inland are being captured.

"And though hardest hit at first, villages still stand near the sea," he said. "Villages like yours, where your people live wary, yet self-determined."

This morning, returning home on the oceanside, Akosua could see a soldier silhouetted in the east corner of the fort where four cannons— as the preacher called them—sat pointed away from the sea toward the nearby village of Abandze and the surrounding forest. They sat poised to kill intruders who might try to sneak up from the east side of the hill. She turned the notion through her mind; intruders killing intruders.

A piercing scream came from the part of the fort nearest to the sea. One scream, a woman's.

Akosua peered through the dim; she focused on the fort—gray, cold, and more frightening than ever before. She had seen slaves at the market, one or two, seldom more than four being sold at a time. Like those slaves from the other day, she had seen some in shackles being taken into the fortress, but she believed they paid their debts that way; then they'd be free again. Slaves were an allowed part of life; mistreatment of them was not.

She took careful steps from the ocean view around her hill to see the side opposite the fort. She'd never heard anything that fixed her attention like that scream, not in nineteen blustery *harmattan* seasons since their *ayefro*, when she came to live in Kormantse as Kwabena's bride.

*Was the wind carrying the sound?*

She shivered with indecision. Her birthing time was near. She did not want to bring her baby into the world under some awful omen.

As more light opened the day, her gaze traveled from Fort Kormantin down the path through the green to the sand where fishing boats sat, then over to the other path that wound its way up toward her through scrub brush, tall grasses, and wide spreading trees that dotted the countryside surrounding her tiny hilltop Fanti village. She saw trees bending low and leaves shaking and shimmering.

A strong tightening surged across her belly and lingered. Her six sons—five still living, and the twin brother born dead—had announced their coming with similar birthing pains.

She turned toward her house, held the gold tight, pulled the *etam* warm around her shoulders and braced her way to safety against early gusts of the year's autumn winds—the harmattan.

The wind grabbed her etam and sailed it into the sky. She reached up and tried to catch the long wrap, before she realized she had chased her etam too close to the edge. She watched it fly out over the valley between her hill and the other one.

Bam! Bam!

It sounded like doors slamming against walls inside the fortress. The wind howled, but she heard voices, women—more of them screaming—and men. She could see rooftops all around the outside walls. Yes, there was an open air adiho, atrium, in the center, like in village houses. It seems like women were outside now in the *adiho* of the fortress.

"Get that door! Man the doors!" Voices rose from inside the fort. "Shut the doors!" The voices' intensity threw frightening images up for her to grasp. Were they at the door closest to her village?

A gruff voice shouted above the melee. "Who left that door open? How many times I got to stop you from letting lust rule your brains? I ought to bash your heads in. Whoever did it is a dead man! A dead man! Get 'em back into the women's dungeon!"

More screaming, frantic, spilling out of one place; ten, twenty, thirty voices. Scanning the roofs, Akosua noticed two lights, then three, four soldiers up on the top level holding torches over each wall shining down into the adiho. Other soldiers stood shadowed beside the long black cannons.

She leaned forward, straining to hear. Many footfalls raced louder toward the main entrance on Akosua's side. Pounding from that hilltop's stonewalled circle, the stampede magnified.

The gruff commander shouted, "Get that door; they're pushing it!" Two soldiers left cannons and ran down to help. Women were jamming against the wooden doors, but she could hear hard fist strikes, and screams and Fanti shrieks being stifled.

"Get 'em! Get 'em!" the gruff voice hollered. "Stop the noise. No noise!"

"Get that one over there by the stairs." The man shouted with fevered alarm. "Stop her!"

Akosua could hear a woman's voice coming nearer to her, up the stairs, screaming. She thought she would be silent, but the woman charged toward the cannons nearest the sea. The woman climbed in the shadows, and ran between the cannons, crying out, "Help me! Please, help me!"

Akosua could barely see. The woman struggled up onto one cannon. Three men yelled at her, attempting to reach her. She tried to jump. She slipped.

One man threatened, "You will fall! That is two halls down to the ground. You'll break your neck!"

The djembe in Akosua's chest throbbed frantically. It was hard to catch her breath.

"You'll break your neck!" the man repeated.

Akosua gasped. Where were the woman's clothes? She had nothing on—her hips and legs were uncovered. Waist down was only for the husband's view, no one else.

Akosua's hand pinched her two cloths that covered herself. She knew her own tightening pain would subside, but her chest heaved with remorse for the woman.

The woman looked down and hesitated. Akosua understood that she would not want to be found dead outside the wall, down there at the foot of the fortress—naked. What shame it would bring on her family, on her ancestors.

In that second of doubt, another soldier grabbed the woman, and pulled her back inside the wall. Akosua could hear his fists pounding—no, she could see his head and from his grunts, she realized it was his feet—kicking the woman.

The wind howled above the fortress and out up into the sky over the woods.

Akosua stood, trembling. *How is it that I have never heard ... that I never knew?*

She burst into tears. She shook violently. Then the gush of water poured from her baby's path. Still sobbing, she looked down at the puddle. Water ... life ... truth—the proverb that began every Akan baby's life came boldly to her mind.

At that moment, she knew she had not lived the truth, had seen and not seen, watched, but not wondered. She had ignored the fearful faces and discounted the reality.

The preacher spoke truth; she could never do less—ever again.

She struggled head first, clasping the gold stone in one hand, holding her garments tight around herself with the other, and pushed into the wind. She braced against a tree during another spasm. They came faster. She was halfway home when Kwabena found her.

"Where have you been?" His tone was strained.

"Did—" Her raspy voice surprised her. "Did you hear it?"

"What? The wind?"

"The women screaming in the fort."

"No." His brow wrinkled.

"Kwabena." She swallowed. Her throat hurt. "Please take us away. Take us to someplace, somewhere else—somewhere safe."

He looked at her. At the fort. Then back at her, but said not a word.

Two houses away from theirs, she tried to ask him again, but she doubled over in pain. "Aahh! It is different than the others. Ooh! The pains are too fast, too soon, too soon."

He carried her into their house, calling his elder sister, " Serwaa! Serwaa!"

The gray-haired woman rushed out of her sleeping room, beckoning for him to bring Akosua in there and at once maneuvered Akosua into the birthing squat.

"Kwabena, promise me." Breathing erratically, Akosua pled, searching his face.

He did not answer.

Refusing the message in his eyes, she gripped his wrist. "Kwabena, will you take—"

"Your fingernails will squirt his blood." Serwaa pried her hand loose and shooed Kwabena outside.

Akosua grimaced with the long spasm, crying through clenched teeth. "Kwabena!"

Akosua's whole body, wet with perspiration, endured intensifying pains, more rapid than any of her previous births. Like today, most of them started before the early crowing of the cocks, but some lasted until after evening crowing. This seventh baby surprised them all, crowning before the sun reached its highest point in the sky. As the morning's mystifying events merged into memory, Akosua sighed and smiled at the first lusty cries of her long-awaited infant. She held her breath for the pronouncement.

Serwaa saw first and rewarded her with the words, "Akosua, you have brought to the world a girl child!"

Tears of gratitude spouted as Akosua exhaled and watched Serwaa pour a libation and pray, giving thanks to the Supreme

God, who came near on *Kwamemeneda*, the last day of the week, *Onyankopon*, Creator of all.

⊙──⊷

From that moment, Akosua's husband put all other responsibilities aside. For seven days he had one task.

During the days of contemplation, he spent much time in prayer, thinking. Then he consulted with clan griots and advisers. He presented to them ancestors or a living person he admired, they recalled character, skills, and ways the ancestors help strengthen the village. They also suggested other names for this most necessary child in his family. He first thought of his own name Kwabena Kwantunyi Mensa. Kwabena meant a male born on the third day of the week, Kwantunyi, a traveler, and Mensa, a third-born son.

While he considered the newborn's future, his house bustled with women cooking for the naming day. He thought about the two most important women in his life, his sister and his wife. *Serwaa's* name was a female form of the male *Osei*, which meant kingly, and *Akosua* meant female born on the first day of the week.

The wives of his three eldest sons were pounding purple cocoyam and cassava, then molding the sour mixture into *fufu* rounds, and grinding and boiling white corn maize into balls of *kenkey*. Serwaa was mashing ground nuts into *nkatie*, and peanut butter soup, *nkatewan*. By the time they finished cooking, they'd filled large bowls of banana plantain slices fried in palm oil and piled platters high with mounds of deep fried whole fish. Five of the baby's brothers had made and purchased many gourds full of palm wine and *akepeteshi* to quench the guests' thirst.

⊙──⊷

In the black of the eighth morning, their way lit by the twinkling stars, villagers trekked toward the Kwantunyi house. They gathered outside where Kwabena and Akosua whispered welcome to them.

Just as the first filters of hwaani hwaani light revealed the thatch-roofed, mud and straw-walled house, the ceremony began at the command of an elder. Another elder lifted a gourd full of water and hurled the water up onto the roof. Kwabena hurried to the place where it dripped down and raised his baby high over his head, letting the water trickle onto her tiny, bare body. The baby caught her breath and whimpered and wiggled until her Papa spoke.

He raised her up. "I lift our daughter to You, Most High, Onyankopon, the Supreme God,

*Creator of earth, seas, and air,*
*The sky with sun, moon and stars.*
*The trees, plants, birds, fish, animals—and mankind.*
*These things, O God, did not create themselves.*
   *Out of you, they came.*
*You send us the rains of life.*
*You have blessed us, at last, with this girl child.*
*For only a girl can prevent the unspeakable.*
*Through her our clan will live on.*
*Most humbly, we honor, we praise, and we thank You.*
*We receive Your gift.*

Akosua stood close with two cups.

Kwabena brought the baby to his chest and reached for the first cup. He tested it, to see if it was water. It represented the water of life. He dipped his finger into it and then placed his finger into the little one's mouth.

"Ama, you were favored to be born on God's day, Kwamemeneda, the Lord of Life's Satisfaction Day, the seventh day. Your day name is Ama—the female way to say Kwame."

He shifted her closer, "Now, Ama, this is water. Let your 'Yes be yes.' Water is truth. Let nothing come from you that is not truth.

"Know what a lie is. Let your life be as pure as water. Today you have been told to stand by truth, and reject that what is not truth. Do not allow your life to be diluted with lies."

Akosua handed him the second cup. He tested it; it was palm wine. He looked at his baby, held her close to his heart, and said, "Ama, this is wine. It is water diluted with wine. Let your 'No be no.' Learn the difference between truth and mixed truth. Mixed truth is a lie."

Kwabena had the gift of the storyteller; the breathless crowd listened as he spoke her second name to her with an explanation about her ancestors, sixty-four generations of travelers; then, her third name, especially for her, a name reflecting characteristics he already observed in her or desired her to have.

He told her how when traveling in Yoruba land, a water buffalo attacked him. Some men rescued him and took him to a Folayan; she nursed him back to health. Her name meant "one who walks in dignity." The throng hung on every word. Kwabena looked into the bright eyes of his beautiful, mahogany baby girl, and in a regal tone that no one in the stillness could miss, he whispered, "For you, my Fanti babe born on Onyankopon's day, born in such troubled times, I chose a name to encourage, to comfort, and to strengthen you on life's journey."

He spoke her name in full to her, then to the joyful crowd who repeated after him: "Ama Kwantunyi Folayan—the child born on the seventh day, daughter of the traveler, is one who walks in dignity. Welcome!"

The naming done, he kissed Folayan on both cheeks, handed her to her mother, and urged the people to join in the celebration.

The drummers struck the first notes and the dancing began. Some clapped and a woman danced up to Akosua, took the baby and moved throughout the people, singing to the child a story about one of Akosua's ancestors. Others followed suit, with songs about how well they respected Kwabena. The baby passed from one to the next.

Many spoke of knowledge they had learned from the Kwantunyi family about places where Kwabena had shared philosophies and experiences with other merchants, wisemen and griots—the tribal historians who kept centuries of genealogies and events in the clan's oral tradition. The festivities ensued—music, games, food, conversation, and laughter.

When the last guest left, the sun had set. Two-year-old Akonor wanted to know if he could play with his new sister tomorrow. Serwaa told him no, but he could kiss her cheek instead. He smiled, pleased with the thought. Then she took him with her into her room.

Kwabena and Akosua sank down on their pallet. They had waited nineteen years for this naming day. Exhausted and with full hearts, they fell asleep.

Between them lay their blessing—*Ama Kwantunyi Folayan*.

# CHAPTER 3

# *Age Mates*

*I dream of seeing behind the mountains.*
*When I think about myself, I know I am different.*

## February 1789, Village of Kormantse, Fantiland

*E*ach year when he returned from a trading journey, Folayan showed her Papa, the Kwantunyi merchant, new skills she'd mastered.

At three, she could bring cups of water to guests without being reminded. By six, she could do most household cleaning tasks, including polishing with *ntwuma* dust. It brought the solid earth floor to a burnished gleam. By nine, Folayan earned the honor of lighting the torch from the *bukyia*, fire place, outside the kitchen and carrying the fire to the bukyia at the women's fields where, after gardening, she cooked vegetables, etsew, and cornmeal kenkey.

When she was not learning from her mother, Serwaa, or her sisters-in-law, she often enjoyed the company of her female age mates. They had first met while wrapped in etam tight at their mothers' backs. From months to three years apart, none wanted to be the last to learn the newest task that showed they were growing properly through each passage of life.

Being the youngest of the group, Folayan tried extra hard to keep up with them. These accomplishments were attached to support, joy and praise from all the mothers and each other—most of the time.

*They will not let me hate Afua.*

*Even after she pinched me so hard it broke my skin when I was five.*

*Papa showed me with his Ashanti gold weight scale how my thoughts about her were like sharp gray rocks, putting me out of balance. I am out of harmony with the world. He said my nine-year-old soul does not have room enough to take a big space up with bad feelings. I asked him, "What about her harmony?"*

*He said she was accountable for herself.*

*Maame said I must keep searching my heart until I find gold in her.*

*My other maame, Serwaa, my father's sister, told me Afua is in my life for a reason. She will help me learn much about myself.*

*I do not want to learn anything from her. I do not care if we are age mates. One day, if she does not stop being mean to me, I shall give her what she deserves.*

*Afua sometimes says things about my family. She says my Maame talks too much about the fort over there, and how we should not sell slaves, and to let them work off their debt and be free. Afua mocks my Maame, and says my Papa is different, too. And that instead of traveling away so much, he should spend more time teaching his sons to be men. I told her they are men except for Akonor, who is two years older than me.*

*She says my Papa is teaching me things only boys should know, and he disrespects our traditions, and he probably eats his meals with women. I told her that was not true, and to hush her mouth. She is hateful. Hateful.*

*But I thought about it. Maybe travelers are different. My Papa learns much about many places and people and customs. He gave me his grandfather's name, Kwantunyi.*

*I am the daughter of the traveler.*

*I can count over 700 ancestral leaders of my Maame's family and over 900 on my Papa's side. For those ancestral leaders, I must know at least two ways they made their village stronger and better, as well as if they did anything to disgrace the family. When I think about that, I shudder. I do not want to do anything bad that children will be telling the whole family or their village about hundreds of years after I die.*

*I must learn much more than that about all sixty-four of Papa's special ancestors who were Kwantunyis—travelling merchants—I am still learning more about them. Papa requires my brothers and me to know about their travel routes, names of villages and cities, and important events that happened while they were journeying.*

*Kwantunyi. Maame said it was no surprise that my brothers would have that name, but me? My Papa gave me the name, too. He has taken all my brothers trading except Akonor. Maybe one day I, too, will go on a journey with him.*

*I dream of seeing behind the mountains. When I think about myself, I know I am different. I think about things the other girls never mention. When Afua picks on me for being the youngest, Adwoa, my best friend, speaks for me. Adwoa tells me I am different, too. When she says it, she chuckles or sighs, wondering about my thoughts and the things I do, but her words are soft. She is that way with everybody. Sometimes she comes out here to my special place on the side of the hill to wait with me for my Papa to return home from a journey.*

*My age mates and I visit each week, completing chores together and playing, but Adwoa knows me best. Sometimes we just sit arm-in-arm, not even talking. Sometimes we think the same things and Adwoa will*

*start saying it, I will finish it, or the other way around. Then we laugh. I
have no other sisters, except for my age mates.*

*But not Afua; she is not my sister.*

*My Papa has been away with my two brothers, Kwesi and Ekow,
much longer than he planned.*

*I see far-away worry in my Maame's eyes.*

*Yesterday, Afua told all my age mates that my Papa might not come
back. I do not tell her about my fitful sleep—bad dreams in which I
follow Papa to tell him that something in the bush makes a small noise.
But Papa never notices. Besides that, there is a big snake trying to kill my
Papa. I always wake up afraid and sweating with my heart beating fast.*

*That is why I come to sit on the hill edge, waiting for him.*

*Before they left, I told Papa I wanted to watch them travel out of my
sight. Papa brought me to this place and showed me the path they would
follow down into the valley, up the next hill, and then on to the highest
point as far as our eyes could see, throughout the whole land of the Fanti.
He told me it would take about three days to get beyond that peak.*

*Down on the other side, they would travel along the Volta River,
through forest valleys, until they came to the River Niger, which they
would follow a long, long way into Mali.*

*Papa said he would return after six new moons. I want to see him
and my brothers coming over those furthermost hills that are so green now.
They will come—the size of ants at first, then grasshoppers, then men.*

# CHAPTER 4

# The Ofram

*It stretched three times taller than the rooftops,*
*a proud fisherman with strong arms lifting to the sky*
*a basket overflowing with a mound of dark green herring.*

**Late June 1789, Village of Kormantse, Fantiland**

Kwabena Kwantunyi Mensa, the traveler, had been away six months.

Cloistered amidst stands of kola nut, palm and plantain trees, his *akura,* village, settled under the last of the Friday sun.

Neighbors trickled into streets lined with square houses: thatch-roofed houses with walls of straw and copper-colored clay. The afternoon's last light flickered golden, purple, and red onto the faces of Fanti citizens who strolled toward the town center. After bathing and eating, they came to celebrate the end of six days work.

Most of the people arrived by the main road that stretched from one end of the akura to the other, straight through the town square. At the south end, the road divided where an ancient ofram tree, the tallest tree in the area, stood.

One path went to the right, toward the sea. The traveler's family lived along the second path that led to the farms. Folayan and Akonor walked behind their mother and brothers, Kwamina and Emissah, and their families. When they neared the tall tree standing in the fork of the road, Akonor pointed.

"See that ofram tree, Folayan?"

She nodded. It stretched three times taller than the rooftops, a proud fisherman with strong arms lifting to the sky a basket overflowing with a mound of dark green herring.

"If you climb to the top, you can see all the way to Jenne, and Walata, and Timbuktu."

"Where Papa is?" exclaimed Folayan. Her eyebrows scrunched. She wanted to believe Akonor, but experience with his teasing urged her not to.

"Uh-huh," he continued, "and you might see if Papa and our brothers are on their way home."

Folayan stared into his large deep-brown eyes. So many people told her that her own thick-lashed eyes matched his. "Are you speaking truth, Akonor?"

"Emissah told me."

Their second eldest brother, Emissah, would not lie. Folayan looked up, leaning so far that she lost her balance, and stumbled backward, falling onto her behind.

Akonor laughed and pulled her up. "We must go. Everyone is leaving us."

A whirl of dust skittered dry leaves across the children's path and around the trunk of the tree. Akonor circled it and grabbed a leaf three times the size of his palm. Its colors matched the horizon. He cradled his prize in his hands, protecting its curled edges.

Folayan, too, followed the wind, arms flailing, leaves eluding her. She returned to Akonor's side with her head down, bottom lip jutting discouragement.

"I could not find one as big as yours."

"That is because you are so little. I am supposed to have bigger things than you."

She frowned at him. He was taller, but her long legs gave her height well above other girls her age. He always tried to make it seem like there was a great difference between them.

Akonor smirked. "When Papa returns, he will bring me a gift."

"Yes. Something for each of us."

"My gift will be bigger than yours, Folayan."

"I do not care what size it is. It will be something special for me."

Akonor pondered a moment. "Kwamina and Emissah have gone on many journeys with Papa. This time he took Kwesi and Ekow. Next time he will take me."

"And me!"

"No, Folayan, you are a girl. He will not take you." Akonor pointed to the tallest tree again. "The most you will see of those places is what you can see from the top of this tree. You will grow up and marry and have many babies. You will never travel anywhere."

As if tapping on a door, he knocked on her forehead with his knuckles. He leaned into her face and said, "Papa will not take you anywhere. Only me." Cocky Akonor pounded his chest with his finger three times.

Akonor darted ahead a few yards, turned, and stuck out his tongue at Folayan. The grin on his face teased her to chase him, but she didn't feel like playing. For a moment, she stood still looking up at the tree. Then she saw how far behind her family she was and ran to catch up.

At the square, families nestled around another important tree—gnarled and grand, the *Onyamedua* was probably the oldest in the village. Graceful fingers stretched in four directions, beckoning all to rest under its umbrella. Women who came early brought the *oto,* a mixture of yam, eggs, and palm oil. They spread it on a clean white cloth at the base of the ancient tree, giving honor to God and to their ancestors.

Friends sat beneath its wide green boughs and shared events of the past six days. Women chatted, men debated, youths flirted. Akonor coaxed Folayan and other children their age to play "race and chase" until in the dimness, someone lit the fire, and everyone circled around for a story, then another.

On the way home, Akonor entertained Folayan with a story of his own, walking backward while acting out parts. When they turned onto the path at the fork, Akonor whispered, "There is your tree." He chuckled and continued with his tale.

But Folayan did not hear any more.

Before she stepped inside her house, she glanced back again at the giant, its silhouette looming in the moonlight.

# CHAPTER 5

# *Adventurer*

*She remembered his smile and open arms,*
*and how easy then it had been to let go of her fears.*

**Late June 1789, Village of Kormantse, Fantiland**

*F*ive days later, Folayan's mother and aunt and several other ladies left at dawn to go to the market, down at the beach between their hill and Fort Amsterdam. There, they would spend the day selling vegetables they had grown in the fields, and fried fish their husbands caught the night before. Some had foods they had cooked at home.

They also sold scrub sponges, cooking tools, painted calabashes, baskets, cloth, clothing and other items they and other townsfolk made. Folayan and her friend, Adwoa, were too young to go to market, so they stayed home. After they finished their work, there was plenty of time to play. The girls often included El Mina in their games.

El Mina, the first trading post that the kwesi broni built, was the biggest and oldest castle along the Gold Coast. The Bakatue Festival took place near El Mina.

Sometimes Maame told Folayan stories about how she met Papa at the Bakatue and all the exciting things that happened during the celebration. People came from far and wide once a year to the lagoon for the fishing, contests, music, and dancing. Since it was so much more fascinating than the fortress across the way that they could see every day, the girls often played "El Mina."

For about an hour, they built their own little marketplaces in the soil, using sticks as tiny people. They imagined what went on in the castle. Then Folayan said, "Adwoa, let us play a different game."

Adwoa's eyebrows rose. "What could be more fun than El Mina?"

Folayan went to the backside of the house and reached up under the wide thatch eaves. She carefully took down the ladder made of vine and poles, then coaxed Adwoa to follow her out to the giant tree. Setting the ladder against the brown trunk, she started up.

"What are you doing?" Adwoa exclaimed.

Folayan paused, looking down. "Akonor said if I climb this ofram tree and look to the north, I can spot my Papa coming."

When she was high enough to stretch to the nearest branch, Folayan grabbed hold with one hand, then the other. With a quick twist she swung her legs up, locked her ankles around the branch, and maneuvered herself upright. Before proceeding, she stood, holding onto the trunk while she peered up through the deep green sea of leaves.

Folayan glanced down to see if Adwoa was still looking. She was, with her mouth gaped open as Folayan crept higher and higher until she was one-third of the way up. Folayan felt proud of herself. She knew Adwoa wished she was this brave so she, too, could have such an adventure. Papa was Kwantunyi, "The traveler, the adventurer." She had his name, and this was her adventure.

Fierce pinpricks peppered her legs. Folayan screamed and looking down found a wave of tiny red ants swarming over her, biting, stinging.

"*Nsetsea! Nsetsea!* Oh, oh, oh!" Slapping and brushing, she tried to rid herself of them, but lost her balance and fell crosswise with legs askew, clinging to the tree trunk.

"Adwoa, go for help. Get my brothers. Hurry!"

Adwoa raced toward the beach, then a moment later, came running back past the tree and Folayan's house, then up the path toward the farms. She did not stop when Folayan cried out her name.

Folayan scanned the road for Adwoa's return. Then from the other direction, she heard girls' voices. In dismay, she saw several of her age mates turn onto the path that went right in front of the ofram. Afua was explaining something to Esi, Ekua, Abena, Yaa, and Fatima.

Watching them, it seemed to Folayan like one of Afua's good days. Afua could be nice sometimes and make you smile. She had interesting stories to tell. Folayan wished she would stay that way, but Afua could change in a blink and make you feel uneasy or strike you.

Folayan stayed still and prayed that not even a bird chirped to draw their attention up the tree. Afua would poke fun at her for the rest of her life if she saw her caught like this.

By now the nsetsea ants were up to Folayan's waist, scattering over her body as she scratched, squeezed, smashed, and swatted them. She wanted to cry out, but dared not whimper. The girls continued on, laughing at something Esi said. They turned onto the path that led into the bush. Folayan breathed out.

The fiery bites on Folayan's legs started throbbing. Fighting the ants with one hand, gripping the trunk with the other, she could see nothing but her tiny enemies. At last, she heard Adwoa's excited voice.

"That is the one, Kofi. She is up there in the ofram tree!"

"Folayan, we are back! I brought my brother. I remembered he was clearing brush in our field today."

Foyalan sighed in relief that Adwoa had brought a rescuer.

The youth rounded the tree and started up the ladder. He told her, "I am coming. Just hold on."

When Folayan looked down, her stomach lurched. Strange that she should be afraid of the height now. She hadn't been when she was gloating to herself about Adwoa not climbing the ofram tree with her.

"Umph!" She pinched an ant off her neck.

"Folayan? Can you see me now?" He lodged in the crook of a large limb.

"Uh-huh. Ouch!"

"Can you slide down to me?"

"I am afraid. Ow!" She slapped at a column of ants trooping around the back of her knee. Her right arm hugged the tree so hard the bark cut into her skin.

"I need you to try so I can help you down. The ants are on me now. Can you try to take one step? One little step at a time?"

Folayan hesitated, then moved herself until she found a niche for her right foot, then the left. Inching her way, fingernails piercing the wood, she eased down.

"That is good. Just one more and I can reach you."

He moved his body into position. "There, now come to me. Open your eyes."

Folayan peeped through her eyelashes, afraid to open them any farther.

Kofi smiled at her and opened his arms. Folayan let go of everything and slipped into them.

"Now hold onto me tight," he said, shifting her onto his hip. "We will get down safely."

In moments, they were on the ground. Adwoa brushed away ants from Folayan's legs. Folayan took care of the ones on her arms and upper body. Kofi got rid of his own.

"We better get you home," he said. "Look, your skin is already blistering."

Folayan stepped forward and stopped. Even the bottoms of her feet pained her. She began to cry. She wanted to lie down right there and take off all her clothes to get at the rest of the ants.

Kofi came to her side. He smoothed the tears from her cheek, swept her up in his arms, and carried her home. She kept her face buried in his chest, not sure if she was crying more from the pain, or the embarrassment, or from fear of what her Maame would say, and Papa, if he found out.

When they reached her house, Kofi put her down in front of her sleeping room, then retreated to the center of the courtyard as his sister took over.

Inside her room, Adwoa helped her crush the rest of the ants before helping her over to the sleeping pallet. Folayan's head throbbed, and she was so drowsy.

⊙⸺⚷

Folayan woke to the sound of voices coming from the courtyard. Maame and Serwaa were home. Adwoa was explaining what happened.

"We knew you would be packing up before my brother could get down the hill to the market, so we waited."

Maame lifted the curtain to Folayan's room, letting her friend step in first.

Adwoa's eyes brightened. "You are awake. How do you feel?" she asked.

Adwoa pulled the cover over Folayan. It felt wet. Her whole body felt wet, her stomach hurt, but the maddening stings had lessened.

"How is your head?"

"Better." Folayan remembered what she wanted to ask, "Adwoa?"

"Yes?"

"Please. I, uh … I saw Afua and some other age mates going out to the bush. They came by the tree while you went to find Kofi. Adwoa, may this day be our secret? Forever? Please?"

Adwoa patted her hand. "Afua will not enjoy that torment."

"*Meda wase,* thank you. And your brother. Will you tell him, too, and thank him for me?"

"I will. Do not worry about him. He is very trustworthy."

Maame checked Folayan's forehead. "Meda wase, Adwoa."

"You are welcome."

Serwaa came in with a small calabash bowl. "Your brother says he must go."

"Oh yes," Adwoa said. "I will come back tomorrow."

Folayan waved. "Meda wase."

Both women followed Adwoa from the bedroom and Folayan heard them thank Kofi. When Maame returned, she peered at Folayan's mahogany skin, caressed her welted face and patted her thick, short cropped hair.

She clicked her tongue. "My pretty little girl, all speckled up like this."

When Serwaa returned, Maame asked, "What am I going to do with this child?"

Folayan looked back and forth at her mother and aunt, but didn't say a word.

Serwaa spoke. "For one thing, the ash will be a lesson she will not forget. Here, it is cool enough now."

She handed Maame the calabash full of ground charcoal. The two women talked to each other above Folayan's grunts and gasps. The child winced as they coated her entire body. When they finished, Folayan looked at her body. It was gray with black streaks all over, and she wondered what her face must look like.

"Maame?" she whimpered.

Maame covered her with a wrapping cloth. "Yes, child?"

"How long do I have to stay like this?"

"Until your blisters go down. Close your mouth, or your jaw will lock." Maame smiled. "The bites hurt, but the ash works fast. Tomorrow or the next day, you will be your old self again."

Serwaa chuckled. "Um hmm. Then you can be about climbing more trees."

"Do not encourage her. She gets into enough trouble already."

Serwaa winked at Folayan. "I will bring your meal."

Maame sat down beside her only daughter.

"Maame, how am I to be chastised? You never told me not to climb the tree. I did not disobey you."

"No, child, I will not chastise you this time, but when are you going to remember the name your father gave you and what it means?"

"Kwantunyi?"

"No, dear, you are his little one who walks in dignity."

"Oh."

"You think about it," Maame said, as she left the room.

Serwaa returned with a plate full of boiled cornmeal kenkey and fried fish. "Eat. Eat!" she said.

Folayan obeyed, making no complaint when ash fell into her food.

Serwaa watched her eat. After a few minutes she said, "That boy, Kofi, Adwoa's brother … he is a good boy."

Folayan nodded, but kept her silence. She remembered his smile and open arms, and how easy then it had been to let go of her fears.

# CHAPTER 6

*Brothers*

*She lay back on her pallet, smoothing her fingers*
*around the edges of his leaf and imagined that*
*from the top of that tree, she could see all the*
*villages of the people who would be at the Bakatue.*

**Late June 1789, Village of Kormantse, Fantiland**

Folayan woke up the next morning to someone whispering her name. It was her eldest brother, Kwamina.

"Come in," she answered, and shifted under the cover.

"How are you feeling today?" he asked.

"A little better," she whispered, hoping for some sympathy, since she had not received any yesterday.

"Do you feel well enough to get up?"

"Nooo," she whined.

"Then you want me to call Maame to put more ash on you?"

"No!"

"So be it, but get well before three days."

"Why?"

"Did you forget the Bakatue?"

"The Bakatue. But Papa is not back."

"He told us to take you this year, even if he was not home. He and our brothers may come by a different route and meet us there."

They were to travel to the Benya Lagoon for the final week of the festival near El Mina. The Omahene, the paramount chief, and the queen mother, along with village chieftains from each of the Akan tribes, would be there.

Emissah stepped into the room. "Did I hear someone speak of the Bakatue?"

Kwamina nodded. He said to Folayan, "Your blisters are already healing."

Akonor knocked on the door frame and came in. He had a twinkle in his eye and his hands behind his back. She wondered if everyone had talked about her after she fell asleep last night.

"You are laughing at me," she said with a pout.

"No," Emissah said. "I was just thinking about how I wanted to climb that tree myself when I was about your age. However, I saw the ants first. But about the Bakatue, do you remember that you and your age mates will be able to take part in some activities this time?"

Her eyes widened. "Yes."

"There will be much to see. Each village tries to outshine the others with music, drums, dances, food, and clothing. People who have not come for a long time will be there to reunite with family and friends they have not seen since they were children."

Kwamina interrupted, "And to look for life partners."

Emissah agreed. "That is where I first met my wife." He smiled.

Akonor asked, "Are we going to see them re-route the sea into the lagoon?"

"They did that several weeks ago. Early enough so the fish they put in will mature in time for the festival."

"How many times have you helped them build the dam?"

"Twice," Kwamina said.

"I like walking on the bridge with all the people," Akonor piped up.

Emissah looked at Kwamina. "Maybe next year, we should take him early to stay the entire preparation time with our Maame's family at Edina."

"And he can see all the different rituals happening each of the six weeks. Some are serious, others fun, like the wrestling," Kwamina said to Akonor. "Would you like that?"

"Yes!" Akonor turned a smug 'just me' smile at Folayan.

Folayan said, "I want to go early next year to that lagoon, too."

The two elder brothers looked at each other. Kwamina spoke, "We all know Maame will not let that happen. Never. Even as I think about it now, she would not let Akonor go alone, either."

Akonor protested, "But I am almost eleven *afenhyia*, years."

"Noooo." Emissah shook his head. "Maame's fear of kwesi broni slave-catching is too strong."

Akonor cast an accusing stare at his sister.

"Remember to respect all our women, Akonor."

"She is only little and she spoils my fun."

Kwamina tapped his shoulder. "Treat your sister with kindness and protect her like we all do, and it will be well with you, Akonor. Remember, she holds inside her the future of our clan."

Folayan pondered those words. She had heard it said before, but did not fully understand why it was only her and not her brothers, too. Why not Akonor? She studied him, then wondered why he stood sideways. *Is he hiding something?*

Emissah said to Folayan, "Get yourself well so you do not miss it. Otherwise ...." He shrugged. "Let us see, there are at least one hundred homes in our village. There may be only enough people left here to fill two houses. Perhaps you can stay in one of them." He chuckled and kissed Folayan on the cheek.

"We must go now," Kwamina said. "There is much brush to burn today." They waved to her as they left.

Akonor stayed behind wearing a sheepish look. He thrust his leaf at her. "Here," he said, and ran out of the room.

Folayan clicked her tongue. "Akonor!"

She picked his prize up off of her lap and smiled. She lay back on her pallet, smoothing her fingers around the edges of his leaf and imagined that from the top of that tree, she could see all the villages of the people who would be at the Bakatue.

The years before, she'd had to stay close to her mother's knee. This time she would have more freedom as long as she was in eye-view of her Maame.

Folayan sat up straight. She must get well.

Folayan reached for the calabash of ash. She spread a little on the back of her hand. It was not painful like last night. Determined, she covered herself.

# CHAPTER 7

# A Stone's Throw

> *You have brought dishonor on your self*
> *and the family. Always use wisdom, Folayan.*
> *That is the way of dignity.*

**Late June 1789, Village of Kormantse, Fantiland**

Folayan's skin healed in time for the journey to the Bakatue. Each day, Maame allowed her to walk around the festival with her age mates, as long as one of her elder brothers was with her. This year she toured, next year she would be able to sit and learn skills with the crafts people.

Folayan loved to draw in the earth. Her family members admired how well her images compared to the item she had copied or brought up from her mind's eye. She was anxious to spend more time watching the artists who painted pictures of people and animals and trees on cloth.

Two days after they returned to Kormantse from the festival, Papa's caravan arrived.

The next year, during the Bakatue fishing festival, Folayan was three weeks past turning ten. Her brothers kept their commitments to her, and Papa took her around the lagoon to where artists painted calabashes, drums, and cloths. Fascinated, she asked many questions.

As soon as they came back home, she collected coconut shells from several neighbors. Keeping half of each coconut for herself to mix her colors in, she scraped the hair-like layer off the other half, leaving the woody skin smooth. Then she painted designs on the hairless coconut shells and gave them back.

The neighbors told her family members and village friends that she was a sweet girl and how much they liked her artwork. One woman even paid Folayan to paint more bowls for her.

Seven moons later, Folayan stood trembling, trying to hide behind the ofram tree, wishing she could stop her twelve-year-old brother who ran from her, bleeding and yelling, "I am telling, I am telling!"

She wanted to flee in the other direction; way across the village, maybe down to the sea, anyplace but to face her parents.

It started ten days ago. She'd come upon her brother tossing small stones at the giant tree he had tricked her into climbing to see their Papa coming home.

This time Akonor gloated. "Folayan, everybody knows I am the best stone-thrower of all my age mates."

Just to be contrary, she argued. "You only count boys, how do you know I am not better?"

Before she left him, he challenged her. "I will give you a chance to prove your boast. We will have a match in one nnason, one seven-days week. The loser will grant three wishes that the winner wants."

She stopped and grinned at him. It felt good to tease him for once. "Two nnason. One wish."

He would not agree, except for two concessions— ten days and the requests had to be in the loser's ability or power to bestow.

Akonor spent his days goading Folayan. "I think I want a tree cut so I can make a big drum. No, I think I want you to make the drum."

Every spare moment, Folayan practiced. Akonor tried to get out of her what she wanted. She would just smile and say, "You will see."

The week sped by. On the day of the contest, Folayan stood next to her brother. Each had a pile of twelve rocks. Akonor scooped up several. Folayan imitated. They alternated. Small flat stones sliced through the air rebounding off the giant tree. "Seven! Hah!" Akonor slapped his thigh in triumph. "So far I only missed one!" He swaggered around in a circle.

Folayan's brow knit in frustration. She had missed two. "It is not over yet."

He came nose to nose with her. "It is over."

Folayan squinted, aimed and tossed. "I hit it! Akonor I hit the tree!"

To her shock—and his dismay—he got one out of the final three. Folayan hit the tree three times straight and won, ten to nine.

Akonor's head dropped. He went a short distance away and sat on the ground, pouting. Elbows on knees, head in his hands, so that his eyes squinted up in slants. She felt sorry for him. He was two years older than her, yet sometimes he seemed younger. He'd try almost anything to get his way, but this day she would not give in.

"Brother. Are you not going to ask me what I want you to do for me?"

He looked forward.

"Akonor?"

Still not talking, he turned to her.

"I want you to make me a book like the one Papa brought you back from Timbuktu and teach me how to read it."

"No!" he exploded. "That is not fair! You have many gifts. Papa brought it for me. He is teaching me … *me!*"

She just stood there, watching her brother. Was she wrong? "I am not asking for your book, just one like it."

"Girls do not read. They make babies."

Her mother had said similar words when Folayan had asked her about reading.

"I can have babies and read," she told her brother.

"Well, girls are not smart enough to read," he sneered.

"I, too, am smart. I can learn to read just like you."

"No, you cannot. I will not do it." He started to walk away.

"But you promised!"

"Well, I am not doing it. You better think of something else."

She watched him leave. A hot rage surged in her. She grabbed up a stone and threw it. At the moment of release, she realized she could hurt him badly.

"Akonor!" She called a warning to her brother.

He turned and looked back. The stone struck his cheek, just below his right eye. Blood spurted out. He clasped his hand to his face and ran for the house. "I am telling. I am telling!"

Folayan was afraid to move. She stood by the tree, paralyzed, as he ran inside. Moments later, Maame and Papa came out. She could not hear his words, but she watched Akonor tell his story while pointing at her. Maame led Akonor inside the house. Folayan hung her head.

Papa came and stood over her, hands on his hips.

"Did you throw a rock and hit your brother?"

Folayan nodded, then stammered out her side of the tale. By the end, she was sobbing, "And when he said I was not smart enough, I … I … threw it at him."

"Why did you not ask me to teach you?"

Folayan looked up at him, eyes wide in surprise.

"Because I thought you would say books are for boys only."

"Have I ever said anything like that?"

"No. But you did not bring me one, only Akonor."

"It never entered my mind that you would want one."

"Then you will teach me?"

"I will. But, first, you have another lesson to learn. Violence never settles disputes. Some way, somehow, it comes back to destroy you."

He picked up a rock and placed it in her hand. "Sit down here by this tree until you think of a way you can use stones to help and not harm. Do not move until I come back."

Papa's disappointment was more than she could bear. Living with his words was worse than punishment. "You have brought dishonor on yourself and the family."

Folayan felt like he had shoved her against the tree. But he had not touched her with his hands. Her body sank with the weight of his words.

Folayan sat and thought and thought.

Papa returned. She had nothing to say.

He paused. "Who is Onyankopon?"

"He is the Most High God ... Almighty."

Papa stood up, "And?"

"The I am that I am." Her head dropped.

"Yes. Do you remember when we talked about Him and the stones?"

She nodded, picturing God writing His Ten Promises on two big flat stones, each nearly as tall as her body. She imagined God writing on them with His finger, the powder puffing up from the stones as He pressed the words into them. When finished, God handed the two tablets to Moses. But then Moses threw them down and broke them to pieces when he saw the people breaking their promise. She scrunched her mouth to the side and turned her head.

"Do you remember the proverb about the stone in hand and strength?"

Her eyes looked up toward the top of her right eyebow, searching her brain, envisioning stones, broken promises, problems of acting before thinking. "Yes, Papa."

"What do these two thoughts tell you about Onyankopon?"

"He is patient?"

Papa nodded, then lifted her chin and looked into her eyes "He suffers long with us before taking action."

"Yes, Papa."

"Strength will hold a stone in hand, and avoid the consequence of picking up the shatterings of unwise decisions."

"Yes, Papa."

He left her again. "I will be back after supper."

Her stomach ached. Her head hurt. She was thirsty.

When he returned the third time, she said, "I could sew some of the stones in a pouch and make a musical instrument. Music makes people happy when they sing and dance." She looked up at him, her eyes pleading for him to accept that.

Papa stood, pondering her offering. "That is weak, Folayan. Your mind will not be free until you have a more powerful idea."

Folayan hid her face in her hands. She had disgraced herself. *Weak. Dignity is not weak.* She released a deep breath.

"When you have thought of a better plan, come tell me."

Papa took a few steps toward the house.

"Papa!"

Papa turned back.

Folayan stared up at him. "My plan—my plan is to think before I do, and to help and not hurt in whatever I do."

"Daughter, I believe you have enough understanding now to know that it takes wisdom and thinking to solve problems. And wisdom takes time. It is easy to strike first and destroy."

He studied her.

"Always use wisdom, Folayan. That is the way of dignity."

Her bottom lip quivered.

"Yes, Papa." She fingered the stone held in her hand for hours.

He reached for her other hand. "Now, we can go home. Your Maame has food and I have business to tend to with Akonor."

A tense whistle escaped Folayan while she uncurled aching fingers and let the stone drop.

# CHAPTER 8

# *Who Will be King?*

*When our griots repeat our generations to us,
I ask questions. Then when I travel to different
places. I ask more questions.*

**January 1790, Village of Kormantse, Fantiland**

*U*pon entering the house, Folayan immediately apologized to Akonor. Later, she helped her mother bathe his face with herbal water. Before bedtime they were laughing together, she felt forgiven.

The next morning, although she had made peace with her brother, Papa was not finished. Holding a rolled parchment in his hand, he said, "Do not go to the gardens today, Folayan. Come with us."

She exchanged glances of 'woe' with Akonor, and they followed Papa out to the tree where they had the disagreement.

"Answer me, my son. You seem to want to rule over your sister—like a king. How does a prince know if he is prepared to be a king?"

Akonor's mouth dropped open. "I do not know."

Papa turned to Folayan, "My daughter who walks in dignity, can you name five great women who walk in dignity?"

She winced, and stood straight. Her palm felt sore from having gripped the sharp stone for hours yesterday.

She knew generations of names when reciting her ancestral roll, but at this moment her mind resisted. He had said "great." He waited. Anxiously, she let two names stumble out, "....Uh, Serwaa and Maame?"

Papa unrolled the map of the world that he bought in Timbuktu which he used when telling travel stories. "See children, here is the mighty Alkebulan, the kwesi broni call all of it Africa."

"The same as they say Fort Amsterdam; we say Kormantin?"

"Yes. They say Egypt, we say Kmt." He smiled and pointed, "This is the Atlantic Ocean and the Gulf of Guinea, but this map is too small." Papa broke a waist high limb from the tree.

Akonor held the map, while Papa drew the outline of a giant Alkebulan on the ground across the road, even behind some trees. When he finished, he said, "Now, it is large enough for us to walk around it. Over here, I drew the seashore with these fishing boats and palm trees between our village hill and the fort. Children, today I want you to help me draw. Lead me on a journey. Start here at the two hills, and trace the line backwards to where our people came from. Folayan, you begin."

Folayan looked up at her Papa, and took the stick. Adoration swelled in her chest. Out of the corner of her eye, she peeked at her brother, who looked miffed. She giggled, tracing the path, adding waterfalls, oases, rivers, and buildings, while Papa coaxed. She marked the line that went from the Atlantic gulf up to Mali, and across the Sahel over to ancient Kush, on back up the Nile River to Kmt with the pyramids, and across to Canaan land.

In the Canaan space, Papa drew a box, "Long ago when our ancestors were in Canaan, they were always reminded that the Most High God had rescued them from slavery, and guided them out of Kmt. He had them build a place—a wilderness tabernacle—where His presence could be there with them. It was like a big tent with three parts: a fenced outside space with a large square altar to confess what they did wrong, and to ask God to forgive them. The priest held the animal they sacrificed. It died in their place."

She was glad she had asked her brother to forgive her. It felt good.

Papa said, "Now Akonor, one of the duties of a king is to lead his people to connect with God. Draw the furniture that was in the tabernacle. There was a laver, a stand with two big water bowls, one on the ground, the other above it waist high where the priest washed the blood away from his hands and feet.

"Then there was a wooden building with walls overlaid with gold. It had two rooms. The first room had a small table with twelve flat loaves of bread which was a symbol of the Word of God. In God's scrolls, it says we should learn more truth about Him each day.

Next was a smaller altar of incense, a symbol of sending daily prayers going up to God.

The third item of furniture was a seven branch candle stand, it reminds us to tell people each day that God loves us and wants us to love Him back and receive the happiness He wants to give us. These three items show us how to stay close to Onyankopon every day.

As Akonor finished drawing, Folayan asked, "These—the bread, altar of incense, and candle stand? The people were supposed to do these each day: read, pray, and tell others about God?"

He nodded, pointing to the second room. "Here the merciful God's Firelight rested above the seat on the golden box—the ark of the covenant. Inside it were two stone tablets on which God wrote Ten Commandments. They show us God's character, as well as, how to treat Him and each other kindly." He paused.

Urgently she asked, "Papa? How do you know all this?"

"When our griots repeat our generations to us, I ask questions. Then when I travel to different places, I ask more questions. I listen for stories that are the same. My confidence is strengthened from mouths of many witnesses about the history."

Folayan peered at her father's face. Then with a sharp nod, she said. "I will ask many questions."

Papa cupped her chin in his hand, "That will help you go far in life, daughter. Remember their answers, but always think for yourself." Akonor looked at his drawings, but said nothing.

Folayan pondered his words as he began to draw again. "What are those buildings Papa?"

"These are churches in the land of Kush. It is also called Ethiopia. When I travelled there, in a city called Lalibela, I walked down into four of the twelve churches that the Christians have carved out of rock mountains, like hollowed caves. They are shaped like the sanctuary that was in Canaan land."

Folayan whispered, "I wish I could travel to those places." She held her breath, hoping that Akonor would be silent.

Papa said nothing. Had he heard her? She was too timid to say it again.

"Daughter, have you thought of any more great women?"

She hunched her shoulders. "No, Papa."

"I will help you. Some of the queens lived amidst the pyramids. Stand on the place I speak about."

Folayan looked over the map lined on the ground. The Nile River curved a long way through the land on that east side. He had drawn many mountains in the middle area around the Nile, but fewer hills down where the river fanned out in several streams that spilled into the Great Sea.

Akonor finally found his voice, "Papa, do you mean the pyramids up there in Kush or down here in Kmt nearer to Canaan?"

"Right there where you are with the big pyramids. During a famine, the Hebrew people were welcomed guests, but they stayed for many generations in the land of Kmt. When a new king, called a pharaoh, said there were too many Hebrews, he forced them to be slaves and told his soldiers to kill all the baby boys."

"No!" Both Akonor and Folayan gasped.

"One day Hatshepsut, the pharaoh's daughter, went to bathe in the river. She heard a baby crying and told her servant to fetch it from the river. She held the baby in her arms, loved him, and chose him to be her son. She named him Moses and hired a woman to care for him until she took him to live in the palace, wanting him to learn and become king and rule with her."

"A king?" Akonor's interest peaked. "What kind of things must a king know how to do?"

"A king's palace is usually in the center of his kingdom, his heart should be centered in God. He leads his people in worship of God. He must know his purpose and be confident and balanced so his people will look to him and feel secure in his ability to know the condition of his people and buildings, and to care for and lead them.

"He must study about his kingdom and the world, choose wise and trustworthy counselors, and make good decisions on how to make it better, stronger.

Papa paused, "He must know what is right and stand for right though he may have to stand alone. He must protect his kingdom from intruders and be skilled in war, physically strong, and able to lead his army into and out of battles successfully."

"I am strong Papa." Akonor raised his arms to show his muscles.

"A good king keeps his territory in order. This requires laws that keep life running in an organized manner, productive. So everyone has food to eat, houses, work that makes the kingdom a peaceful place to live. When a king has creative ideas and inspires and encourages his citizens to share their ideas that cause his kingdom to grow, then his people are happy. If you were king, would Folayan be happy?"

Akonor side-glanced at his sister and his wrinkled brow showed his bewilderment.

Papa continued, "A king leaves a legacy of laws to keep his kingdom in order. Happy citizens help a king that improves lives. They want a king who constructs buildings even empires which people from other lands desire to be part of rather than to be captured enemies, unhappy, hungry, and hopeless."

"Ooo!" Folayan blinked and wondered what would she do if she were a pharaoh like Hatshepsut? *Would people want to come to my kingdom for help? Where might they come from? What would they look like?* Then her brow wrinkled, "Papa did the Hebrews look like the people of Kmt? Were they brown like us?"

"In temples and tombs--paintings of pharaohs and most people are dark brown. Why do you ask?"

"Because I might paint a picture of them. I think they looked the same, otherwise the pharaoh would have known the Hebrew boy was someone he was trying to kill."

Papa said, "Hmm. Good thinking. What about Hatshepsut will you remember?"

"She was kindhearted when she saved the baby Moses from being killed." Folayan recalled Akonor's bloody head. Her shoulders drooped. "Papa, I am very sorry I hurt my brother."

Papa watched her. After a moment, he said "That is good. Now, let us walk up the river where Queen Tiye lived. Her parents were commoners, temple priests. She became the Great Royal Wife of Pharaoh Amenhotep III and her son was Akhenaton, and her grandson Tutankhamen, two pharaohs. She was very important to the kingdom because leaders from other lands chose to talk with her about problems.

What does that tell you about her?"

"She was wise, too. Even though she was a commoner like us, out of her came two great kings. Kwantunyis are not royalty, but the chieftain respects you, Papa, for your good advice."

He nodded, "Queen Tiye was a Nubian Kushite, it is likely that she also was a valued co-ruler with him, uniting the two nations of Kush and Kmt. Nubians were long practiced in respecting women for their knowledge, and understanding about rulership and getting along well with other nations."

"Was she beautiful too, Papa?" Wide-eyed, she looked up at him.

"The statues I saw of her were beautiful. The people of Kmt say they are 'kissed by the sun' and Nubians are known to be very beautiful."

"Papa will I be kissed by the sun when I grow up?"

"I am sure of it."

"But Papa, why is my skin …?"

"Chh." He stopped her. "People of Alkebulan are like a handful of flowers with many shades in them. Some are very black; others have a bit of broni. Where I have traveled, I have been surprised to see many differences." Folayan examined her hands. Papa continued, "Not everyone is the same, you have seen other people at the Bakatue from many villages, and Serwaa." He paused. "I started to name you Serwaa, but chose Folayan. When you were born, I saw her in you. Your skin is like hers, only slightly different from mine."

"But Papa, why can I not be kissed by the sun like you?"

"The difference in shade has no respect with God. Remember the Gye Nyame: "Except God …" He pointed to her to finish the statement.

She pursed her lips, "Except God, nothing happens."

Papa said, "You are far more than your skin color, you are kissed by the One who lives beyond the sun, Onyankopon, the Most High God."

He waited until she looked up at him again.

"Folayan, always know that many women are beautiful." He pressed two fingers on her forehead, "It is what is inside the head that saves the nation."

"I want to be able to do that, too." She took steps along the river line. "Papa, who else are you going to talk about?"

"Kandakes, but I have some new questions for which I seek answers. What I want to tell you will have to wait until I return from my up coming journey, but," he tickled her chin, "it will be full of surprises about the Kandakes and more?"

"Khan-dah-kes?" Her bottom lip jutted, he was going away again, so soon. "But Papa that is a long time."

# CHAPTER 9

# A Gracious Hostess

*On this day, she was to be a hostess. Just like a grown woman ...*
*she was the hostess. But though Afua was her guest,*
*she did not have the right to disrespect Folayan in her own home.*

**October 1791, Village of Kormantse, Fantiland**

"Papa! Watch out! Please watch!"

Folayan struggled to open her eyes.

She felt Serwaa rubbing her forehead and whispering, "Wake up, little one."

Folayan's heart pounded, as if she were in a foot race.

"Did I wake anyone else?"

"No, I do not think so. I was not asleep yet, and reached you quickly."

"Oh. Good." Folayan sighed. "It frightens me more when I wake up and several of you are here in the room. I do not like rousing them—or you—from your sleep."

Serwaa said softly, "Do not worry about that. You cannot help it. Was it the same dream again?"

Folayan nodded. "I scream loud, but Papa never sees the snake."

Serwaa wrapped her arms around her.

"Why does it keep happening?" Her head lay on Serwaa's chest.

"It is probably only because your Papa and brothers are traveling. You will outgrow it. And many journeys will pass, then one day you will wonder how many years ago the dream stopped troubling you."

Veiled in a verdant grove that graced the crest of the mountain, the village of Kormantse waited for Folayan's father's return from his journey.

Every five years, Papa traveled far beyond his yearly destinations. This time he decided to go all the way back to Ethiopia—ancient Kush.

People frequently asked Folayan about him, such a long time away. Meanwhile her twelfth year began without him. Almost every day, she went to her special nest near the edge of the cliff, looking for Papa.

She did not intend to go today, though. She stood in the doorway of their house, waiting for her friends. On this day, she was to be a hostess. Just like a grown woman.

Folayan looked around the adiho, a large square open-air court-yard. Each room around it had a curtained doorway and a window on the inside wall. The entrance, with its solid mahogany door, opened into a short hallway with a room on each side, her parents' room on the left, Serwaa and Folayan on the right.

Next to them, Akonor slept in a longer enclosure that the family gathered in when the weather required the protection of the thatched roof that encircled the adiho. The family gathered here, but they preferred to enjoy the fresh air and sunshine available in the adiho. In the rear corner, the women prepared food in the room with a door that opened outside to where the women cooked on the three level mounded bukyia behind the house.

On the inside back wall of the adiho, her elder brothers' wives and children occupied two chambers. Kwamina had four babies, Emissah three. Papa said they would soon be building their own homes, leaving a personal space for Akonor. Her two brothers who went with Papa on this current journey slept in the two rooms on the fourth wall. Maame expected soon they would bring wives to live in the house, too.

Folayan loved their open adiho. With seats grouped near the table by the tree that grew in the far corner for shade, it remained a peaceful, relaxing place where the family and guests enjoyed instruction, serious conversation, music, stories, and much laughter. They also entertained guests in the adiho.

One day Folayan hoped to have a fine house where she might receive guests and friends. Now, she was learning what she would need to know for the time when she became a married woman. Besides housekeeping, cooking, and clothing care, part of her training included gift-making.

For the past two weeks, she had been focused on presents for all her age mates. Because her friends had been as excited as she with the beautiful bracelet her Papa brought from Benin last year, Folayan wanted each of them to have something similar.

With colors and dyes she made herself, she had bored small holes and painted many seeds. There were red flowers on yellow seeds and brown fish on pale blue seeds. And she had added something extra.

In black on white seeds, Folayan painted two of her Akan people's adinkra symbols; her favorites, the Gye Nyame, meaning *Except for God, nothing happens*, and the sankofa bird, representing wisdom. It was important to *go back and fetch it*. Even her Papa's gift did not have these. Her friends would have very special bracelets.

Hearing laughter, she went to the entry door. Opening it slightly, she saw all eight of them, all giggling girls, ages twelve through fourteen, making their way down the road that led to her house. She hurried to the kitchen.

"They are coming, Maame!"

As her mother smiled and went to greet them, Folayan sped into the adiho to assure herself again that all was ready. Nervous yet excited, she smoothed then tucked the top edge of her etam where it crossed her chest and wrapped under her armpits. It was her favorite, striped yellow and green, with the Gye Nyame design on the hem. Folayan watched Maame's gracious welcome to her friends.

Upon arrival they stepped inside the entryway. Each ebony brown girl greeted Folayan's mother, "*Wo ho te sen*, Maame. How are you?"

"*Mehoye*. I am well. Wo ho te sen?"

They asked about the health of her family members

Maame returned the courtesy by asking about each of their mothers, grandmothers, aunts, and other family members.

When the greetings were over, the girls proceeded into the adiho. It did not surprise Folayan that Ekua said, "I am excited to hear another of your Papa's stories."

Folayan smiled, "He was going to tell me about the Kandake Nubian queens who ruled in their own power without kings."

"What?" exclaimed several of the girls.

"On their own?" Amba asked.

"Yes. He will tell me about them when he returns, but I can talk about Hatshepsut of ancient Kmt. She chose to be called Pharaoh, but she remained wise, self-controlled, knowledgeable about her kingdom, and gracious—and she had a beard wig made for her chin! So, the men would respect her and not ignore her commands."

"A beard wig?" Yaa's eyes opened in wonder.

Folayan nodded, "Her father, Thutmoses II, knew she was very intelligent and capable of ruling Kmt. He educated her in all the ways a son would be prepared to become the Pharaoh. When he died, she was twelve. Some men defied her father's plan and caused her trouble.

"She also had a young half brother, Thutmoses III. For the kingdom's sake, she gave him knowledge and responsibilities that would prepare him to be a strong king, knowing he might grow up and try to overthrow, even kill her.

"When she found a baby boy in a basket in the Nile River, she kept him as her son. So, he might become a king and rule with her if necessary. She answered her enemies' question of 'Who will be king?' As her father wished, she reigned as the Pharaoh."

After the girls' chatter about Hatshepsut subsided, Folayan shared Maame's words, "A queen must be wise, and knowledgeable about her realm, as well as gracious.

Folayan's hand delicately pointed as she described, "A queen's hair, face, ears, teeth, whole body, and clothes must be clean from head-to-toe."

Yaa said, "And wear pretty dresses."

Afua blurted, "With many jewels!"

Folayan continued, "But more than beautiful garments  and the jewels—her goodness will gleam from her heart, beautifying her face."

Afua looked around and spied the beads, "You finished sooner than I thought you would."

"Yes." Folayan pointed to a table near the north wall, by the tree. There, rows lay lined up according to design.

"There are twelve beads for each of you."

Most are natural. I painted pictures on a few seeds. You will not all have the same pictures but I did make a sankofa and a Gye Nyame for each of you. We will string them together with this." She handed a length of thin cord to each of her age mate. Then she held up five bracelets that she planned to sell at the market. She told her friends, "I made these in different patterns. You can make yours like them or however you wish."

"Oh, how pretty," her best friend complimented. "These have flowers, and look at this butterfly. You truly have a talent for making things look so real."

"You are very kind." Her reply sounded quiet and gracious, but inside Folayan brimmed with pride. *"Meda wase."*

Most of the girls exclaimed their appreciation as they picked out the colors they wanted. Only Afua remained silent in her choosing. Though Folayan was the youngest yet she already stood taller than all of them save Afua, who was the oldest of all the age mates.

Even though the top of her shoulder came to Afua's armpit, still Folayan felt much shorter when the other girl came close to her.

She wished she were old enough to wear her own duku on her head like Maame—that would make her stand over Afua if she was not wearing a headdress. Folayan drew a long breath. She would not think on such things for now. Today was to be enjoyed with her friends.

They sat on the gleaming floor working. Folayan had two piles of beads for special bracelets for Maame to take to the market, along with the metal tools her brothers brought back from their travels. They took them apart, examined them, then created more, and many new tools.

Serwaa, came out of her room with a sewing basket. After the greetings, she and Maame watched the girls begin their artwork, then moved away to sit in the front corner to share women's talk and sew.

Afua said, "I thought you were going to make the beads like yours."

"Like mine?" Folayan looked at her, shaking her head, "No. I said I would paint seeds for you."

"You said our bracelets would be like the one your Papa brought back from his last trip. Where is it? Go get it," Afua demanded. "I want to put mine together the same way."

Folayan hesitated. The rest of the girls sat silent, concentrating on their work, half-glancing up to see and not see the expressions of Afua and Folayan.

Ekua spoke, keeping her voice low. "These are just right, Afua. We will each have our own design. That is better."

Folayan's two sisters-in-law came out of their rooms. They greeted every one and Serwaa joined them in the kitchen.

With her basket on her hip Maame asked, "Will you girls be all right if I go to help the others with the meal?"

"Yes, Maame," Folayan said.

"Yes, Maame," the rest of them chorused.

Maame smiled and went to put the sewing in her room.

Afua leaned close. "I want to see your bracelet. Go get it now."

Folayan sighed and stood.

In her room, she took a small, red cloth bag from her storage basket in the corner. Her father had brought it also from Benin in the south.

Folayan took the bracelet out and studied it. The designs she painted were similar, but not the same. The bracelets did not have the best part, the regional Akan adinkras.

*Why does she always have to have her way? I did the best I could. I was just trying to do something nice for everybody.*

She remembered the many conversations she and Adwoa often had about how they would handle Afua's arrogance, "the next time." But the "next times" came and went again and again. This would likely be just another one of those.

Folayan clenched her teeth and started back. Stepping out of her room, she met Maame, who looked at her curiously.

Folayan held up the bag. "Afua wanted to see Papa's bracelet."

Maame nodded and hurried to the kitchen.

When she rejoined them, the girls were in a close circle trying on the bracelets Folayan had made to sell. Their hands pressed in over each other as they admired her bracelets on their wrists.

Yaa said, "Folayan, come see! Put your hand here, too."

Folayan smiled, happy that they were enjoying themselves. As she reached into the circle, Afua snickered, "Look at how different Folayan's hand is from ours." With disdain Afua said, "It is so, so …."

Folayan snatched her hand away.

A sinking feeling swirled inside her. She swallowed hard, and blinked back the water in her eyes.

She furtively glanced back and forth comparing. *My hand is almost as beautiful and deep and kissed by God as theirs.*

The muffled voices in the kitchen rose in laughter. Then in her mind Folayan heard Serwaa's often repeated words: *…lift yourself up. Girl, stand up straight! Never eat someone else's foolishness. Poison may be stirred into it.*

Folayan cleared her throat, and spoke boldly, "My father was gored by a water buffalo. He saw his skin is layered in different colors. He realized that this top layer is thinner than a strand of hair. His nurse-maid told him all people look the same under that thin, thin top layer which is God's special design for each of us. Each one of us is His special creation.

"I mix flower petals, stems, bark. and leaves to get just the right color I want. God is the Great Master Artist.

"You point at my hand. I say look closely--and see that we all have some special design about us—God's gift.

"Do you dare snicker at the handiwork of the Most High? Are you that wise to try to restrict the plan of God?

"You snicker, Afua ... I rejoice!"

In silence, the other age mates gathered their materials and went to sit down to work on their bracelets. Only Folayan and Afua remained standing. Folayan did not look at Afua when she handed her the bag.

Afua examined the bracelet. "This has sixteen beads. You gave us twelve. I am the chieftain's daughter so I need at least five more."

"There are not any more," Folayan said.

"What about those?" Afua was pointing at her two sets of beads.

Folayan shook her head. "I am making two more bracelets. Maame is going to sell them for me at the market with the ones you all tried on."

Fatima's eyes sparkled with admiration. "Oh! A merchant. How splendid. You will be the first of us."

Afua cut the girl a hard look. "Of us?"

Fatima blinked and glanced away.

Afua turned back on Folayan. "Besides, you can make beads any time. I need more now."

All the girls watched. Folayan knew she had to be gracious. She was the hostess. But though Afua was her guest, she did not have the right to disrespect Folayan in her own home.

"No." Folayan swallowed.

Soft though her reply had been, Afua's face hardened as if Folayan had shouted.

"Then keep your beads," she sneered. "And mine as well. You will have eight to sell. I will just take yours."

Folayan reached for the bracelet. Her hand closed around it. "I cannot give away my Papa's gift."

Afua did not let go. Instead she tightened her grip and twisted. Something popped. Several beads skittered across the floor.

Everybody gasped.

Folayan yanked back. As the broken cord slipped from Afua's hand, more beads fell. Silence held as Folayan fought a strangling rush of anger rising from her breast.

She almost gave freedom to that fury, before she saw the smirk of triumph in Afua's expression as she glanced toward the kitchen where the muted conversation of the women could be heard.

*So, that is your game. But you will not force me to disgrace myself in front of Maame.*

Folayan swallowed her retaliation and returned to the group. In silence, she held out her other hand for the beads remaining in Afua's grasp.

The pinch of anger on Afua's lips was sweet balm to Folayan as she saw in her eyes the wavering of a battle lost.

Afua dashed the beads to the ground.

"Take your old bracelet. I do not want it. It is ugly, anyway." She scooped up her beads and twine from the table and stomped from the house.

Fatima hurried after her, apologizing to Folayan all the way to the door.

Watching the two girls until they turned at the end of the road, Folayan was torn between elation and dread. She had stood up to Afua. She looked at the beads in her hand. It had been a costly victory.

When she rejoined the girls, they had gathered all the scattered beads and piled them in front of her place. Everyone sat down and continued working. In quick time, they had completed the bracelets. Folayan told them she had wanted them to all wear them and act like ladies at the Bakatue. They attempted it, but with the different mood, soon all were ready to leave.

At the door, Adwoa whispered, "You were brave. I am proud of you." She stepped back and smiled.

Folayan said nothing. She could not release her wrinkled brow.

Ekua said, "Do not worry, your Papa will bring you another bracelet or something else just as special."

"Yes, even better," Yaa said. The others agreed.

"And thank you for making our beads." Ekua touched her wrist and smiled.

"It is very kind of you to share with us." Abena hugged Folayan.

After they left, Folayan sat looking at the three piles of beads. Of the sixteen on Papa's bracelet, five were broken. She placed the good ones in a line next to the ones she had painted.

Hers were just as pretty. She could use hers to make Papa's as full as it was before, but that would leave only one to send to market. Too bad Afua had taken her beads after all.

Folayan examined the seeds. Maybe she might use a longer cord and tie fancy knots in between each bead to give it the original length, but her parents would notice and how would she explain that?

A tear ran down to her chin. She angrily swiped it away. She did not want to try to explain that either, if Maame walked into the adiho.

*Oh, Papa, return home soon.* If he were here, he'd tell her a funny story and make everything good.

She sighed, staring down at the broken pieces. Perhaps she could just hide it away and never wear it again. Afua would be pleased with that.

She picked up the twine and new beads she'd made. Folayan began restringing Papa's gift.

This business of becoming a woman was hard work. She decided she would rather remain Papa's little girl for a while longer.

# CHAPTER 10

# Her Honor
# the Queen

*The Kandakes were warrior queens.*
*They fought not because of moments of anger,*
*but when intruders refused to reason,*
*they fought to protect their people.*

**October 1791, Kormantse village**

A few days after Papa returned from the long journey, he called Folayan to him.

"While I was away, I learned much more than I knew about the queens. See—I have redrawn the map of Africa." Folayan looked to the ground. "The word Kandake is a title, it means queen. In the same way that the Pharaohs were the kings of Kmt, at times, the Nubians of Kush were ruled by a line of powerful Kandakes.

"One of them, Makeda, the Queen of Sheba, heard news of an Hebrew king named Solomon who lived in Jerusalem, in Canaan land.

King Solomon was known in many parts of the world to have great wisdom granted to him by God. Rulers came to see him from far and wide, bringing rich gifts, asking him questions.

"The Kandake wanted to test him with some hard questions, too. So, she went to see him and took a caravan of servants, animals and examples of the abundant riches of Kush.

"When it was her turn to ask her questions, indeed they were very hard, but King Solomon answered them and she was impressed. He was likewise impressed with her own intelligence, power, and wealth."

"And beauty?"

"And beauty. When she went back home, she told people all about King Solomon and new things she learned about his God, our God whom she and her people chose to serve."

Folayan said, "She asked questions. That means she was very wise, like you Papa."

He laughed. She grinned. She loved hearing his laughter.

They walked further on the river line, studying it. She asked, "What are these slashes along the Nile?"

"They are cataracts, places crowded with jagged rocks and huge boulders and waterfalls. Many boats and people have been destroyed trying to get through them.

"They also protect from invaders who want to battle and take land from citizens."

"The cataracts are good then."

"Good for the people who stay put, trouble for travelers."

"I see six cataract markings."

"Those are the biggest ones. There are many more, just as there are more Kandakes who raised their hands to protect the people of Nubia. By this time the Nubians ruled Kush."

Folayan slowed. She rubbed the sore in her hand imagining huge jagged cataracts.

Papa kept walking. "A legend is told about the Kandake who sat atop her elephant leading her mighty army also on elephants, ready to prevent Alexander the Great from crossing the cataract, but he decided to go fight another battle in Asia. Alexander was the leader of the Greek army. The Greeks called the Kandakes, Candaces."

She marveled as she caught up to Papa when he stopped.

She looked around on the map, "What about these other pyramids!"

He told her, "This is where the Nubian Kandakes' had their capital of Meroe in ancient Kush."

"What is the difference between Kush and Nubia?"

"They are much the same territory. It is now called Ethiopia. Writings on the statues, tombs, and walls tell that earliest Kandake queen of Kush was Shanadakhete. Like the ancient kings she was an important religious leader of her people. In Meroe her statue stands at her temple showing her wearing her crown and royal garment draped in three parts. She is beautiful, and jeweled. Her strong body appears to be well able to bear children. In some images she is seated on her throne holding a spear and palm branch. A prince stands by her side, but it is said that she had no king ruling with her.

"The next few rulers were kings, then, ten years before Jesus Christ lived in Israel, Shanadakhete's descendant, Amenirenas was the queen. For five years, she fought Augustus Caesar and prevented Caesar from taking the land into his control."

"Papa, are you telling me the queens fought intruders?"

"Yes. The Kandakes were warrior queens. They fought not because of moments of anger, but when intruders refused to reason, they fought to protect their people."

*Akonor would not reason with me, but he did not hit me.*

Hoping to thwart Papa from the same thought, she asked, "Who was Augustus?"

"Augustus Caesar was the emperor of Rome, who had conquered many nations and was coming after Kush. Many of the Kushite kings and kandakes and their armies fought the Romans."

"Did they fight the Jesus Christ, too?"

"No, Jesus came in peace. I have been told that He came to teach the people of the world about Onyankopon. He came to show that the Most High is good, kind, merciful, and loving, but also that He will not let those that cause suffering and pain go on forever. Those that hurt others and do wickedly will be destroyed."

Folayan glanced down, then to the sky. Her thumb rubbed the bruise in her hand from the stone.

Papa said, "When Augustus Caesar wanted to know the total of people who had been brought into the Roman empire, he had a count taken. That is why Jesus was born in the village of Bethlehem."

"I do not understand?"

"Each man had to go register in the village of his ancestors. Joseph had married Mary and his ancestors came from Bethlehem. Joseph had to obey the emperor's command and go register in the census although the baby might be born on the wilderness journey."

"Was he?" Folayan was anxious.

"No, but the town was so crowded they had to sleep in a stable with the cows and sheep. The baby was born there."

"How do you know so much Papa?"

"Our family talks shook up my curiosity. I wanted the answers to so on this last merchant journey, I went back to Kanem Bornu and other places around Lake Chad. I did not have to go all the way to Lalibela again to get my answers. I had friends on the Sudan side of the lake. One of the men I talked to for many days was a priest in the Ethiopian churches.

When he was captured and forced into slavery. It was many years before he was able to get back home. His wife of his youth that he loved so much had remarried at her father's demand, and she now had children with the new husband. But the priest was not allowed to marry another because of his priesthood. Brokenhearted, he returned to Lake Chad and I was able to ask him many questions about the Christians and their Jesus. The kwesi broni call this land Ethiopia. Lalibela is in Ethiopia, and the people have been Christians for hundreds of years. Using hand tools, they have hollowed out giant churches cut out of mountain sides." Using his hand to show, he explained, "Inside each of those churches are three rooms just like in the portable Hebrew tabernacle that was built in the wilderness on the way to Canaan, and later King Solomon built an unmovable tabernacle in the city of Jerusalem. In each of the churches in Lalibela, the priests dress in garments like the ones in Jerusalem. The Ethiopian priests answered most of my questions."

Folayan listened intently as he spoke histories so vividly as if she was in a crowd of hearers.

Papa explained, "The Queen of Sheba told the ancient Ethiopians the prophecy she learned from King Solomon of a Savior who was expected to come to his Jerusalem.

"The prophet Balaam tried to curse the people of God, but God only allowed blessings to come out of Balaam's mouth, including the prophecy that a Star would come out of Jacob. God changed Jacob's name to Israel.

"And another prophet named Micah foretold that the ruler of Israel, whose 'going forth have been from old, from everlasting' would be born in tiny Bethlehem."

Folayan said, "So, the Nubians were waiting for those prophecies to happen. Did the Romans leave them alone?"

"They did for a long, long time, but the Kandake Amanishaketo gave the Romans the worst defeat they received by all the kandakes and she managed to negotiate a treaty that left Kush in peace from the Romans for three hundred years. A kwesi broni from Italy hired men to break into her pyramid and steal great wealth in gold, bracelets, jewels. They sold them across the Great Sea."

Folayan walked among the pyramid pictures. She found one that reminded her of what she might have looked like to Akonor, when she was about to throw the stone at him. She sure did not want to bring it to her father's attention, but her curiosity won, "What about this one Papa? Who is she?"

"She is Kandake Amanitore who ruled Kush during the time when Jesus Christ was born. During her reign, she had temples built, and water reservoirs, and pyramids.

Folayan looked down at the pyramids Papa had drawn.

"Amanitore was one of the great builders of Kush which had over two hundred pyramids," he glanced over his shoulder, then crooked his finger. "Come over here between Kmt and Israel."

Folayan followed him up to the narrow space rounding the Great Mediterranean Sea.

"This passage way is called Gaza. Phillip, an apostle of Jesus was told by an angel to go down here at midday. Phillip obeyed and that is where he saw a wealthy Kushite man reading a scroll while riding in his chariot. Phillip ran up alongside the chariot to greet him. The man had been to Jerusalem to worship and was now trying to understand the meaning of a prophecy in the Scripture scroll that was written by the prophet Isaiah. Phillip asked if he wanted help understanding it."

"Papa? You said they had their own writings. This sounds like the Kushite man could read the prophet Isaiah's different language. Wait. Remember you told me the Queen of Sheba went to Israel to see King Solomon. She must have been able to speak that language. I want to speak—and read—different languages, too. What was Isaiah's called?"

"I suppose it was Hebrew. The Hebrews live up there in Israel which they conquered from the Canaanites. Canaan is the land where our Akan people came from and still practice a number of customs that the Hebrews do."

Papa walked up to the area east of the Great Sea and stood. "From here they travelled down to Nubia then west across the Sahel all the way to Timbuktu and ancient Ghana, then south to the Gold Coast. God led them all the way."

Folayan stared at him, her thoughts popping, "How do the Hebrews say God?"

"I have heard the word Yaweh—but the Hebrews are careful to use other names." Papa stopped to ponder. "Folayan do you hear it? Ya-weh. Ya. That YA is in the center of our name for the Most High. Say it out loud with me—Ony …"

Folayan leaned toward him. They said it together, "O-nYAn-ko-pon."

Papa reasoned, "If Onyankopon the Most High, is the Father, and as the Christians say, His Son is Jesus, the One the prophet Isaiah wrote of would …" Papa rejoined Folayan down in the Gaza space.

They both stood deep in their thoughts, until Folayan asked, "Did Phillip explain the prophecy?"

"Yes. He told him that those Scriptures had just been fulfilled during the days the Ethiopian man had been visiting in Jerusalem. Phillip told the man all about Jesus. Isaiah had written down God's messages about Jesus. He wrote when and where Jesus would be born and that He would grow up and teach, and heal, and repair broken hearts and help them understand God's character and commandments … And that Jesus would suffer, be rejected, beaten, and killed and be raised from the dead … but one day He would become the King of Kings."

"The King of Kings? How can that be?"

"That I do not know, but the Nubian, who was high in his Queen's royal court, was so happy to understand these things that when they came near a river, asked to be baptized like Jesus."

"Baptized?"

"Yes, on my recent trip, I was told that right then the man got out of his chariot. As they stood in the river, Phillip lowered him down under the water, as though he was being buried. But instead of soil covering him, it was water. When he came up it was like he was given new life to follow Jesus."

Again Papa stared down at the map spot of the Gaza strip.

She said, "It seems like Onyankopon wanted people outside Canaan land to know about Jesus."

"Yes. It does. Before Phillip helped the Nubian treasurer, God made it so thousands of visitors who had come to Jerusalem would know about Him. It happened fifty days after the Passover and the crucifixion and after the resurrection. They say that Jesus kept teaching until angels took Him back to heaven in a cloud."

Folayan said, "What?"

Papa hunched his shoulders, "After that, His disciples preached to several thousand people who had come from all over the world to celebrate the Passover, probably like the Kushite Nubian treasurer had come to worship. They told the crowd the same thing Phillip had told the treasurer that Jesus Christ was the Son of God and for them to go back home and tell their people Jesus was coming back the Second time to rescue and bring His followers to live with Him in heaven.

A question formed on Folayan's lips, but she held it seeing that Papa paused like he was thinking about something else. He rubbed his forehead then continued, "They say the preaching was so powerful that over 3000 believed and the Christian church began. The new Christians went back to their countries and started churches over the world."

Folayan asked, "I wonder if anyone told people in Alkebulan about Jesus?"

"Yes there were people who did, three that I know about."

"Who?"

"The country of Cyrene is in the north part of Alkebulan. Up here by the Great Sea." Papa showed her the home place of Simon the Cyrenian who was forced to carry Jesus' cross. He said, "Simon and his two sons, who were Jesus' disciples, had much to report to the people in Cyrene.

Folayan listened with raised eyebrows, "Alkebulan is Africa?"

"Yes. And we know of another person who took the news back to Alkebulan and to Queen Amanitore's daughter, the Kandake Amanitere who was ruling when Jesus' was crucified. Her treasurer—"

"The one that Phillip baptized? "

"Yes. He went back to Kush and taught what happened while he was in Jerusalem and travelling home. In time the Kushite Ethiopian territory became known as a Christian nation. I wonder why I am just now realizing this this way?" He plopped down by a tree like he was exhausted.

She leaned against the ofram to watch him. Then she remembered the ants, and went to sit on the backside of the neem tree with him. He seemed to have burrowed into a cave of his thoughts, not likely to budge soon. From the tree she looked out at the map and thought about all that Papa had told her. She rehearsed the questions he had asked, her answers, and the advice he had given:

The queens had much to think about. Their children and citizens needed a strong queen who was wise, and nurturing. So many people depended on them. They had no room to be hot-headed. They had to sankofa and know their history, and how their ancestral leaders helped and hurt the people.

*If I were queen how could I improve my nation and not repeat mistakes of the past?*

*How could I figure out who my enemies are and rid them from among my counselors or officers? I would have to pay attention to who ignores my wishes. And who listens and helps me make wise decisions. I would have to be stern, yet caring and merciful.*

*I would need to search carefully for wise, humble, capable linguists, counselors and other helpers to support me in achieving my goals to improve the nation and to build a strong, well trained army of warriors to protect the kingdom.*

*Papa said, "A queen sets goals and her scribes write them down, so they can be announced to all her people." I would have to develop the habit of learning what other societies do well, and like the Queen of Sheba, travel seeking to gain more knowledge to help my people be healthy and strong, and to build houses, and temples.*

*As queen, I need to also be strong, and walk with dignity. I must guard my character, and always be thankful for blessings. I must keep to myself words, plans, and secrets. I must hold my tongue until necessary to inform others. I must reject pride in myself, because the King Solomon said "Pride goes before destruction and a haughty spirit before a fall."*

*I want to be creative and learn how to achieve my dreams and to inspire my leaders and helpers to do the same. If praise comes to me, I will accept it gracefully, and I will search for opportunities to praise the citizens so they will feel free to grow ideas and create things that make the monarchy great.*

*A good queen keeps her word. Her people rely on her to not get distracted. Papa said that helps them trust her.*

*A good queen takes great care to always be beautiful with her hair, face, teeth, skin,--her whole body, her clothing, and to ever be dignified. Along with the tasks required of a king, she still maintains her womanhood, gentle yet strong and powerful, and respected. In all ways she is diligent to represent herself to be deserving of her title of Her Honor, the Queen.*

*To accomplish all this responsibility, a queen must seek God and stay close to Him. She needs divine guidance to be the spiritual leader of her children and citizens connecting them to the Most High.*

*Those ancient kandakes had to figure ways to solve problems, not cause them. I too, must think to solve my problems and ways to be strong, and a peacemaker. I am twelve afenhyia now ... like Hatshepsut, but with only one life to rule. What kind of person do I want to be ...?*

A breeze rustled the leaves through the trees. Clouds moved across the sky. Folayan pondered the heavens and was glad she was not a princess, then she thought of the gifts her Papa had collected for her in his kwantunyi box. He did not count royal blood as the only rule of dignity. He expected his sons and daughter to think and act as though they were children of a king, and subjects of the Most High God.

"Papa?"

"Yes, Daughter?"

"Are we Christians?"

He was silent.

She did not ask again. When he wanted to talk to her he would. She waited.

"I think your Maame is one. We do not talk about it."

Silence again.

Finally, he said, "Me. Everything turns in my head—Ancestors, Muslims, Christ. Each adding to and leaving out something from the other. I need to know more."

Silence.

She knew that for hundreds of years her Akan people had resisted becoming Muslim. It was one of the reasons they migrated from the east to here, but they had friends and Papa read the Quran. *What is it that he wants to know more about?* "Papa?"

"Hmm?"

"When people brought knowledge from Israel into Alkebulan, did our ancestors learn about Christ?"

"They speak of one who is our kinsman. We have a custom that when we have times that are so hard that we have no other choice, we can sell a part of the land, or sell ourselves into slavery to pay our debts and protect our family.

"Then if one of our kinsmen earned the money, he could come and pay the debt and buy the person or the land back. He is the kinsman-redeemer. The things I am told about the Jesus Christ make me think He is that One, who will restore us to our happy home the way it was for our first ancestors."

Folayan thought about her friend. She whispered, "What if one of my brothers or I had to go work off the family debt, like Fatima? Papa no one has come for her! If it was me, would someone come for me and be my redeemer?"

Papa shifted to look at her, then into her eyes. "Daughter, I would come for you. I would not stop working three, four, five additional tasks each day until you or any of my family was back home safe."

She smiled briefly, then her brow wrinkled. She wondered if the Christ would come after her, too? "Papa? Why do some people not like the Jesus Christ?"

"Folayan?"

"Yes, Papa."

"You must get wisdom, get knowledge, get understanding. Then decide for yourself."

"Yes, Papa."

"Folayan, tell me who you are?"

"I am Ama Kwantunyi Folayan."

"What can you do to bring honor to your name? Name some of the queens and tell me what you learned."

Folayan thought a long while. "Queen Hatshepsut saved a baby and trained him to be a leader, and solve problems, and to help others."

"Yes, Daughter."

"The Queen of Sheba was very smart and sought more wisdom from King Solomon. And she went back to her country and taught her people what she learned."

"What about your name is like what the Queen of Sheba did?"

"She traveled?"

"Yes, but more importantly, she returned." He paused, and came face to face with her, lifted her chin and asked, "What did I say?"

Folayan answered firmly, "She returned."

"Remember if for any reason you are ever away from the village, remember to always mark your path, ever be thinking how to return to your village. You must return. That is what Kwantunyis do. What can you tell me about how to be like the kandakes?"

"To watch and be ready for what may be coming, to stay healthy and strong, and … and not be the one to cast the first stone." She looked sideways at him. He waited. She added, "They built buildings, and temples for worship, and houses. I learned that there are times when I must stand up for myself, and for the good of other people, too."

"Um hmm."

She swallowed, "Even though they were warrior queens and fought against their enemies, I learned that to talk together and make peace treaty is better than war."

"You have mentioned several ways to walk in dignity. What about the other part of your name?"

"Ama?"

"Yes, you are very special because you have the same day name as Kwame. The day Onyankopon draws near to us. Why do you think He does that?"

"Because … because He likes us?"

"What else do you think He wants?"

"For me to like Him?"

"How can you show Him you like Him?

"I do not know that Papa."

"He wants you to want to know Him better."

"How can I do that?"

"Become interested in Him. His creations. His character. The more you seek to know Him, the more you will bring honor to Him as well as bring honor to your own name—Ama."

She looked beyond the trees, and the map on the ground, pondering his words.

"Ama Kwantunyi Folayan will you keep the promise of your name?"

Folayan swallowed. "I want to try Papa."

"Is that water or wine?"

Folayan blinked several times. "I do not know?"

"Trying is a twin of lying. Trying is saying you will, while planning that you will not put your whole might into a task. So, if you do not intend to do it with your whole heart—what is it water or wine? It takes decision and daily effort. If you make a mistake. Stand up, correct it, and go forward. Like you did with Akonor."

"I … I will, Papa. I will keep the promise."

# CHAPTER 11

# Womanhood

*It will come. It will come right on time.
Then it will all begin for you. Most of our age mates
have completed their festivities or are in the middle of them.
But you still have the gift of looking forward to it.*

*Maame has told me the good news. I have been saving and preparing for this time for many afenhyias. You shall have a most wonderful celebration.*

**May 1793, Village of Kormantse, Fantiland**

Since Folayan was the youngest among her age mates, once in a while she felt left out. She was thankful Akonor was now age fifteen, and though two years older than her, still sometimes enjoyed her presence.

Nine years earlier, when he was six, Akonor joined his next elder brother in caring for the family's goats and donkeys. Except on the seventh day of the week, Kwamemeneda, Folayan would wake up to the daybreak tinkling of the bell around the biggest goat's neck as it led its fellows out of the corral made with vine tied branches. Herding had now become Akonor's sole responsibility.

So, in the dim of morning, Akonor, with staff in hand, followed his charges out to the location where they would spend the day. Later, after gathering eggs from the guinea hens, working in the women's farm, and preparing the first meal with them, Folayan took her brother his portion. Sometimes she stayed and Akonor let her help him care for the animals, especially on Wednesday, when Adwoa went with her mother to sell their wares at the market.

Folayan enjoyed sitting outside the akura walls with Akonor while the animals grazed hither and yon. Akonor's favorite topic: looking forward to the time when he would go with Papa to interesting places beyond the village and Fantiland.

Folayan daydreamed of going on merchant travels, too. She was interested in meeting many merchants and learning about the unique talents of different tribes such as building styles, and special skills they acquired, such as the Fulani people who provided much of the animal products like cheese and leather for people who came from near and far to buy them. She wanted to know about new and useful tools different groups made, and fabrics, and personal care items. Folayan had always been fascinated by the animals her brothers told her about.

Papa told Folayan about sights seen before she was born. "It was in the land of the pygmy people, near the Congo River. It had stripes on its legs like the zebra, yet it looked like a horse, but more like a brown giraffe with a long head, and deep black eyes."

Folayan liked to imagine the animals. She drew a picture of Papa's description of the animal, he called okapi. "Its purple tongue was as long as my arm, from my elbow to my fingertips."

Folayan wondered aloud what it would be like to have an okapi as a pet, like her zebra. She laughed to herself now, remembering the day—when Papa returned from a journey with a surprise.

"Papa! Oh Papa, a baby zebra!" Folayan exclaimed.

Papa and her brothers grinned, then chuckled with each of her squeals and giggles at the colt's snort, or shiver, or stamp of foot.

"In Songhai," Papa said, "some hunters had brought this orphan back to their village where we stayed for a few days. They found him standing beside his mother. Apparently, she died birthing. In the few days that they had him, he became more trouble than they expected.

"None of their cows or goats would adopt him. None of them had time to care for and get milk from them for him. Their wives were grumbling that he would be more valuable in stew.

"So, your brothers put their heads together."

Kwamina explained, "Papa told them his sons had an idea that could solve their problem. We needed a milk goat and although we know zebras cannot be tamed, or ridden easily, and they can be mean; even so we knew someone who might get some use out of the zebra."

Kwesi added, "Papa paid second price. And the people were so surprised, they whispered, laughed out loud, and quickly took the money and handed over the nanny, kid, and zebra."

"Second price, Papa? You said you never pay above fifth price for anything," Folayan asked.

Papa shrugged with raised eyebrows and smiled. "My sons convinced me that my girl child would be happy to help him survive."

"The little fellow was weak." Kwamina rubbed the zebra's head, then left side, "Ribs showing. Big possibility that he would not live long. But we made a leather teat to feed him. Each day as the sun set he had become stronger, appetite bigger, and while we camped at night, we poured attention on him. Look at him. Dull eyes, now bright. He almost looks like he's smiling."

Folayan embraced the zebra's neck, "He is smiling. He is." She rested her forehead on his. "Thank you. Thank you for bringing him home to me."

In the weeks and months following his arrival, Folayan took special care of her zebra and he thrived. Each day he showed his love for her, calling her with his silly bark, as she approached the fence. He followed her as she went out to collect materials for her soaps, tooth sticks, charcoal, and so on. Each day he did something to make her laugh, and she could not help telling others about it.

For two years the zebra had brought her so much joy, and now that she was fourteen and her age mates bodies were changing much faster than hers, sometimes he was her only companion.. He went practically everywhere with her.

Over the next year, Adwoa tried to include her as much as possible.

Folayan's fifteenth afenhyia arrived the first week of August. Within that same moon, Adwoa invited her to spend the day sewing *kaba* blouses.

Stitching the straight lines of the simple front-to-back garments gave them an opportunity to talk about rite-of-passage activities.

Some of the age mates reached their time when *Nanabesia* would test them to see if they had learned everything from the women in their family about how to be a cook, hostess, wife, and mother.

"When it is your time, what are you going to do with Zebra?" Adwoa asked.

"Zebra?"

"Well, when you play Kings and Queens, you will have much greater responsibilities than a village chieftan, you will be like the Asantehene in Kumasi, King of the Ashanti, or Mansa Musa, Emperor of Mali. You will not only rule over villages, but also towns, and cities like Mopti, and Djenne. You will have thousands of people to protect. Whatever calling life may bring you, the game prepares you by giving you a bit of experience walking in the shoes of different people who do all kinds of work. They provide for the needs and make a village or even a kingdom prosper. Whatever position you are given, you must learn to solve many problems. Each player will either be a king or his queen, or be one who helps him. Everyone will also be a husband or wife and have to solve family problems. The game is fun, but also serious. You must concentrate.

"You will play the game at your own house, or outside with Serwaa or your Maame sitting nearby or other places in the village. So, if you are outside, Zebra will see you. Can you picture you and your partner in the middle of discussing a problem and Zebra calling out for you to come and play?"

Folayan giggled. "He might just do that. Especially since I have been painting gourds, and not been able to spend much time with him lately."

"Down at the market, more and more people have come by our space carrying your cloth designs, too," Adwoa said.

Folayan nodded. "Yes." She made seven or eight stitches in her blouse before hearing the rustle. A bird hopped on several branches, then flew up and out of the adiho. Folayan muttered, "I hope my life will keep on being happy like that bird."

Adwoa remained silent for a long while. "I hope so, too."

"Is my womanhood ever going to come?" Folayan whispered.

Adwoa put her blouse down and took Folayan by the shoulders, and turned her to face her directly. "It will come. It will come right on time. Then it will all begin for you. Most of our age mates have completed their festivities or are in the middle of them. But you still have the gift of looking forward to it."

Adwoa's mother entered the adiho. After greetings, she went into her room then came back out with sewing of her own. She sat down on the other side of her daughter and said, "My Maame says coming of age is the most special time of a girl child's life—crossing over into womanhood."

Folayan asked a few questions about the rituals. Adwoa's mother explained things Folayan didn't quite understand from what Serwaa and her own Maame had told her.

Nodding, Folayan could feel relief from some of her anxieties. She smiled, and turned to Adwoa. "How many celebration games and events have you played so far?"

Adwoa thought and counted on her fingers. "Four."

"Which one is your favorite?"

"So far, Kings and Queens. I learned a great amount during the six weeks."

She became animated in demonstrating how the village honored a girl who was ready to be presented. Her age mates who had already been presented as marriageable would join her in playing the game. Adwoa explained more about how they would be matched with an unmarried young man to deal with business, political, social, and household difficulties that leaders and husbands and wives faced in life.

Folayan anticipated the time when she would be allowed to play the game after her womanhood announcement, and completion of her forty days.

Meanwhile, she doubled over in laughter as Adwoa reenacted one of the problems she and her partner had experienced.

The humor was contagious. Adwoa's mother wiped a joyful tear and said, "My stomach hurts from so much laughter. How I wish there was a way to remember this day, you two as you are, before Adwoa begins her seclusion." She paused. "It is only three weeks away."

"Maame." Adwoa moved to her right side. "What is wrong?"

Folayan put the kaba down, scooted to Adwoa's mother's left side and rubbed her back.

"It is just that life will change. You will marry and go to live in another woman's house. Your husband will command your attention, and I will be lonely without you."

"Oh no, Maame, my brothers' wives are with you. And we will see each other at our farm, like we see my sisters every day."

Nodding, Folayan added, "And cook supper together."

Adwoa's mother put her arms around each girl. "Do you know what I wish? I wish there was a way to keep this moment forever, with both of your faces so full of joy, like you have been all your lives, growing up together."

They were interrupted when Adwoa's four brothers came into the house, all tall, all married, except Kofi, the youngest one. In the age group above Akonor, Kofi was five years older than Adwoa.

After greetings, Folayan grabbed up her kaba and became intent on sewing. Ever since she was nine, when Kofi saved her from being eaten alive by the ants in the ofram tree, she had watched for him whenever groups came together.

He was always kind to her—to everybody. But today something different stirred inside her, a strange swirling, and she could not look at him like she wanted. She told herself to stop it, certain that to him, she was only his little sister's best friend.

When she went home, Folayan talked with her mother and aunt about what Adwoa's mother had said. Both women were silent for longer than was comfortable for Folayan, so she added, "I am trying to think of something to help her feel better."

"You can paint a picture of you and Adwoa for her," Maame suggested.

"Oh, Maame, I can. Yes, I can do that." She hugged her and ran to get her tools.

Serwaa followed her and stood in the doorway of the sleeping room they shared. It was a moment before she spoke. "Make a picture for your Maame, too."

Folayan blinked. "What? Oh, yes, Serwaa. I will."

⊙┅┅┅┅⚷

The harmattan season, stronger than Folayan ever remembered, made that November worrisome. Papa told them to be thankful that they lived near the sea and not up in the north, where fierce winds shifted Saharan sands into everything.

The huge orange sun hung low at evening when they were bathing at the Etsi lagoon.

Maame asked, "Folayan, what are you doing?"

She looked up. "I am trying to see my face, but the water is too rough."

"Do you not know what you look like by now?"

"I never paid such close attention. For this painting, I want to be as truthful for myself as I am with Adwoa."

After the womenfolk were back in the house and mealtime was over, Folayan sat on her pallet trying to paint the portrait. Adwoa's image was all finished. Except for a lined oval above her neck, Folayan remained headless.

Maame came in and handed her an elegant golden comb shaped like the sankofa bird—with its long neck it reached back to take into its mouth an egg. "Maybe you can see yourself in the mirror here."

Folayan looked into the mirror set inside the wide golden breast, and saw her face. "Oh, thank you." She smiled at her image.

Maame patted her on the shoulder and went back to her room.

As her fingertips polished the comb, Folayan mused the meaning of the sankofa—symbol. Papa said it was not an adinkra.

"*Go back and fetch it.*"

It—the egg. Did it mean never forget your heritage, or protect your children? Maybe it meant teach your children who they are. How would she do that for her children? When would she have her first child?

The mighty wind distracted her. She got up to put an etam around her shoulders. The long etam, the third part of her garment, draped three times around her, covering all but one shoulder of her kaba blouse and much of her waist-to-ankle wrapped skirt. As the winds buffeted the house outside, Folayan sat down and examined her balanced features, wondering how the frustration did not show in her expression.

She noted that Adwoa's face was a little squarer, her own was longer. Her dark brown eyes were wide and thick-lashed, cheekbones high, nose narrow and straight. Her bottom lip was much fuller than her top, both of which had a slight pink tint, while her teeth were even and white. She thought herself fortunate that her skin was unblemished, unlike some of her age mates. Still, Adwoa said that was a sign of changing from girl to a woman.

Folayan sighed. She was changing too, wasn't she? She looked a little older. But she had not yet received her womanhood. All the other girls in her group had. They were looking at young men who were marriageable.

"What if someone gets Kofi," she moaned, "before I come of age?" Hoping no one heard her, she pressed the cool metal comb against her warm cheek. Sometimes she embarrassed herself with the constant thoughts she now carried for him.

Eight more moons grew, and waned before Folayan completed her fifteenth afenhyia, before she earned reward from her wistful watching.

She discovered it one afternoon when they returned from the farm. She showed the spot to her Maame, who then took her to the house that women in their family group go to during their time of impurity. Maame showed her how to prepare and fit the *amoasa* cloth and told her how to care for herself.

The next morning Maame boiled an egg and mixed it with mashed yam and gave it to Folayan.

"This means you are now of age."

While Folayan chewed, she thought about "go back and fetch it." Her body had grown up. It was now her responsibility to—sankofa. She studied Maame's smile that crinkled the corners of her eyes. Then Folayan saw some feelings hiding in them.

"Is something wrong, Maame?"

"No." She looked away. "Well, it is just that I wish Papa was here." She caressed Folayan's face, lingering at her chin. "I will go get your food and paints. In a few days when Papa comes back, we will announce your accomplishment to the village."

Folayan walked around, discovering the little house. Yet lingering thoughts whispered that Maame had not told all of her concern. Drum talk had summoned Papa and several of the council to a neighboring village. Why would they call them away like that for already nine days? They had told them to come with *asafo* flags. Why would they want each community signified? Asafo were to fight and protect the villages. She shrugged. Maybe they were planning some new contest or games. Whatever it was, it could not outshine her news.

The next day Serwaa came and explained what was happening to Folayan's body and how she must carry herself now. She told her how a child is conceived.

Then she said, "A woman is very important. Our people hold women in great respect. We have power to keep the clan alive and to determine kings."

"Kings?" Folayan responded her mind still envisioning Serwaa's explanation of a man and a woman and childbirth.

"Do you know what it means to be a king maker?"

"A woman in the king's household." Watching Serwaa shake her head, Folayan's eyebrows knitted and she stopped talking.

"You know that we have possessions and lands, such as our farm, that are passed down through mothers to daughters and nieces, while fathers pass their parts down to their sons and nephews."

Folayan nodded.

Serwaa continued, "A woman is protected by her father, brothers, and uncles … but …" Serwaa held up her pointing finger, "… men cannot make kings. An Akan king must come down through the line of the queen mother and she sits on the throne with him."

"It could be his sister, too, can it not?"

"Yes, it can."

"But Serwaa, why does he need her when he also has a linguist to speak his words?"

As soon as the words left her mouth, Folayan remembered how a chieftain or a king needed to be kept safe from strangers or villagers who might wish evil on him. Serwaa explained, "It is because as he sits on the throne, his sister will sit by his side when he meets with his council or petitioners or visitors from other places. She listens and also must be a shrewd thinker. The king needs someone he trusts more than anyone else, someone who can be his eyes and look at the people, because he cannot."

"I know it is because they are plotting to harm or cast a spell on him, but has it always been a law that forbids us to look directly at the king or chief?"

"All I know is it has been from a time long ago, but his sister's task is to listen, watch their eyes, and see if they try to look at him."

"I know another reason, Serwaa. She is not afraid of him."

They laughed. Serwaa added, "And she has his best fortune in her mind, where other men, even brothers, might be advising him for their own gain."

"I could do that for my brothers." Folayan nodded with surety.

Serwaa said, "Yes, you could, although becoming a king maker is not likely to be your lot, but one of your age mates may have that chance."

Folayan screwed up her nose. "Afua?"

Serwaa raised her eyebrow.

Folayan grunted, "Her son would be a frightful king."

They sat with their own thoughts for a while. Then Serwaa cupped Folayan's lithe, soft hands, into hers, knotted with life, and commanded in a whisper, "There is something truly frightful that you must know."

Serwaa's back straightened and her tone changed. "It is taboo to find yourself with a child growing inside you before you have been publicly proclaimed a woman and prepared for marriage."

Folayan's breath caught and turned away from the stabbing words. *Why did she speak so harshly?*

Serwaa waited. Silently, Folayan rehearsed her sentence several times. "It is taboo …"

Finally, Serwaa took her chin and calmly guided it until they were face to face. She looked directly into Folayan's eyes. "Until your family and friends have come together for your *ayefro* to walk with you in the wedding procession, and bless the beginning of your new life with your husband."

In that women's house, during the cleansing ritual, Folayan had several days to ponder the import and consequence of Serwaa's words, especially the warnings. The images repeated in her head: Serwaa's grim stare at her, making sure she understood every point about the last girl many years ago who was "banned from the village, sent into a hut in the forest with lurking wild animals, all alone until many months after the baby's birth, with no visitors."

Serwaa shook her head, her voice low and harsh. "No visitors except her Maame in shame bringing her food. To that, add all the scorn the mother suffered as the girl stood in front of the chief and villagers pleading to be returned into society." Folayan sat with eyes wide until the dryness forced her to blink.

Though always full of questions, Folayan could not make her mouth speak one. As if Serwaa read Folayan's thought, she blurted, "And the boy! Chh! Although he could have been banned to be out there with her, he fled to another village. Yes, left her to be out there … all … by … herself."

"Why, Serwaa?" Folayan exclaimed. "Why was he not command-ed to be with the girl?"

Serwaa stared hard at her. "The only truth—is that her growing belly will show everyone *she* is the mother."

Folayan shuddered each time the thoughts assailed her. She sat on her pallet, massaging her temples. Her age mates had not spoken of this. Could it be so? Not even her Papa would come rescue her?

Folayan looked up to the sky above the adiho atrium rim. Tree tops quivered in the breeze as leaves gripped tight, proving their strength. She lamented that her testing time had not even come to pass yet. Not to begin until Papa had been told about the arrival of her womanhood. How long would it be before she would be taken to the clan leader's house? Oh, how glad she'd be at the end of her forty-day examination.

*Maybe … maybe then I could hurry up and marry Kofi. Kofi?*

She hoped.

The next evening she returned to the family house. After her brothers had been served their meals in the adiho, Folayan studied the faces of each of the women sitting together in the kitchen area. Six women. *Seven now*, she thought. *Almost.*

"It is a good thing when a girl is obedient to her mother," said Serwaa. She reached for more kenkey.

"Yes," said Maame. "And it is good for her to be industrious."

"Very good," said Emissah's wife. "One who helps the village with her talents."

"One who cleans her house spotless every morning before going to the gardens," said Kwamina's wife.

"One who controls her temper?" Maame's words jabbed Folayan's heart.

They continued back and forth with their wisdoms while Folayan listened.

"Whoever finds a woman like that has been blessed by Onyankopon. Do you not think so, Folayan?"

"Yes, Serwaa."

"Are you ready to be a wife like that?"

"Uh, well … yes, Serwaa?"

All the women giggled.

"Shall your Maame watch for a flower to be plucked from my garden?"

Folayan blushed. She had finally come to the stage of bloom. How soon would someone's female elder come asking questions about her. "Yes, Serwaa." She held her head down, her heart tight with excitement. Since the ants, Serwaa had teased her about Kofi. Folayan wanted him to know she was now a woman. Her smile remained through the evening.

Two days later, as soon as Papa entered the house, Maame took him into their room. When they came out, he was wearing a smile that matched Folayan's.

"Maame has told me the good news. I have been saving and preparing for this time for many afenhyias. You shall have a most wonderful celebration."

"Papa, we must take smaller steps," said Maame. "There are several girls who have had their celebrations, and no one has come knocking yet."

"But you are not talking about my Ama Kwantunyi Folayan."

Maame just smiled to herself as she hurried through the kitchen room, and out the back door. She returned with a hoe and a thick stick. She stopped to select a painted calabash from a kitchen shelf. With the three items in hand, she proceeded out the front door.

Family members followed her outside to the front of the house. She filled the smaller jug with water from one of the large rainwater calabashes sitting outside near the door.

Maame poured a libation into the earth honoring the ancestors and with the stick banged on the metal of the hoe alerting the village. People began to emerge from their homes with smiles, nods, and clapping in joyful acknowledgment with Maame that this house had received the blessing of a girl child come of age.

# CHAPTER 12

# Zebra

*She thought of it being like the rituals that kept the village strong,
each one doing their part. Maintaining the togetherness of marriage.
Showing that men and women need each other. Children needing parents.
Women teaching girls how to spin the cords that flow
throughout the home. Men teaching boys how to weave
and bind the house and family together.*

*Trying to be brave, to show that she, too, was a strong Kwantunyi, she willed
her legs to stand. The tears still streamed.*

**October 1794, Kormantse Village**

As people approached Maame with congratulations, Papa turned
to Folayan. "I have much work to do before our next journey.
We will leave before the harmattan season."

He took her by the elbow and guided her back into the house.
They sat beside each other at the table in the far corner of the adiho.

"I have been planning for this time since the week of your birth." He
reminisced about her sayings, antics, and accomplishments, growing
up rite by rite.

She smiled, watching his moonlit face as he laughed about this and that, until a sentence muffled in his throat.

"Papa?" She spoke softly and rubbed his forearm.

"Now, you have come of age," he said.

He looked up at the stars for a long while, then sighed. "How suddenly you have come of age."

She rested her head on his shoulder, gazing with him at the tiny lights in the black expanse. "Look Papa," she pointed to the sky, "the Drinking Gourd."

Papa chuckled. "You had just passed four afenhyia when I told the story about the gourd and how our ancestors used it and other stars to help us in our journeys. Your brothers contested who found it first that night.

"You kept saying, 'Show me. Papa. Show me, too!' I lifted you up and described it several times, until you cried out, 'I see it!' Your brothers teased you. You asked me to put you down and drew the gourd on the floor."

"I was right, was I not? Its bowl looks like a box with three stars in its long handle, does it not?"

"Yes. Your wobbly drawing proved you found it in the sky."

Folayan laughed.

"I want to acquire enough provisions to hold your celebration and marriage soon after the harvest."

Marriage! Folayan counted to the harvest—nine moons from now—and after that would come her sixteenth afenhyia.

Papa lit a torch on the wall.

A shadowy thought emerged, flickering like the light.

Would her new life be just as she imagined? Hoped?

Her hand closed over her mouth. *Has Papa already picked a husband for me? What if he is not thinking of Kofi? Will another girl cast a net and catch Kofi's interest before he notices me?*

Papa peered at her. "Where did the smile in your eyes go?"

"It is a short ... and long time."

"Yes, and much to do."

She watched Papa pace the adiho, making plans, asking her opinion, or agreement. Her own thoughts wedged between so that she did not respond when he asked another question.

"Folayan? Did you hear me?"

His voice was distant. He stood silhouetted in his sleeping room doorway. *How long?*

She retraced his last words, and smiled. "Yes, Papa. A chest the same size as your box will be very special."

Papa beckoned her. Once she stepped in the room, he pointed at his box. "It has secret parts. I want to make sure I do not leave even one out."

As he pulled out the contents—her gifts from before she was born till now—she sorted them by varied sizes on a two-foot space of the wall.

Each time she'd taken out the items before this, she always noticed something different. Today she was grateful that they were not only women's housewares, and cooking utensils, but also tools—some of them that a man would use. And of course, the pretty fabrics, as well as the woven straw bag half-filled with jewels.

When the box was empty, Papa began to examine its compartments and noted its exact size using his elbow to fingertips as a measuring rod. Maneuvering himself into a narrow space, he bumped the wall. Folayan lurched to rescue the toppling stack of cloths. She shook out and refolded them; two warm goat hair covers, a woven silk kente, a smooth hide ....

"Ooh!" Folayan jerked her hand away, then hurried back into the adiho to inhale long draughts of the fresh air. She stayed until sad memories mixed with those bringing smiles sifted through her mind and she returned to look at it again ... for the first time since she begged Papa—not to leave him.

It happened about two moons before Maame announced the arrival of Folayan's womanhood. She had joined her age mates at Yaa's house.

The women and girls had picked the cotton from their farms. And now the girls were nearly finished spinning the raw cotton into yarn, to be woven into cloth by the men. Folayan admired the men's artistry. The beautiful cloths they designed, she would never be able to do. Only men were allowed to weave.

But, as she pulled and combed the cotton from the boll, twisting it thin and long, winding it into a round of thread, she thought of it being like the rituals that kept the village strong, each one doing their part. Maintaining the togetherness of marriage. Showing that men and women need each other. Children needing parents. Women teaching girls how to spin the cords that flow throughout the home. Men teaching boys how to weave and bind the house and family together.

"Folayan!"

She caught the round of yarn slipping off her lap.

"Zebra thinks you have been gone too long, he has come to fetch you," Yaa said, pointing at him trotting toward them. "I wonder how many houses he has visited looking for you." The girls' giggles swelled.

Folayan peered around them for her pet. Sure enough, the familiar high-pitched warbled bark grew louder each moment. She and the other girls went out to meet him.

Zebra was so happy to see Folayan. She laughed and gave him a good long neck rub.

Afua stood back, unusually quiet, while different ones told their stories about Zebra.

Shaking her head, Abena said, "He jumps the fence whenever he wants, no matter how high they put the rails."

Esi agreed. "And he likes to walk down the road talking to people."

"Do you mean barking?" Abena asked.

"Well, I can tell a difference in his voice when he is playing or is anxious." Esi said.

With her back to Folayan, Afua told them, "Animals are for work, not for play. A zebra is not a pet for a girl. And by the way, I still believe her father thinks he has six boys."

Folayan's mouth pinched. She stared at Afua.

The other girls were silent for a moment. One rolled her eyes, another sighed.

Ekua pretended Afua had not spoken at all. "I have seen Zebra at Sunday market, here on the hilltop, trying to sweet-talk the merchants. Most of the time they give him a morsel or chase him because he has snatched one."

"Yes, he is quite friendly," Yaa said, "but one thing I know, Folayan is the only person he will let ride him."

Afua said, "I want to ride him."

"That is not a good idea." Folayan said.

"Are you telling me I cannot ride him? He is just a donkey with stripes," she said sharply. "I can ride him."

Folayan said, "Zebras are not as strong as donkeys."

"You ride him." Afua snapped. "Why can I not?"

"He gets nervous, and he trusts me to be careful with him. I do not want him to get hurt."

Afua pushed Folayan aside and tried to put her arm around Zebra's neck. He reared up. Afua slipped and fell.

Zebra barked shrilly and ran, back-kicking, toward the rear of the house. He stood watching, with ears twitching in opposite directions back and forth.

"I will ride him if I want to," Afua grumbled while Fatima helped her up. After brushing off her garment, Afua turned to glare at Zebra.

He stamped one foot and stepped backward twice.

Afua started toward him again.

Folayan demanded, "I said NO."

The other girls warned Afua.

"Girls. Calm down." Yaa shushed them. "I think its time for us to enjoy some hibiscus tea. We will go back inside."

After tea, they all packed up and left. Three went to the south road, four to the north. Straight ahead to the west, Folayan walked beside Zebra until her last two age mates turned at the ofram tree.

When they were out of sight, she mounted Zebra and rode him the rest of the way home.

The next two days, the girls finished the spinning. Afua did not join them—to Folayan's relief.

On the third day, Folayan decided to go herding with her brother Akonor. As the sun began to set, the donkeys and Zebra started to trot home. Sheep and goats milled nearby, but their leader—where was he?

It was nearly dark when Akonor returned with the he-goat. "I found him tied to a tree."

"Tied?"

"In the valley near Abandze … I barely heard his bell."

"He was not bleating?"

Akonor pointed; the goat rasped a hoarse cough. Folayan's stomach shuddered.

Akonor's jaw clenched. His eyes looked worried. Folayan gazed at him. They ran to the corral. The he-goat's bell tinkled behind them with goats and sheep following. In the dark, they counted the animals. All of them were there except Zebra.

"Papa! Papa!" Akonor and Folayan rushed into the house. They poured out the day to their father. Folayan burst into tears, as Akonor wiped his away.

Their father gave no reproof, but he called all his sons, then paired them: Kwamina with Kwesi, Emissah with Ekow, Akonor with Papa.

She watched her brothers ready their weapons. Fanti warriors. By now, Zebra would have come back on his own. No one said, yet all knew. Was their enemy in or outside the village gates? Papa said, "We will go out now to every home in the village. If we do not find Zebra, then in the morning, by twos we go, one searching for Zebra, the other guarding against predators who will be hunting for food. We will depart at hwaani hwaani light. Be wary. Remember sunset and sunrise, the two most dangerous times of the day. The predators are hungry. Be vigilant my sons. Do not become prey.

"Folayan, you stay and keep checking on the animals in the corral, in case your charge comes home." Papa said.

Folayan winced. *My charge. My charge? I was careless! How? How can I ask him to please take me, too?*

Several times during the night, Folayan slipped outside to the animal enclosure, whispering, "Zebra?" Then louder: "Zebra?" She felt her way to the donkeys. They snored soundly.

In the black sky, stars of the Drinking Gourd shone bright. *Does Zebra need water, is he somewhere out there parched for water? Is he looking for me? Did he think I was following right behind him as he came home with the donkeys? Did he wander so far he cannot find his way back? He has never been out alone at night. Is he afraid?*

She returned to the house, dressed for hunting, went back into the adiho, and waited.

Soon she heard stirring. The men came out and rehearsed their plan, then moved to the door. Folayan leapt from the shadows, and held onto her father. "Papa, let me go, too. He will come more easily to me. Please, please!"

Papa was speechless, shaking his head.

She waited to hear his words, "Absolutely, not!" but she held tight with her head in his chest.

Instead she heard Akonor speaking, "Papa? May I speak for my sister? I ... I have no words to prove the pain I feel. I just know I must find him, now. We ... I .... We must do our part to find him ... and she ... is Kwantunyi, too."

Papa looked at his sons. They all nodded agreement with Akonor. Papa said, "Stay by my side."

"Yes, Papa," she whispered.

At the gate, a gathering of men waited to help them search. They all spread out surrounding the hilltop, then worked their way down.

Beyond the grazing meadow, one hour of daylight from their village, Papa stopped, then stepped in front of Folayan. Papa bird-called the signal while he and Akonor shielded her from the sight.

Unable to see around them, she looked up. Three vultures circled in the sky. Not far away, her brothers sped to the spot birds marked and on to examine Zebra laying in the midst of trees.

Papa held her back.

Kwamina returned. "Lions! We must go. They will be back. They are not far away."

Folayan ripped around Papa and raced to the site. Her brothers stood or crouched around Zebra. His hide had been sliced straighter than the sharpest knife could cut, she could not tell whether from claw or tooth. Half of his ribs, belly, and hind leg had been eaten.

Her chest hurt so hard, she barely breathed.

"Daughter." The voice was tender behind her.

She whirled around to plead. "Can we take him back? He must return home. You made me promise that if I ever got lost, I must return home.

"You taught me to always leave markers, follow the stars, to know which direction I came from, and how to get back. He did not know, Papa. He did not know. I must take him, Papa!" She bowed her head. Her voice waned to a whisper, "... And bury him safe at home with me."

"No, Daughter. The lions have claimed him. They will follow his scent. Too close to our village."

She stared at her Zebra, tears running. Trying to be brave, to show that she, too, was a strong Kwantunyi, she willed her legs to stand. The tears still streamed.

Finally, she asked, "Then at least cut some of his hide that I may have it."

Papa nodded, and Ekow and Kwesi quickly cut away a section from the grassy side. Kwamina embraced her until she finally relaxed into his chest.

On the way home, the brothers watched her, and when she appeared to be losing heart, they came alongside, they held her up, holding tight. Encouraging her, reminding her how proud they were of the way she cared for the little orphaned zebra and how she'd proven she would be a very good mother some day. And how she would always carry good memories in her heart of this friend, and of the many ways Zebra had brought comfort and joy into all of their lives.

⌖——⚷

Now, Folayan stood in the adiho, deciding to go back to help Papa with his box. He looked up as she re-entered the room.

Folayan had not seen the hide since that day they brought it back. She sat down beside the stack of cloths, lifting each one until she spied again the thin one peeking between two thick quilts.

She swallowed and took out the black-and-white hide. She unfolded it, placed it on her lap, and began to smooth her fingers over it. Memories floated in her mind.

She felt grateful that she was able to go with her brothers to find him. It helped whenever she thought about her special friend who came to her—newborn, still with tan and white stripes, long-legged and motherless.

She recalled the speculations her neighbors and friends put forth as possible answers to the puzzle. Though the family talked about it, they had no definite answer as to how Zebra ended up an hour away.

Nevertheless, Folayan believed that sooner or later, the truth would peek and reveal itself. Until then, there were suspicions, but no confession, no answer. The village walls had not spoken.

# CHAPTER 13

*Salt*

> *Many eyes watched everything at the market,*
> *and since he took half-year merchant journeys,*
> *his wife was especially watched, and had never*
> *given any cause of comment, but for honor.*

*Many of our Kwantunyis had slaves carry the bundles. But we stopped doing*
*that eleven generations ago. We pay each carrier with cowry shells now.*

**October 1794, Kormantse Village**

aame came into the room. "What are you doing?"

Papa explained, "I want to look for a box just like this one for Folayan and I am studying some of its special parts. See the little box built in this back corner?" He lifted the lid.

He frowned, "What is this?" Papa held up a thumb-sized knotted cloth with a cord on it.

"Uh, it is mine," Maame stammered. "I mean, it is Folayan's." Her voice went higher.

Folayan's head jerked from her mother to the pouch. She had never seen it before.

"I did not give her this," he said. "This box only has my things and gifts *I* brought for Folayan."

Maame said, "I know. I … but you … it is …" Folayan saw her mother's eyes flit, searching. "It is just a bauble from—from someone."

"A bauble? A bauble?" Papa said. "Who gave it to you? Why is it in MY box?"

"It is a story from long ago." Maame glanced at Folayan. "It was a few days before she was born. I was at the market selling goods. And the preacher, he …"

Papa interrupted, "The preacher?"

"Yes, the preacher from the fort." She looked up at him, his eyebrow raised in question. "He bought some things and … he said it must be near time for my baby to be born and did I want a girl child. I said I prayed every day for a girl child."

Folayan smiled.

"He paid me for the food with this … this pebble. I kept it three days until my pains started. It troubled me so I took it out to our spot by the hillside." Maame swallowed hard.

Folayan felt her own forehead wrinkle and her mouth turn down to match Papa's grimace.

"Just as I was about to throw it into the sea, I heard screams coming from the fort." Maame looked to the left, leaning as if she heard the cries again.

Folayan watched her father's face change from annoyance to disbelief to anger.

He glared at his wife and mumbled, "So, they were right."

*Who?* Folayan bent forward, trying to understand him.

"Kwabena." Maame stepped in front of him, her hands clasped his forearms, her voice tense. "I asked you! I asked you that day to take us away from this place, with all the slave-dealing everywhere we turn. I begged you. Do you not remember?"

Papa's mouth formed to say *No*, but he did not say it. He stomped to the door. "I do not want it in my box!" He thrust the pouch at Folayan, and growled, "I do not know what happens when I am away—working!" Maame wrung her hands. Her brows knit together. Serwaa pulled the door curtain back. She looked at her brother and his wife. Papa gave her a *Do Not Speak* scowl. She turned on her heel and left. The curtain swayed back into place.

Folayan's stomach trembled. What was happening? She had never seen her Papa like this? *Who was right? About what?*

Not looking at Maame, Papa muttered, "And you talk like him more and more. About slaves. The men have mentioned it several times over the years. Now, they say their wives have been troubling them and that you are the one who stirs them up. I wonder … has he ever been up the hill? Has he been in this house?"

"No! No, Kwabena. What are you saying?"

He stared at her. "Are you telling me the truth?"

"Kwabena!"

Papa stormed out of the house.

Folayan's heart matched Maame's wrenching face.

The gold stone cast a shadow over the joy that should have been.

Papa returned later that day and talked to Maame in their room for a long time. After that, he did not appear to be angry, but laughter left the house.

Folayan worried. Papa had gotten upset sometimes, and Maame had been upset with him, one time or other. But this was very different. Maame hardly talked to anyone. The pall lingered. Folayan worried if her Papa might decide to bring the joy back by taking another wife.

Folayan's fears began to calm when she overheard Serwaa telling Maame that Papa had spoken to the elders, not his age mates. Those old men had helped him see that he was wrong. There were witnesses who had seen the preacher give Akosua the gold pebble. No kwesi broni had ever been up to the top of the mountain. Many eyes watched everything at the market, and since he took half-year merchant journeys, his wife was especially watched, and had never given any cause of comment, but for honor.

Still it was many weeks before the smile crept back to his eyes. Folayan watched her brothers with their wives. She noticed that they, too, had times of consternation with each other. Was it because of the strain between her parents? Or had it always been, and she never noticed because the joy was too great for disagreement to remain?

Had the gold pebble brought disharmony to their house? But she disdained that thought, for it had been in the house for nearly sixteen years.

Papa was not home much, spending most of his time at the sea. September through November, he let his sons focus on fishing, while he garnered salt. "How do you do it, Papa?" Folayan asked, after meals one evening when he was tallying his store.

"With much patience." He demonstrated. "First, I build my dikes. I let the seawater come in. Next, it dries in the sun. That leaves a wide flat of salt. Then, I break it into chunks, like this one."

He was good at it, and also at bartering with travelers from the interior who paid well for a supply. Enough one-color cloth to make a dress could be traded for two large rocks; a fabric with several colors of dye, four rocks; and fifteen rocks of salt would buy a trunk the size of Papa's, but plain, not carved or gold decorated.

Then one day, Papa told Folayan that he had searched the nearby villages to buy her a box like his, but found nothing that matched what he imagined. The day approached for him to go on his merchant expedition with Kwamina and Kwesi. Papa purposed to find a box for Folayan—the one in his mind, or one even more beautiful.

As always, Papa had hired porters for the loads. Most often, they balanced the parcels on their heads with perfect posture. He paid them to transport goods made by his family, as well as items he purchased from others in Kormantse and nearby villages.

His carriers appreciated Papa. Folayan had heard a number of them say he took them to interesting places they never would have known about. Some had travelled with him many times, others only once or twice. Five were new this year.

Some carried food, tools, and supplies needed by the caravan when they stopped for the night or had to wait several days until bad weather subsided.

Akonor asked, "How long will you be gone this time, Papa?"

"The journey should take about two moons to get to the furthest stop. That includes five to seven weeks walking, then narrow boats will ferry us, the horses and the donkeys across the River Niger, then we continue on land to Djenne, or Walata, or Mopti. Further up in Timbuktu, we should remain about eight to twelve weeks selling and acquiring goods as other traders come in with different products."

"Lots of traders? Every day?"

"Not every day, Folayan. Sometimes a week may pass before a new one arrives. After all our bundles have been refilled, I allow another day for the carriers to barter one more time with their own goods if a new trader comes in, and after that we start our journey home."

"Papa, are you going the same places as last year?" Akonor asked.

"Last year we went south to the big market in Benin; this year, north to Timbuktu."

Folayan glanced at the many bundles lined up. The three large bundles at Papa's feet each held Folayan's wares: painted cloths, dishes, and calabashes. Would they be traded along the way? Would any reach the fabled city? If so, where in the world would they end up? In a home in Mali? Out east to India? Or north across the Great Sea?

Just after all the bundles were matched with carriers, Papa asked, "Son Number Six, where are your bags?"

Folayan always blinked when he said that. Then she remembered her baby brother number four, Ekow's twin was born dead.

"Sir?" Wide-eyed, Akonor wrinkled his brow. "I have none."

"Well, perhaps you better ask your brothers to help you get one together if you are going on this trip with us."

Akonor stuttered, "Kwa-Kwamina?" Then he looked back and forth at all four brothers, searching for help.

Kwamina told him to follow. After a few minutes, they returned from the house with Akonor's full pack that had already been prepared for him and hidden in his parent's room. Four horses were brought around and draped in decorated bridles and beautifully ornamented back coverings that hung to their knees.

Akonor was fully dressed in new traveling ntama, wrapped under his arms, around his body below his knees, and the end draped over one shoulder down to his waist. His rite-of-passage knife was sheathed in a leather pouch secured at his side.

For the first time Folayan realized, the top of Akonor's head came to Kwamina's ear and his jaw now had a manly cut to it. She threw her arms around him. He did not protest. "I am very proud of you, Akonor. How do you feel?"

He whispered, "I am so happy, I cannot even spit."

He looked as dignified as his brothers and Papa. Folayan followed the men to the side of the hill and perched on the family spot, watching them leave.

Many years ago, Folayan saw a caravan of camels belonging to traders doing business at El Mina. They had slaves, but the camels carried many of the wares. She'd asked, "Papa, would it not be easier with camels? Why do you not have them?"

"Our ancient Kwantunyis used camels on the Sahara and Sahel, but there were no camels down here in Akan land where our people migrated. We found that it can be more profitable for us without them."

"But they can carry much more than men or horses or donkeys," Folayan said.

Papa explained more. "Camels in a caravan were led by a man on camel back or who walked and pulled the first camel by a nose hook only as fast as the lead person walked. It is true that the camel could carry greater loads, and hold water, but they had to be cared for, fed mostly with food that had to be carried along, too, and the camels had to be watched so they did not eat any poisonous plants."

Her mouth pursed in disagreement, but Papa said, "For our family depending on the trade route, it became easer to use the donkeys, several horses, and we chose to hire men because it gives more of them money to provide for their families."

That's when she asked him about slaves, but she was only seven years old then, not realizing Fatima's condition. Now Afua reminded them often that Fatima was not like the other age mates.

Papa had patiently answered her. "Yes, Folayan, many of our Kwantunyis had slaves carry the bundles. But we stopped doing that eleven generations ago. We pay each carrier with cowry shells now. And we allow them to put an additional bag of their own goods on top, if they wish. They can sell it and come back with an additional profit."

Folayan thought then that was a good plan, and her pride swelled, because her Papa was a good man.

A horse whinnied. Others hooved the ground. Folayan whispered, "He was and is still a good, kind man." Folayan surveyed the carriers, smiling with anticipation. Excitement filled the air. She watched the families give farewells and hugs to their men.

The last three men lifted her bundles to their heads and took their places in line.

Folayan felt someone close behind her; she glanced back.

"Maame?" Her mother usually stood as the first person in their family's cluster, but not today. She held onto Folayan's elbow.

Folayan searched for her father. *Is he going to leave without saying goodbye to Maame?*

Then she saw him coming toward them. He scanned his family, then in three giant strides he was next to Folayan—wrapping Maame in his arms.

# CHAPTER 14

# Waiting ...
# to Remember

*Soon she would be dressed in special garments during her
six-week seclusion time, and the best ones she'd wear for the
last seven days, her Coming of Age week, when she'd sit
in the chief's compound near Nanabesia, like a princess,
and the entire village would come to celebrate
that she had become a woman.*

*Ama Kwantunyi Folayan, we wish to hear you recite your traveler ancestors.*

**October 1794, Kormantse Village**

Folayan's heart sang again and again, as she pondered her mother's
joy in Papa's long embrace, not letting her go—twice—before
the caravan descended the hill, crossed the valley, and disappeared
from her view.

The next morning, the family continued their daily chores and
preparation for Folayan's celebration. From their farm, Folayan and
Maame selected gourds of different sizes. Wide-bottomed ones they cut

almost flat for dishes. Smaller and taller round ones were for drinking dippers, vases and bowls, and large calabashes for carrying water from the lagoon, down betweeen Abandze and the akura. After she'd scooped, cleaned, and dried them to a thin woody texture, Folayan painted the gourds. Someone also said she needed clay pottery.

All the women in the house helped Folayan sew. In a large basket next to Papa's trunk went household items she would use when she married and moved away.

Folayan pictured Akonor in his travel clothing. Soon she would be dressed in special garments during her six-week seclusion time, and the best ones she'd wear for the last seven days, her Coming of Age week, when she'd sit in the chief's compound near Nanabesia, like a princess, and the entire village would come to celebrate that she had become a woman.

Whereas the days usually slithered like the giant snail when Papa was away, these skittered like the redheaded lizard from the last of October to … February, March, April.

The men returned, laden with bigger bundles than when they left. Papa's reputation as a shrewd trader was always confirmed at each return.

Standing at the hilltop, Folayan spied them. She ran back to the house and brought the family to the edge, with everybody laughing, talking in anticipation.

Folayan saw Kwamina in the lead, halfway up the hill now. Kwesi was in the middle. Papa and Akonor were alongside the line near the end. She cupped her hands over her forehead scanning the carriers. They drew closer, yet nothing trailed behind on a travois.

Nothing resembled a box like Papa's.

As his custom was, on the first night of his return home, after bathing, and eating a hearty meal in the adiho, Papa settled onto his carved, curve-topped *egua,* and beckoned the family to relax in a half circle around him.

"Please Papa! Tell us stories," the children coaxed.

After he filled the evening with fascinating Kwantunyi travel adventures, he yawned and made as if to stand.

"Papa! Do you not have any gifts for us?" The children never forgot their part in the game. Papa blinked. "Ehh, what did I hear?"

"Gifts, Papa! Do you have any for us?"

"Well, now that you mention it, I believe I do. Perhaps my sons will bring them in here." The three who travelled with him went to his room and brought out the bundles filled with presents for all.

On the second day back from journey, Papa usually remained in the house resting. Folayan's brothers always went about to see their friends. The women did a portion of their tasks, then spent a few hours of the day gleaning details about women's activities Papa had observed in the villages he visited. Since he was a storyteller, he paid attention to objects and events that most men would not see, or retell.

The second day was the best of all for Folayan. Her Papa was home. Her nightmares ceased. She hardly left his side. Even when he snoozed, she found some quiet task to do until he wakened.

But this morning it was still dim when she awoke, and looked over to greet her aunt. To her surprise, her aunt's bed was empty. She had smoothed her covers up, and was gone.

The adiho was empty as well.

"Maame?" No answer. Folayan went out the back door to the bukyia. Coals burned still. "Have they left already to the gardens—without me? My brothers' wives, too?" She looked up at the sun's position.

She rubbed her eyes. She had not overslept. "What is going on?" she mumbled.

Folayan went back into the house. Everything was swept and clean as they left it last night. She decided to polish the floor.

In the kitchen, she got some ntwuma dust and a sponge and dropped to her knees, sprinkled some dust and began to rub it in circles into the hard-packed earthen floor. An hour later, she stood to admire the soft sheen over the entire surface.

As the front door opened, she spun around. "Serwaa! Where is everybody? You went out so early."

"I cannot be sleeping away the day. They went down—"

"Aah!" Folayan clapped her hand to her forehead, "To the lagoon to get clay for pottery making!"

"Yes." Serwaa held up one finger, "I too, must must remember to remember. Your Papa left something for you in the corner by the window in their room. Go fetch it. Your Papa wants you to stay here and practice all morning."

Folayan went to her parents' room and brought the large leather bag into the adiho. Serwaa said, "Your Papa wants you to tell him what you remember about the things in it. Tell him a story about them."

While Folayan loosened the long cord around the bundle, she felt her aunt watching her. Folayan paused. "Serwaa? Why does he want me to—?"

"Oh! Aduweki is waiting for me." Serwaa opened the front door and scooted out.

Folayan reached into the bag. There were three sacks inside. The smallest one held jewelry that Papa collected for her for years. Sometimes he let her play grown-up woman with them. *Here's the bracelet I used as a pattern for my age mates to make their own like it. Afua broke mine.* Folayan grimaced, then smoothed her finger over the four small cowry shells she'd added to lengthen it.

She divided the items into two parts: the first pile for the seventeen ornaments that Papa had brought each year after he married Maame. *While they waited for me to come. How hard it must have been, every year hoping for a girl child.* The second pile was for gifts brought since her birth and kept in his Kwantunyi box. Thirty-two presents plus the ntama of lace he gave her last night.

She dropped the items into the small bag. *When did he take them out of his keepsake box and put them in this? And where is the nugget?*

She sat back on her heels. Were things really normal again with her parents? She looked up through the adiho opening. In the blue sky, large white fluffy clouds slid past, slow and peaceful, but her thoughts would not calm.

She walked around the adiho, languidly running her fingertips along the walls, then stopped at the tree planted in the corner, and snapped a thin green twig off. She sat down on a nearby seat and pulling each still-attached leaf into strips, she pondered.

*What else do I not know about this thing called marriage?*

Folayan finally returned to the gifts and examined each piece of jewelry, the rainbow of stones, and the fancy combs. *Is it these that make the queens look pretty? Or is it something else?*

Folayan enjoyed designing her hair by twisting, rolling, braiding, and placing one, two, or several combs in her hair for each different style. She peered often at herself in the gleaming copper-colored floor, but it was too blurry. She wished she could see herself in Maame's sankofa mirror comb. *Would she mind?*

Folayan hesitated a moment, then went again into her parents' room. The sankofa mirror comb was on Maame's shelf. Back in the adiho, she could only smile at her reflection. She felt pretty. She returned her mother's comb to the shelf.

The middle-sized sack held items that all the women in her house kept in store: a calabash about the length of her forearm, three different thicknesses of cording, a hand-span wide pouch of charcoal ash, some healing herbs, a fire rock, a sharpening stone, and many pouches of different kinds of seeds.

She unrolled the third bundle, a Tuareg tarp spread out the floor, it was twice longer and wider than her body with her outstretched arms and legs.

Inside the roll, she discovered a red blanket with three gray stripes. Under the blanket lay a carving knife, and a machete.

*A machete? Like my brothers? Of my very own?*

In her prancing around the room, she sliced a branch off the tree with such ease she gasped, "Oooooh!" She hurried to put the machete back down on the blanket, next to the hip-high digging stick.

Guilt flamed inside her. She went back to the tree and tried to fit the cut branch to its stalk. The tree looked lopsided. She examined the branch; maybe she could make another digging stick. In the meantime, she wedged the branch in the tree so it did not look so unbalanced. She sighed. *I must tell my parents what happened as soon as they come home.*

Folayan picked up the carving knife, the length of her wrist to her elbow. Her thumb tested the sharpness of the blade. She would give it and the machete the same respect. She whispered "I must have been ten afenhyia, when Papa brought back this knife."

*It is not so fancy like Akonor's, or Papa's with the sankofa handle, but it has this pretty pearl handle. It is useful. And it is mine.*

Folayan put everything back in the small sacks and then in the big bundle. It was bulkier now. She had have to learn how to roll tight like her brothers. She took it to her room.

When she returned to the adiho, she looked up. All but the edge of the sun had passed the opening. She decided to go find the other women. *Where are they? They should have been back by now, on Papa's second day home.*

She went to the fields. *No family anywhere?* Dumbfounded, she meandered down the road toward the ofram tree, then on to the special spot on the side of the hill and remembered Serwaa's instruction. She sat down to focus on the family story. Her thoughts went back to their beginnings in Canaan land. She pictured each item in the box and practiced her heritage story again.

She looked behind herself toward the village. "Maybe they are visiting their friends," she muttered, then resolved to go to Adwoa's house. *I know, I will gather some plantains to share.* Folayan went back to her house to get a basket. While there, she looked in each room. Still no one.

On the way to pick the plantains, she became distracted by beautiful hibiscus bushes and picked two kinds, white and lavender.

She headed for Afua's first to get it over with, but knowing how Afua could keep her there until she was ready for her to leave, Folayan changed her mind.

However, her best friend, Adwoa, was quite involved with her mother pounding fufu.

Abena was making soap and had a basket full of plantain peels. "I have nowhere to put the hibiscus right now. It will only die."

Yaa said, "I am too busy frying fish today, but here, I'll take one stem of hibiscus for some tea later. After putting the flowers in water, she mused, "They are so pretty." She broke off another one and inserted it in her hair. Then took a third flower from the basket and secured it behind Folayan's ear. "Now, we both look beautiful."

Folayan wished she could see herself ... and that Kofi could, too. She grinned.

Since most of her friends had no time to visit, Folayan stayed only a few minutes at each house. *Maybe Ekua will have time to visit.*

Ekua was not home.

Finally, she approached Afua's house. She hesitated, but knew it would slip out from any one of the girls that she had come by. Waiting for Afua's attitude would be worse than dealing with it now.

When Afua came to the door, Folayan lifted the basket and blurted, "I wanted to make tea and thought I would share some with my age mates."

Afua frowned. "Is that all you have?"

Folayan stared at her, then spoke carefully, "My Papa is back from his journey only yesterday. I will come again when we can visit longer."

Folayan reprimanded herself on the way home. "I will. I will go again ... when I am not alone." She felt exhausted. Still finding no one in the house, she practiced her story once more and decided to take a nap.

"Girl!" Serwaa pulled the curtain back. "Are you going to sleep forever? We have already prepared the meal!"

Folayan wiped her eyes and looked beyond Serwaa to the sky. Only a few stars twinkled in the cobalt blue sky. *They prepared the meal without me?*

"Get up, we are eating." Serwaa clicked her tongue on the roof of her mouth twice. "Up! Up!"

Folayan rolled out, backed upright, and spread the cloth over her pallet. Serwaa waited at the doorway. As Folayan came to her, Serwaa caressed her cheek.

*Why did she do that?* It was an action she had often done, but today.

When Folayan asked everybody of their whereabouts, all day, they answered, "Working."

When she asked again, they seemed to lose their hearing, even the four children: two six-year-olds, the seven, and the nine-year-old. After the meal, Papa called the family around him. When all eighteen were seated, including the three babies on their mother's laps, he announced, "This is a time of achievements, a time of Passage. My last son, Akonor, has completed his first journey, and in a few months, we will all march in his sister's long-awaited wedding."

Folayan's face felt warm from the family's chuckles and appraisals.

"Now is the time, my daughter, for you to show us treasures of your mind and abilities that you have mastered these fifteen years."

Folayan gulped. She searched her parents' faces for a twinkle of humor. Nothing. Then panic struck! *I should have practiced more.*

Papa waved her up to stand by his side. "Ama Kwantunyi Folayan, we wish to hear you recite your traveler ancestors."

Relief eased the tightness in her neck. *At least he did not say all nine hundred forty-six generations of his people.* Neither did he say Maame's ancestors. *He only wants me to recite the traveling merchants, the sixty-four kwantunyis.*

By her ninth afenhyia, she had learned them all, beginning from when each patriarch reached age forty. Still it would be a long story.

She cleared her throat, placed her feet together as if ready to march, with upright carriage, and head high, she began her six-week Rite of Passage experience.

# CHAPTER 15

# Ancestral Journey

*Many thousands of other students came from all over*
*Africa and beyond, from faraway lands,*
*even across the Great Sea.*

*"Daughter, my only girl child," he said with a smile, pride lighting his eyes.*
*"I am satisfied. You have exceeded my hopes. I am well pleased."*

### April 1795, Kormantse Village

"*I*n the old times ..." Folayan hesitated.

Kwamina cupped his palm to his ear.

Speaking louder, she pointed east, "Forty-one kwantunyis led our people from Canaan, across the Gaza of Arabia. She moved into the land of Kmt and the mighty pyramids, through Kush, the Nubian land of Ta Seti, following great river Gihon, also called the Blue Nile. Our next sixty-four ancestors led families of our clan from the Nile Valley into the desert—the huge Saraha Desert.

"He was Kwamina the first. Neighbor families trusted his skills, began to call him Kwantunyi, 'the traveler' and asked to come along."

"Folayan, help the children see it." Papa said.

Maame sat beside him nodding agreement. *Where has she been all day?*

"They journeyed through the Sahara. Kwamina sent his sons ahead as scouts. While camped at an oasis, merchants told them of the way bordering the desert. After Kwamina died, his sons Yoofi, Osei, Kwaku, and Yaw in turn guided our people west through the Sahel where land is more flat, savannah with trees, but not thick forests."

Papa leaned forward, "The children, Folayan."

She blinked trying to figure out how to make it thrilling, like Papa's stories. She decided to mimick him and began to lumber side to side, then stretched her arms to her knees, clasped hands, and pointed to the ground.

"Our people saw many animals in the Sahel, like giraffe, antelope, wildebeests grazing, baboons leaping from tree to tree, and elephants snapping branches off like twigs." She lifted her "trunk" and pretended to grab a branch and bring it down to her mouth and chew.

The children giggled.

"They trekked onward each day, waiting until Yaw gave the call, 'The sun will soon set,' he would say. 'We must stop, and prepare our meal, but first—our shelter.'"

Folayan unrolled the Tuareg skin tarp. "We need some poles." Shading her eyes, she looked to left, then right. The children's heads turned with her.

She stepped back. "With his machete, Yaw reached up like the elephant and knocked a long, nearly straight branch right off the tree. Like this one."

Folayan whacked the air with all her might and retrieved the branch she'd stuck back in the tree earlier. Gasps escaped from the audience. She held her breath waiting for a reprimand.

"Ooh! Ooh!" the seven-year old awe-filled Ama, Kwamina's daughter

Folayan called on all her brothers. "Please go outside and get some tall sticks, bring your walking staffs also. Papa, may we use yours, too?"

He nodded. Akonor went to get it. She used her knife to peel the leaves and the bark halfway up the severed branch.

Avoiding glancing at her parents for approval, she saw that the children's mouths were wide open. Folayan set the knife back on top of the bundle.

Her brothers held their staffs rising to meet the tallest staff at the top, making three separate triangles, spaced about four feet apart at the bottom.

She took cording from her bag and wrapped the grouped poles tight about four inches from the top where they touched. And just like Papa had taught her she spread the tarp over the triangles into a tented covering and secured the sides of the tarp to the rest of poles spaced around the perimeter with cording strung out connecting to the tarp edge.

She cautioned, "Normally, we would dig and stake these outside poles firmly into the ground, if we were not inside our house, but we will do our best to brace our shelter in here, without spoiling our nice shiny, solid packed floor."

When it appeared to be stable, she asked Akonor to crawl in. Folayan felt proud at the short time it had taken to erect it under her direction.

Following Akonor, the children scrambled inside with lots of giggles. While they "slept" in the tent, she continued the story.

"For nearly three afenhyia, our people journeyed through the Sahel's hot, breezy summers, or waited for weeks while wet, freezing weather passed. While oxen, goats, and sheep grazed, the travelers filled their wagons with clay pots, calabashes, and gut skins, stocking water from oasis to oasis, lingering from planting season to harvest."

Folayan crooked her finger. "Ama, go to the food preparation room get some small baskets with lids, and straw sacks with seeds already in them."

Ama returned with her arms full. Folayan asked the family to "Take a basket and stand up."

With lots of laughter, they followed her here and there in the adiho, "identifying" and gathering herb leaves and seed from imaginary flowers, bushes, grasses, and trees.

Folayan explained, "Our ancestors harvested and saved some seeds to plant later. While travelling, they soaked some until little green sprouts opened before adding them to stew. Some they ground for mush or meal for bread."

When everybody else returned to their seats, Ama lingered, wide eyed, "Please, one more thing."

Folayan cupped the little girl's chin, and smiled remembering herself, standing aside, watching the boys, wanting to be challenged with new and different experiences, wanting to learn much more.

Folayan took the little girl's hand and led her to the entry way. Looking into the child's eyes, but speaking loud enough for all to hear, she said, "Our ancestors finally reached Timbuktu about the time Emperor Mansa Musa's mosque was completed almost 400 years ago.

"It was across the road from the beautiful University of Sankore which was already three hundred years old. Papa says the people kept it as well then as they do now. It still looks like a young building because every year the people come together gathering sand to repair and remud it. They do the same in other cities in Mali, such as for the mosque in Djenne.

"When our leader, Yaw, became sick and died, his son, Kwabena, took his place and decided it would be good for the family to settle in Timbuktu.

"During the ninety-six years time our family lived there, we had three Kwantunyi leaders." She named them and told how they helped the family grow strong and prosper in Timbuktu.

"It was a great city where they say over one hundred thousand citizens lived." Folayan spilled tiny seeds from a larger bag out into her hand. "That must be twenty or thirty bags full of seeds—if each seed was a person."

Exclamations erupted from the watchers. Folayan poured the seed back into the bag. Ekow's son, Ebo, leaned over and rescued the eleven seeds that dropped to the floor.

"Meda wase." Folayan thanked him as he gave them to her.

She handed the bag to Ama, then bent down and drew lightly, careful not to mess up her sheen on the floor.

She called on Ekow's other son. "Come ... Akwasi, Ama will pour seeds into your hand and you spread them out on one of the four parts in this rectangle that stands for the University of Sankore."

He covered the section completely.

"Good," Folayan said. "That is how many of the citizens of the city were students in the university.

"The other three parts show us how many people from other places of the world came to go to school in Timbuktu. Many thousands of other students came from all over Africa and beyond, from faraway lands, even across the Great Sea.

"History and law were taught, and every student had to memorize the Arabic language." She recited a greeting. "As-Salaam Alaikum."

Two brothers responded, "Wa-Alaikum Salaam." The children blinked, mouths agape.

Folayan chuckled, "Seven of our ancestors were favored to study at Sankore."

Touching one finger for each ancestor, she listed them. "First, Kwabena studied physics and how things work. He had already learned from Yaw how to build wagons, but at the University of Sankore he learned about other tools that make our labor easier."

Folayan placed her hands on the heads of the two boys, Akwasi and Ebo, who bore the names of two of the ancestors. She explained that, "Akwasi, the first, studied science. Ebo, the first, studied medicine."

As the boys stood in front of their elders, their little chests stuck out and they stretched taller.

Behind them, Folayan patted their shoulders.

"Kwaku studied astronomy. He knew about stars and the night sky like the Dogon people who also live in Mali. Gyasi was a scholar of mathematics.

"Kwadwo loved medicine and surgery. Papa said somebody in Timbuktu dug up some graves and found some dead bodies. The people's bones showed that they had kept living many years after the surgeries.

"The seventh ancestor to be a student at the University was Ekow who learned geography and navigation. He went with a group that sailed acoss the sea. They traded with the people who live in a place called Brazil in the New World." Each time the children heard a different language, they giggled when Folayan gave examples of them.

After the children stopped giggling, Folayan explained that many languages were spoken at Sankore as well as many trades.

She named trades and told the children that people still go to learn in Timbuktu. She asked, "What would you study if you went?"

All the boys vied for and envied each others' choices. One wanted carpentry, another tailoring, the third chose business. Ama remained silent.

Folayan thought, *if only they would allow us—women—to study there, maybe one day*, but she couldn't help giving her niece an opportunity to speak her dream.

Ama lowered her head. Again, Folayan lifted her chin and saw a wish veiled in her eyes. Ama squirmed and glanced at her parents. Folayan waited.

Finally, Ama asked, "What would you like, Folayan?"

"Oh, there is much I would like to learn. Papa once told me about the great teacher Imhotep developed mathematics to engineer and design architecture for Pharaoh Zoser. He also studied and wrote down the healing abilities of plant roots, stems, leaves, flowers, and seeds like what Serwaa and Maame find and use to help people here in our village. Imhotep is called the father of five sciences, including medicine and kmistry. He studied the km—the black earth of Kmt. Imhotep examined its tiny parts the rocks, the grains of sand, the many colors in it. It is called a science—the science of kmistry. Scientists of Kmt used kmistry and made paints for painting beautiful murals on walls, and the wealthy women used the many colors pulled from the earth to paint their faces—eyes, mouths.

"Wet kmistry. Sometimes the km is rough. If they make it wet with water, it becomes smooth and silky. Some stones are used as jewels with many different colors. Some are so hard they can be used to smooth skin, or small stones can hold in a fire. Like our bukyia stones. With the fire and wet km they made mud and baked it and made beautiful vases and urns. Or giant stones for buildings where the people of Kmt were like tiny grasshoppers walking around the giant tombs they built for their pharaohs. Papa told me, if I knew kmistry I could make better paints for my art, paint that lasts thousands of years, too. I wish to study art, and shoe-making and … languages, and read literature about places all the people come from to study there."

Folayan smiled mischievously at Akonor.

She relished the wavering eyebrows of the men and some women in her audience, "Timbuktu was a big bookmaking center and students wrote and brought hundreds of thousands of books to the city, like the book Papa brought to Akonor when he was a little boy."

Folayan sent the boys back to their parents, and pulled Ama close. "Now for one more thing."

She lifted the child into her arms, face to face, and said, "All those many thousands of men of different cultures came to Timbuktu to learn many things from those great black African scholars like Ahmed Baba.

"But it would not have happened without a lady—like you and me."

As the girl's eyes grew huge, Folayan nodded and said, "A very wealthy Mandinka woman paid great riches for the University of Sankore to be built.

"You and I can do something great, too?" Wonder filled Ama's eyes. "What could you learn that will make our village stronger and better?"

Ama whispered in her ear. "Read books, too."

Folayan's eyebrows raised. She pressed her cheek to Ama's before putting her down, and smiled, "We will start tomorrow."

Ama grinned, all proud at her parents, who nodded approval of the good job she did.

Folayan glanced at Papa. She thought she saw a twinkle that quickly disappeared, erasing any sign of how she was doing.

Her tone grew somber. "We might have stayed in Timbuktu forever, but things had already begun to be uncomfortable for our family with the increase in the slave trade by Arabs and kwesi broni from a land they call Europe on the other side of the Great Sea which is also called the Mediterranean. Its shores touch our Sahara Desert.

She pointed north. "Which way did they come from?" The children and adults all pointed north.

"Besides that, many battles were being fought by the Songhai trying to take Timbuktu from Mali.

"But …" Folayan dropped her head and whispered with her hand cupped to the side of her mouth. Even the babies turned and one loosed the breastfeeding nipple to watch her. "Then Sunni Ali Ber died, followed by the suspicious death of his son."

From her bag, Folayan pulled the Malian wedding blanket—donned it as a robe around her shoulder, and walked tall. "He expanded the empire all the way from Gao—" Folayan took giant steps across the room, "—to the the Atlantic Ocean and Goree Island. When Askia the Great became emperor he expanded it to Lake Chad and lands on both sides of the Niger River.

"One of the boys asked, "Including the Yoruba land?"

"Yes, that was the time when ..." then she removed the robe.

She stood in dignified silence facing her family for a moment. "Our pain was unbearable when we lost Kwadwo and eight other members of our family in one day."

"Boys, will each of you recite their names for us?" The little boys stood up. Akwasi made the first sound, the other boys caught up with the rhythm. Their solemn little voices were like drum beats on Folayan's heart.

"Berko."

"Mansa."

"Annan."

"Anum."

"Essien."

"Afon."

"Botwe."

Folayan looked at each person sitting there in that double half-circle. She knew that every time anyone recited the history they halted at this point, to give the hearers time to reflect and grieve.

"Our people had confidence in Ekow's knowledge of geography. They wanted to look for better horizons beyond Askia's reach. They were ready to travel again." Folayan picked up her leather bag and enlisted all four of the children to stand again.

"Ekow learned from other traders who were from Mali and Niger about the Brong Ahafo region with its splendid waterfalls, and the Friday market of Tekyiman, the oldest weekly market nearest to us.

She said, "He was looking for better horizons beyond Askia's reach. they were ready to travel once again—further away from slavery."

Folayan stopped. An image flashed in her mind—an image from her dream. Her people trying to get further away from slavery. Shaking her head to fling the image from her brain, she swallowed and looked back at the children.

Akwasi asked, "What about the waterfalls?"

The dream flashed again. Folayan could see a waterfall splashing down upon her Papa as he tried to get out of the water. He seemed to be drowning. She began to tremble. Her breathing labored. Looking to her brothers, "Would you speak about the waterfalls?"

Ekow took over. By the time he finished, Folayan regained her composure. She didn't want any more questions and wanted to get through her first rite.

"Our family lived in Tekyiman four years, before a stranger came—asking questions about us."

Folayan glanced at Papa.

Encouraged by his slight smile, she continued, "Our men determined that no more of our family would be captured and enslaved." Folayan draped her voice with mystery. "The family elders watched the stranger for several days and learned where he lodged.

"They planned how they would take him. Make him tell why he was looking for them.

"Then at dusk three of our men lay in wait as the stranger left the market. Ekow led them, gripping his knife."

"Like mine!" Akonor blurted.

Folayan nodded. "The stranger stopped and pressed his back against the wall, looking both ways." Folayan demonstrated against the adiho wall. Tension in the room made her heart beat faster.

Folayan grabbed her carving knife from the bundle and held it at her waist. "The stranger reached into his belt. Ekow sprang upon him and held him fast. "Why do you ask questions about the Kwantunyis?" She bared her clenched teeth.

"The gray-bearded stranger gasped with Ekow's knife at his throat. 'Look. Look,' he whispered, and held out his hand. Kwamina was at his side now and took the thing from his open palm.

"Kwamina examined it in the shadows. 'This is Kwadwo's knife with the sankofa carved into it! How did you get it? What have you done with our brother? Where is he?'

"The stranger's voice was hoarse now. 'Yaw,' he whispered. Ekow refused to move a hair space away.

"The stranger choked, 'It belonged to my father. His forefathers passed it all the way down from Yaw, who owned it first.'

"Kwamina stared into the man's face. 'Where is Kwadwo? Where did you get this?'

"'My father Gyasi gave it to me,' he squeaked.

"Ekow's knife point dented the stranger's jaw at the earlobe.

"Kwamina said, 'Wait, Ekow .... Kwadwo?'

"The stranger sighed, 'Yes. Ekow. It is I.'

"When they were sure, they embraced him many times on that road, and took him to the rest of the family."

Folayan's listeners burst out in applause. She smiled. When it subsided, she continued.

"Kwadwo told them that he had seen our family members captured and could not come for help, so he followed them. Sadly, he was not able to ever get close enough to help them escape. Finally, they took them into boats that went out to the Goree Island.

"He watched for several weeks. Many ships came and loaded captives. He stayed in the Senegal coast for a year until he lost hope and turned back to Timbuktu.

"When he arrived, we had gone. Finally, he met some traders who told him we headed for Tekyiman.

"Our family remained there in Tekyiman for twelve more years until Kwadwo died." Folayan walked to the edge of the group.

"By then Akwasi the second had become the leader. He thought we should move on. He took us to Kumasi. Still the Ashanti slave trade came close. Too close.

"After three years, Akwasi sent Kwame the second out searching for a new place for us, where we could have more opportunities to thrive. Kwame found a place, where to our farms, and merchandise we make—we added fishing."

Folayan led the children around the room, behind the tree, in between their parents.

"And we came to Fantiland and our Kormantse hill. Since then we have had eight Kwantunyi leaders." Folayan named each one and how he helped build and make the village a better place.

When she had given account of twenty-two of the Kwantunyi leaders, and her Papa, Kwabena the second, number twenty-three, the family praised Folayan's history. But she kept her eye on Papa.

"Daughter, my only girl child," he said with a smile, pride lighting his eyes. "I am satisfied. You have exceeded my hopes. I am well pleased."

# CHAPTER 16

# The Gold-Banded Box

*Stars twinkled bright in the adiho-framed sky.*
*Everybody chattered.*

*The key to remember is that a wise captive may be held in bondage, but is always learning the new language while remembering his own, learning useful skills to make money, studying his holder, planning on how to escape, how to survive, and thrive. A captive refuses to give his mind to the man who holds the chains.*

*The key to making wise choices is to be watchful, Daughter. Be smart. Be careful. Fetch knowledge and understanding from the Most High God and always remember where our ancestors' feet have taken us.*

**April 1795, Kormantse Village**

*P*apa took Maame's hand in his. "Folayan, a few hours before you were born, your mother asked me to continue our ancestral journey to take us away to someplace safe."

Folayan watched her mother's anxious face.

Papa continued. "I have searched all these years to find such a place for my family. My sons can tell you, we sometimes bypass the main routes that our Kwantunyi ancestors always traveled."

Emissah nodded.

Papa said, "I realized that any moment the people in my life can be stolen from me ... whether they take them to the dungeon on Goree Island far away in Senegal, or to any of the hundreds of ports and fortresses that stand from there down to those near here—El Mina, Cape Coast, Fort William, or Fort Kormantin ... even to the fifteen-day walking journey, down to the Bight of Benin."

"If not castles or forts, cannons sit in between a couple miles apart, sixty in the Gold Coast alone," Emissah said.

Ekow said, "Throughout the coastal villages, I often see chained captives ... it is so different from the past, when only a few were sold at a time."

Folayan saw Papa squeeze Maame's hand. He said, "I decided the best way I could help and protect our daughter is through knowledge."

The moonlight glowed on the side of Papa's face, his strong chin, his kind, deep brown eyes. Gratitude swelled, thinking of her family's struggles, bravery, determination, wisdom. And dignity. Then she heard Papa say, "Folayan, you, too, are Kwantunyi."

She repeated the words: *I, too, am Kwantunyi.*

Papa said, "As I have taught my sons to survive, I taught you, my precious only daughter so you can take care of yourself and your children."

She glanced at her sisters-in-law with children in laps, or cuddled at their knees.

Papa said, "Slavery is like a spider's web, difficult to see, even when you are in the midst of it."

He studied each face, released a great sigh and slapped both hands on his thighs. "But I can see that you all are ready for happier thoughts and for—Folayan's surprise!"

Stars twinkled bright in the adiho-framed sky. Everybody chattered. Akonor ran to get a fist-sized bundle for Papa.

Papa explained. "I looked everywhere and found no box with the symbols of our history like I wanted."

*Where is it? He said he would bring back my box! What can fit in that tiny bundle?*

As Papa pulled out a chunk of brass, a stub of silver, and a slice of ebony wood, Folayan's astonished, then bewildered facial expressions sent the children into giggles.

He said, "I could not find the box I wanted. I looked in this village and that town. I was losing hope.

*My Papa losing hope?*

"When we go to Timbuktu, while our men sleep with our goods, some of us switch off staying with friends our family made when we lived there. A group of my friends are merchants who travel out of Africa, across the Great Sea into the land they call Europe. We had a fine time hearing about their adventures in the lands I had never seen.

"I told him my only girl child, had come of age and about the box I could not find for you. I asked if they had anything like what I described."

Anticipation halted Folayan's breath.

"No one had." Papa held up his hand, "But just as our bundles of new wares were loaded, and readied to leave Timbuktu, one friend pulled me aside and gave me this small package.

"He told me, 'Parts are easier to find than a finished box. When I was in France, I traded for these. Take them and make the box of your dream and look for other parts as you journey home.'"

Papa put the little package in Folayan's palm.

"He refused payment, just said, 'It is my gift.'"

Folayan glanced at Maame.

"So, in Mopti, I found silver and had the rods and sankofa handles made. At the Market in Djenne, I purchased more brass for the hinges, and I bought the ebony from merchant men in Tekyiman."

"Three markets, which one is the biggest?" asked Ama.

"That is hard to say, probably Djenne. It is a little older and it is a witness of the persistence and skill of African business. The Djenne market has been held every Monday for over 700 years."

"That is a long, long time to be a market woman."

Laughter rippled through the room.

Papa encouraged her, "There have been many market women down the centuries."

The little girl piped. "One day I will be a market woman."

"Yes, you will." Papa said. "And one day you will begin your Rite of Passage that announces you have come of age like Folayan."

Folayan thought, *but I have not ever been to market except at the Bakatue and the little Sunday market here on the hilltop.* She looked at Maame.

Papa clapped his hands. "What do you all have for my only girl child who has come of age?"

Leaving Folayan with the children and Papa, everyone else hurried off in different directions.

Folayan waited, a half smile played on her mouth. The women came back, hiding items behind their backs. Her brothers emerged from her parents' room and brought out a large, draped object.

Papa beckoned for Maame and then Folayan to come stand beside them. Maame lifted Folayan's chin. "This is why we did not wake you when we left before hwaani hwaani light."

The women showed and refolded pretty garments.

Folayan laughed out loud. "All day. You were sewing all day? Maame, too?"

They embraced her. Folayan touched her finger to the corner of her eye. "I thought … I thought you all did not love me anymore."

Maame hugged her, "Never." She went to sit in her chair. Papa cleared his throat. He stepped beside Folayan's brothers, took a corner of the drape and yanked it off with a flourish.

Folayan's mouth opened in awe. The box, the size of Papa's, had rounded ebony sides and lid. A wide golden leather band wrapped around the chest cavity painted with a world of merchant and family journeys through lands from Canaan to Kush, to Mizraim, and Phut down to lands to the Gulf of Guinea. A silver rod wrapped around the box accented above a strip of zebra hide.

"Ohh, look!" Though she'd seen the hide several times, even folded it, when she saw it on the box, something clenched in her stomach, then soothed immediately as she remembered she had begged Papa for it—to keep it safe. It was her way of not leaving him out there alone. Though this was not the whole hide, it would ever remind her that she went back to fetch him.

She dropped to her knees, and ran her finger beneath the gold band—between silver rods, a narrow panel of black and white graced the box anchored with four brass ball feet. "Zebra … my Zebra," she purred, "what a wonderful way to be able to think happy thoughts about him every day.

She lifted the lid and examined every part of the ebony interior, the three secret compartments, the silver sankofa handles outside on the ends, and the brass Gye Nyame adinkra in the center front of the lid.

"It is beautiful, Papa." She ran her finger over the ebony lid shaped to be a seat, and studied the map of Africa carved into it and painted gold. "What are these lines?"

Papa explained, "The trade route lines are copper and the black line is the path our ancestors took on their journey from Canaan land to Kormantse."

Folayan sat back on her heels and stared at the box. She caressed the black and white stripe again. She looked at her Papa.

He watched her anxiously, "Is that all right? We can take it off if it troubles you?"

"Oh, no Papa. I love it there. He will always be with me. I taught him, and he taught me. He will always be a part of who I am.

She got up and walked around it. Then sat down on the back side, turned around and looked at them. "I never, never could imagine such a beautiful, beautiful box. Just for me. Thank you, Papa."

Papa beamed. "I purchased gold dust and nuggets in each city, but most of it from the Ashantis in Kumasi who crafted this gold band picturing our Kwantunyi journey that you told us about tonight."

Emmisah said, "We are proud of you, Sister."

Ekow added, "You are very important to us."

Akonor interjected, "The box will remind you of our heritage."

Kwesi said, "You are a Kwantunyi and must live up to the honor that the name has earned."

Kwamina smiled. "As the circle of the band never ends, we will love you always."

She cooed.

Papa explained, "Yesterday, after we returned from our journey, your brothers went to the wood master. They cut ebony wood. Today I joined them. We carved its rounded sides and curved lid. Then we assembled the chest with the painted leather hide over the four wooden side panels, fixing the zebra stripes in between the silver rods, and finally, we attached the brass parts: the feet, hinges, and the lock."

*Lock? Papa's box does not have a lock.*

She leaned over and examined the front and sides, then got up and walked around to the front of the box.

*Everybody knew about it but me!* Their faces revealed nothing. She sat down again. "Where is the lock?"

Papa placed the key in her hand. Still, questions stirred in her heart.

He said, "Daughter, your eyes betray your lips. What is troubling you?"

She hesitated, then finally asked, "Are locks not for the fearful?"

He flipped up the adinkra. Folayan's eyes widened. *A keyhole under the Gye Nyame adinkra. Hunh!*

"My friend who gave me the lock said, "time was once that we did not need locks, but the world is changing. Thieves are becoming bolder and will steal anything."

*They stole my zebra, my Zebra who did no harm to anyone. He just minded his own business, and mine, too.* The corners of her mouth tilted, then her lips pursed.

She sat silent, feeling her loss, then said, "Things ... zebras ... and people. They steal people , too."

"Yes," Papa agreed. "And minds."

Folayan frowned. "Minds?"

"By choice. It may look like one thing, but we must ever be ready for the unexpected."

"In our minds we make and hold onto our choices. Whether it is about what we want to do, or do not want; it might cause joy or pain— something stolen, or murder, or slavery.

Papa stopped, and looked somberly at her, "Our thinking can make us weak or strong. We must study ourselves. and know why we did an action that causes fortune or misfortune. Folayan your artist's eye helps you examine things closely, differently, deeply. The rest of you must practice that. Make it a habit. Know-yourself-and-know-all-about-your-enemy."

Folayan winced, and groaned, "Afua?"

"Figure out the causes, conditions, habits, and remedies or solutions. And remember, any problem may look like one thing, but we must ever be ready for the unexpected. Be always watchful. Think through. Choose right."

"How? How can we know the right choices?"

Papa pushed the Gye Nyame closed and tapped it. "This can remind you that God is with you. He is our helper. He is all-knowing, all-wise. We can ask Him to help us be wise and not give our minds over to those who want to trick, kill, or enslave us. Use your mind more than your fists."

Folayan's chin dropped. She glanced at her family and nibbled her bottom lip.

Papa looked around the circle and called each of the children by name. "There is a difference between a slave and a captive. Each person must make a decision which he will be.

"The key to remember is that a wise captive may be held in bondage, but is always learning the new language while remembering his own, learning useful skills to make money, studying his holder, planning on how to escape, how to survive, and thrive. A captive refuses to give his mind to the man who holds the chains."

Folayan stiffened. *This is scary.* One of the little boys climbed into his father's lap.

"On the other hand," Papa paused, "a slave gives up, believes the words the holder uses. Words that are fashioned to destroy him, by tearing down his mind. The first thing a holder does is change the captive's names, then the holder knows he has become the master when the slave starts describing himself and other slaves with his master's words and names."

"So, how else can a captive protect his mind?" Kwesi's wife asked.

Papa said, "Slaveholders succeed by keeping them in darkness. Keeping truth from them."

Kwamina spoke. "Not only slaveholders, but other people in power use lies to maintain control over others.

"Do you see what is on this lock?" Papa asked.

"The Gye Nyame." She traced the adinkra carved in the brass lid covering the keyhole.

"Open it."

Folayan lifted the lid up, down, up.

Papa inserted the key and turned until it clicked. He raised, then closed the box's ebony top. "This makes a comfortable seat, too." He sat down and patted the space next to him.

She joined him.

"Do not be afraid of the lock, Daughter. Locks work until a person is very determined to break them. Also, you do not need a piece of metal to be locked out. I have been locked out for fifteen afenhyia, and I cannot find the key to …."

Folayan had no words to comfort him.

He sighed, "Nothing can keep troubles away if Onyankopon allows them. If you remember that, then you need not be afraid." He tapped the lock. "Nothing happens …"

She finished, "But God!"

"As I told you, the brass lock was a gift, I did not buy it. However, my friend showed me there was a better way to reach my goal. How you choose to think of it makes all the difference. It is not to cause you anxiety, but to remind you to lock out foolishness.

"Daughter, the key to making wise choices is to be watchful. Be smart. Be careful. Fetch knowledge and understanding from the Most High God and always remember where our ancestors feet have taken us. I have filled this gold-banded box with those kind of tools to help you on your journey.

"I will remember." The lump in her throat swelled. Folayan hugged him tight. "Papa. Thank you."

# CHAPTER 17

# *Dreams*

*The discussions of this journey have made me*
*focus on a dream that I have been trying to fulfill*
*for nearly sixteen years.*

### April 1795, Kormantse Village

"Papa! Pa-paaa .... No! Leave him alone. Get away!" Folayan fought the bed cover that tangled her arms. "Watch Papa! In the bush. Listen .... Please listen!" Folayan woke startled. Maame stood over her, Akonor entered the room. Folayan asked, Maame and Akonor, "Where is Papa?"

Akonor pointed. "Fishing. Only our brother's wives and children are here."

Four days after Folayan received her box, the family gathered in the adiho. In his colorful manner, Papa told an Anansi—the spider—story to the children. Sometimes for fun, sometimes for caution, always to teach.

*Has someone been naughty today?* Folayan studied their little faces.

Revealing nothing about the offender or an offense committed, Papa knew how to solve the mystery. Folayan looked for clues. At last, the culprit's body language told on himself, and by the end of the story he had gotten the message.

No one wanted Anansi's trouble to happen to them.

Folayan spied tears of shame that welled in little Ebo's eyes, as he inched his way to Ekow's knee and slipped something into his father's hand. So, with lesson delivered, remorse accomplished, and "lost" item returned, Papa only told one story.

With a smile and relief in his eyes, Papa asked about everyone's day. Beginning with the babies, he asked mothers to share something the infant did this day. Then by age group the toddlers, and children told their news or matter of interest or concern. When it came to the adults, Maame often let them all do the talking.

Tonight she spoke first.

"Kwabena, Folayan woke screaming this morning. It is the first time she dreamed it when you are here at home. I do not know what to do about it."

Everyone looked at Folayan. She squirmed.

Papa said, "Folayan, tell me about the dream."

She began low, but ended high, "It is the snake. You never hear my warning."

Maame gasped. Papa glanced at her, then back at Folayan. "I always stop and listen when you ask me. Is that not true?"

"It is true." Folayan said, "But not in the dream."

"The dreams are fewer," Serwaa spoke softly.

"I wonder why it came again?" Kwamina said, "When you were little, and woke from a dream, we told you stories, because you were afraid to go back to sleep."

"I do not remember that," Papa said.

Family members cast sidelong glances at one another. Yet, no one spoke. Until Serwaa said, "Half of every afenhyia you go on merchant journeys, because of them we live well. Very well. I am thankful. Even so, when you are gone you miss much—and we miss you."

Papa regarded Serwaa, then each son. He turned away, "I do not know what to say."

Folayan thought, *Papa without a word. Without a solution?*

He slapped his hands on his thighs, "Sons, you Kwantunyis have the same problem. Tomorrow we will begin to reason together for a better way. But now," he looked around, "does anybody have a thought on how to stop Folayan's bad dreams?"

Kwesi's wife said, "Should we take her to someone?"

"Over a dream?" Folayan asked.

"I think the fetish priest can help." Kwesi's wife persisted.

Kwamina said, "We should pray ourselves."

Kwesi's wife retorted. "We need to do something to help her. I think the priest's prayers are more powerful than ours? Do you not?"

Folayan asked, "Is there any other way?"

Akonor said, "What if her dreams are about the future like the king Papa's merchant friends told us about? The ... the ... prophecy ... about the statue and the stone.

He looked to Kwamina, then Kwesi. Neither one spoke added, "About the things that have been happening in Europe that started with the king's dream."

Kwamina said, "I am not sure how this can help Folayan, but when we arrived at Timbuktu and settled our men in at the market place, our friends invited Papa and his sons to come to visit and catch up on what has happened in our families in the two years since we last saw them. We enjoyed much laughter over the good meal. One of them asked Akonor to tell about what he had seen on his first merchant journey so far. After Akonor told them, Kwesi said, "He nearly missed seeing everything because his sister nearly blinded him."

"Auhh!" Folayan's face puffed in embarrassment.

Kwesi got up and put his arm around her shoulder. "I explained what happened. Do not worry. Your name is still held in honor. I must say though, your battle of the stones started a long discussion about something our friends had learned on their last journey across the Great Sea to Spain. It was a fascinating story about a certain giant stone, but I interrupted Kwamina. He can tell it best."

Kwamina continued, "I wanted to hear about it because I have been thinking about how bad things were getting here with the slave trade. I wanted to know if these troubling times are going to just keep getting worse. So when they told us about a prophecy that has been coming to pass for over twelve hundred years and that now it seems that we are nearing the end of it, I wanted to know everything they knew about it. The first thing they said was that we must study the Bible and history together, and learn to pray to God for ourselves and He will hear us."

Akonor blurted, "Just like He heard and helped Daniel and his three friends."

Kwamina said, "They showed us chapter two of Daniel's book, where God told the King Nebuchadnezzar what was going to happen in this world until Jesus comes again."

Kwesi said, "Shall I get the book we copied from their scroll with the giant statue picture your friend drew for us?" Folayan leaned forward anxious to see the drawing.

Kwamina looked at Papa. May we?"

Papa nodded, "Bring the two packages, also."

While Kwesi fetched it, Kwamina said, "Study the full page drawing of the statue.

Kwesi brought out two same sized, cloth covered packages, and handed one to Akonor. Kwesi sat down and unrolled the scroll. He held it up so all could see.

Then Kwamina explained, "It was a ninety-foot tall man made of metals. The head was made of gold, breast and arms of silver, thighs of brass, legs of iron, and feet of iron mixed with miry clay. A giant rock came hurtling out of the sky and hit the statue at the feet and the statue fell over and broke into smatters.

"Daniel told the king it meant four big empires would be followed by ten tiny ones, then all the kingdoms would be smashed to dust."

He waited for the surprised comments to subside. Then he told Kwesi to show them the book that Daniel wrote. "Papa wanted the four of us to make it so our whole family can have one of our own to read and learn from anytime we want to."

Kwesi carefully opened the elbow-to-fingertip length book. Proudly, he breathed the words etched in bold, black ink calligraphy centered on the red leather cover, "This Book of Daniel was copied from a Nubian-Arabic language Bible in this year 1795 A.D. by these four men of the Kwantunyi family: Kwabena, Kwamina, Kwesi, and Akonor."

Everybody gathered around exclaiming and admiring its beauty. Folayan touched it. Surprised it was not paper like Akonor's book. she queried, "What are the pages made of?"

"Fish parchment." Kwesi smiled broadly, "Twelve chapters—you can tell by our different calligraphy which two chapters each of us copied in the evenings. The most beautiful chapters one, six, seven, and twelve are by the book maker, Papa hired, who sewed it together in the center and bound it in leather, while we traded at the market each day."

Akonor held another wrapped package in his lap. Folayan stared at it. *When is he going to open that one?* Akonor said, "They showed us chapter two of Daniel's book where God told the King Nebuchadnezzar some of what was going to happen in this world until Jesus comes again."

Kwesi leaned to his wife and baby, "We had many long discussions about this in Timbuktu. I already knew about the fiery furnace and the lion's den from stories passed down from our ancestors, but I did not know Daniel's prophecies."

Little Ama asked, "Who is Daniel?"

Kwamina explained, "He was a Hebrew captive of Babylon who refused to give his mind to the King or customs of Babylon. Daniel's friends trusted God when forced to bow to an idol and pray to someone who was not God. Whoever refused to bow would die. Daniel's friends told the King they would honor God whether or not He chose to preserve their lives. God protected them."

"Captive?" Folayan thought about Fatima. "Do you mean Daniel and his friends were slaves?"

Kwamina said, "Though he did the king's business around the country, he could not go home to Jerusalem. Yet, they made him a eunuch, too, unable to have children."

Folayan murmured with the others. "No babies? What would be the use of living?"

Serwaa said quietly, *"Ade Akye Asa."*

Papa repeated it, "Survive we must, and survive we will."

*Survive.* Folayan thought again about Fatima. *Is there any way I can make her life easier?* "Did Daniel live long? What happened to him?"

Kwesi said, "Sister, I asked many questions like you. Papa's friends had so much knowledge, I wanted to know it all. We spent three weeks studying this."

Folayan looked at her brothers. *They can all read Arabic. I want it. I want my taste of it, too—so badly. Papa is taking so long to teach me.* "Three nnason?" Ekow held up three fingers. He squinted.

"Yes." Kwamina cleared his throat. "We know about our great Sudanese empires, and how Sundiata grew Ghana to be a center for trade that merchants came from many parts of Africa and Arabia to trade for salt, gold, and slaves. And how Ghana merged with Mali under Mansa Musa."

Akonor blurted, "On Papa's scroll map, I saw Mansa's route when he took a special journey with thousands of his soldiers and citizens through the Sahara Desert, Kmt, Arabia to Mecca, he became so famous as the richest man in the world. When he died, Mali waned and Askia the Great reigned and Songhai became mightiest of them all."

"Way over in Babylon, nearly 2000 years before those great African kings reigned over vast kingdoms, Nebuchadnezzar was also a great warrior with a huge conquering army which also captured the Hebrew king and many leaders and wealthy Hebrews. Daniel was one of them."

Kwesi inserted, "King Nebuchadnezzar had the biggest empire the world had seen."

"He had a troubling dream like you Folayan." Akonor said.

"Yes, he became concerned about the future, and the dream came to him, but he could not remember in the morning. He summoned his wisemen, astrologers, magicians, and soothsayers. They could not explain it, unless he told them the dream first. Furious, he said they had been lying and tricking him for years. He gave them one day. If they did not tell him, they and their families would be killed."

"All of them?" asked Kwamina's wife.

"Yes. All of them." Akonor nodded.

Folayan thought, *They had familes, but not Daniel.*

Kwamina continued, "Daniel and his three friends prayed together to the Most High. God gave Daniel the same dream and its meaning. With permission Daniel told the king, "There is a God in heaven who reveals secrets, and He has chosen to show the king what will come to pass in the last days, all the way to the end of the world.""

"The end of ..." Serwaa startled. "... the world? What do you mean? What are you talking about?"

"They said throughout the Bible, it tells about how this world was not created to cope with disobedience. The Creator has given man chance after chance—thousands of years to choose good or to choose evil.

"But this is His world. It belongs to Him. He created it. He will not always let it keep going in wickedness.

"He will destroy the sinful world and then make a new earth for people who love Him and choose to live like He says are the best and safest ways."

"Can He fix it without there being an end?" Her eyes watered.

"I asked that, too," said Kwesi. "They told me that when this world ends, all its sorrow, pain, and heartache will end. People who lie, hurt, steal, and murder will end, too. Peace reigned before our ancestors, Adam and Eve, brought deadly sin on this world. God wants to clean and restore it to how He first created it. But before that we have to get through the endtime."

Serwaa looked from side to side, and began to rub her arms. Everyone sat staring at her. Finally, she said, "I ... then I want to know the meaning of this Nebu'nezzar's dream."

After the king's dream, Akonor said, "Years passed, and God came back to Daniel with a vision about animals in place of the statue metals, and He revealed the name of the next kingdom."

Kwesi said, "Our Timbuktu friends told us that during the time Jesus was here. He had asked the listeners who came to hear him if they had 'ever read the words of the prophet Daniel?'"

*Jesus? Jesus read about Daniel?* Her head switched to each brother.

Kwesi continued, "So, our friends studied all twelve chapters with us. There are keys in Daniel that connect to and explain the last book in the Bible, called Revelation.

"We talked about the world beyond Africa. Our friends said history proves prophecy. Step by step history shows the fulfillment, and gives us confidence in God."

Kwamina cleared his throat. He tapped Serwaa's hand, "Here is the meaning for us."

He turned to their aunt, "Daniel told the king Nebuchadnezzar, 'You, king of Babylon are the head of gold; next will come a kingdom like the breast and arms. Two kingdoms would rule together. They were the Medes and Persians. The belly and thighs stood for Greece. The fourth kingdom is Rome's two iron legs—the Roman Empire was ruled by kings and then the Holy Roman Empire was ruled by popes.

In the dream the feet and toes of iron and clay came next, and history shows us that barbarians attacked, sacking the empire relentlessly, dividing the Roman Empire into ten nations. In Daniel's chapters seven, eight and nine, the kingdoms are not a figure of a man but they are shown as powerful animals. They are the same four kingdoms as in Daniel Chapter 2.

*All these villages and nations, my brothers are so interested that they remember all their names and all these things about them. Does God really care so much about us to show us the future of the world?* Kwamina's voice swelled, she turned to watch him. "Since then nations have made alliances to gain more power and territory. They have tried through different ways such as marriage of a king from one nation and a queen from a different one, but they keep breaking treaties. The "miry clay" keeps them from coming together as solid feet. It has happened just like the Bible promised."

Ekow said, "But what about the big Rock?"

"Time is not full yet for the Rock, but we are close," Kwamina said. "God wants us to know how to understand His prophecies that have times we can count out. Our friends showed us the key to use to understand times in prophecy. God told us in the books—Numbers chapter 14:34 and Ezekiel 4:4-6—that a regular day stands for a year in prophecy. It is easy. Ama, will you help me?"

The little girl sat up straight, and answered her uncle, "Yes, I will."

"If a day stands for a year in prophecy—then when God says something is coming in seven prophecy days, it is how many real years?"

With her mouth scrunched to the side, Ama mumbled, "A day for a year." She whispered, *a day for a year,* then smiled, "Seven days would be seven years."

"Right." Kwamina nodded. "Kwaku, what about three hundred sixty days?"

The boy said, "Three hundred sixty years."

"And Ebo, how many years would twelve hundred and sixty days be?" Ebo had to think a while. Then Ekow nudged him, "Son, remember a day for a year."

Ebo asked, "How many days, please?" Ekow told him, and Ebo whispered, "Twelve hundred and sixty years?" Ekow said, "That is right." Ebo laughed, and the family joined him. Kwamina said, "Good for all of you, Ama, Kwaku, and Ebo! Knowing that clue also helps us understand the other prophecies that connect with Nebuchadnezzar's dream.

"You know that in Timbuktu there are many, many books about Africa and other parts of the world." Papa said, "My friends took us to the libraries and we compared the book of Daniel with history books. I agree with what Nebuchadnezzar wrote in chapter four. 'Now, I praise and extol and honor the King of heaven, all whose works are truth, and His ways judgement ….'"

Kwamina nodded, "Like the Babylonian king, I now see the way God pointed these things out to us, one by one, step by step, in four dreams or visions, shows me that Onyankopon loves us so much. He does not want the giant Rock from heaven to catch us by surprise and He wants us to prepare to be saved in God's kingdom."

Serwaa still looked troubled, but she and Folayan kept silent during the following discussion. Then Ekow said, "Children, do you have questions?"

*I do. I want to know if my dream has a certain time, too? I have to think about this dream of the King and about myself. Why am I having these dreams?*

Kwamina and Kwesi answered questions from the boys. Then Ama asked Akonor, "What do you wish you could have learned more about?"

Akonor's eyebrow lifted, "It would be the settlement of Volubilis in North Africa, above Kumbi Saleh. The Romans and Vandals built homes and shops and carved arches that they marched through when the came back from battles."

"Why do you want to know more about that?" Emissah asked.

"It proves what Daniel says is true in chapter nine. In Daniel's vision of four beasts, the fourth is a strange looking beast with ten horns on its head. Ten kingdoms like the toes of King Nebuchadnezzar's statue. Three horns disappeared, and in their place one stout horn with eyes and a mouth boldly spoke against the Most High. The Vandals were one of the ten horns or little kingdoms that occupied some of North Africa, close to ancient Ghana. The Roman and Vandal ruins remain, but the Vandals are barely a word. Their tribe has been swallowed up or like it was just plucked up almost out of sight. I wish ..."

He squinted up at the stars and muttered.

Folayan strained ... *Onyame? Did he say Onyame? Is he Praying?*

"Son? What are you saying?" Papa asked.

Akonor looked back, still muffling his words. "I ... I said I wish I had one of those books."

*What books?* Whatever he wanted, Folayan wanted, too.

"Akonor?" Papa's voice showed concern.

Akonor stood up. "Papa, your friends had Books written in Arabic —Bibles that were first written as early as 300 and 400 years after Jesus lived on earth. There were several languages including Egyptian-Arabic, in Dutch, and in Aramaic—the language that the Babylonians spoke and Daniel learned. One read to us Daniel's prophecies from his Old Testament book.

Akonor struggled with his words. "Another man had four histories called Gospels, written by Jesus' companions—eyewitnesses giving good news about Jesus who was killed on a wooden cross because He claimed to be the Son of God."

Folayan felt tense hearing Akonor's voice sound hoarse. "Papa I know the things we read in the Quran .... Your friends told us a great amount of it is the same as in the Bible. One of these two books says there is no Son of God, the other says there is and because of God's love for the humans He created, His Son came to the earth to die in their place so that anyone who believed that He is the Son of God should not perish but have eternal life …. I have questions. I want to read what the Bible says about the Son of God for myself."

Folayan weighed every word Akonor said, *I want to know more about Him, too.*

Akonor moved toward Papa. "The third man's book was the Psalms. It has some prophecies written a thousand years before the birth of Jesus Christ on earth. Prophecies that came to pass just like they were foretold."

Akonor crouched beside his father. He just waited—for anger or for acceptance.

Folayan held her breath. No one seemed to be breathing.

Papa put his hand on Akonor's shoulder. "I know, son. I am interested in Daniel's words about the prophesied kingdoms that did rise up, conquered much land, and ruled for hundreds of years. And their power diminished like the Bible said they would. The great African empires were far richer than the ten toes. Riches did not help. They ended in Songhai's disunity—like the ten toes. God will have His way." Papa shook his head in wonder.

He squeezed Akonor's shoulder, "We were told that the Bible is a record of God's people's journey to heaven to live happily with Him. I hired our bookmaker to make us a full Old Testament and New Testament in Arabic to study for ourselves; and until I return to Timbuktu to get them, we can read our Daniel book and write our own famiily history and proverbs on these parchments you were holding. Folayan, I want you and Akonor to be in charge of everybody in the family writing parts of our ancestors' journey."

"Me? Me! Papa, I am weak in Arabic."

"Then you will become strong. My son will be happy to help you." He turned, "Yes?"

"Yes, Papa." Akonor answered, "I will."

Folayan stared at the package. *Parchments. Parchments!*

Papa embraced his youngest son.

After a moment, in a subdued voice Emissah said, "Papa, I missed so much not being there with you on this last journey. I, too want to know more. At supper you and my brothers talked about the time when the feet of broken iron and clay began. You called it a time of darkness. The one that lasted for 1260 years. I want to know about that time."

Kwesi said, "The Dark Ages began before the Arabs started coming across Africa, spreading Islam. Many of our ancestors were still living in Nubia at that time."

Folayan was always quite interested in conversations the men usually had out of the women's hearing. She asked, "Why did the Dark Time end?"

Kwamina said, "One reason is that books used to be made by hand on scrolls or like our new book, then they used wood blocks with letters on them, now in Europe they use a machine called a printing press. Now books cost much less. And more and more people are learning to read. They are reading stories about the world, and history, and the Bible."

Papa said, "And they are reading about the One who wants us to pray to Him to solve our problems."

Ekow looked at Papa, then at Folayan. He opened his mouth, closed it. Then he spoke earnestly, "I am not opposed to studying and learning more, but it seems to me the biggest problem our family needs to be concerned about right now is being taken lightly. Foyalan's dreams are getting worse, louder and her panics are longer after she wakes up."

Kwamina said, "How do you know? You were fishing with us."

"My wife told me," Ekow said. "What will be done to help my sister? Papa has never heard her, but is the village whispering that she may be sick?"

Folayan felt a thud in her stomach.

Kwesi's wife nodded agreement.

Ekow said, "She has her box. Next, she will go forty days to Nanabesia, then the knockings. Will anyone question her fitness? I think the fetish priest might help her."

"No!" Papa said. "It will stir all the village."

Folayan was relieved that Papa made an excuse. She was uneasy to go to the shrine.

Kwamina urged, "We can pray ourselves."

Ekow snorted. "Who has not prayed for her?"

"My voice is young and weak," Akonor halted, "but we have not prayed like Daniel and his three friends, pleading for God's help."

Ekow blurted, "I have prayed to Onyankopon Most High for her. For years!"

Kwesi's wife hesitated, "I just thought maybe the fetish priest can rid the nightmares, it has been put off too long. Something has to be done now. But all we are doing is talking about the dreams of a dead king of Babylon."

Kwamina spoke, "God heard and helped Daniel without the magicians and diviners."

Folayan convinced herself that Ekow and her sister-in-law only meant well for her, yet she felt uncomfortable being in the center of friction, "You do not like talking about the king's dream?"

Ekow frowned, "No, not his dream. I want to talk about yours."

Tension stifled the room.

*Should I ...?* Folayan sat there thinking. *I have not prayed. I will pray for myself.*

Into Folayan's thoughts stepped Kwesi's firm voice, "I will pray for understanding of why my sister has the frightful dreams and that they stop." Folayan jerked to look at him,

Akonor said, "I can pray with Kwesi."

"I will too," said Emissah.

"So will I," Kwamina nodded.

With thankful heart, Folayan lowered her eyes, "Meda wase."

It hung in the air until, Ama squeaked, "Tomorrow I begin to read!"

"Yes, but now it is time for sleep," Kwamina said.

He and Emissah gathered their children go to their own houses.

Papa raised his hand. "Sons, please stay by for just a little while longer?"

They stopped.

Papa spoke in a hushed voice. The discussions of this journey have stirred up in me a dream that I have been trying to fulfill for nearly sixteen years."

He turned to Maame. "I heard you. When you begged me to take us away. I want you to know I have not ignored your worry about slave catchers, but even without them, it does not mean there are no troubles."

Papa peered at Maame. His face softened. He touched her cheek. She looked at him with wide eyes. Folayan saw the love in her mother's eyes for him, but she felt like her Maame was holding something back. Like she was afraid.

Papa said, "I heard you." He cupped her face.

Then he said, "Sons … in the morning, we will begin family prayers for the end of the nightmares." He smiled at Folayan, then again looked at Maame.

She bowed shyly, whispering, "The children."

He said, "I want them to hear … that I heard you the first time, when the birthing pains began with Folayan. I heard you beg me to take our family away.

Maame looked into his eyes.

"I have always been troubled about Folayan's nightmares each time you told me about them. I have felt the lock you put on your heart, because you thought I did not hear your concerns, and I have been in the dark, not knowing how to help you. I have never stopped looking for a place. Never."

Maame turned her head. Still, she did answer.

"I heard you. Akosua." His voice dropped. "I heard you."

She put her fingers up to cover his lips. "I believe you, and I know that slavery is not our only problem. I also want to know more about when it will end."

Papa said, "My friends were very interested  that the religious tortures and persecutions over the last 1260 years are slowing in Europe. But not for us, since 1619, its worse. The Atlantic African slave trade burst open taking African captives to places in the new world. My friends told me to remember the prophecy counts down 1260 years to 1798, and to watch for something very significant to happen in 1798—three years from now."

Maame said, "If the world is changing, do you think things will get better for us, too?"

Papa sighed, "I do not know but I will not stop trying. It takes my friends two months to travel from Timbuktu to reach the Great Sea. They have invited me to travel with them across the Sea and go into the lands of Europe." He raised his eyebrows at his sons in invitation. All nodded.

"Why have not you gone before this? Do you need your friends to go?" Serwaa asked.

"No, but they know the routes. Our own ancestors went up beyond ancient Kumbi Saleh that included parts of Mauretania. They probably saw Volubilis. Across the sea is so much farther and would cause me to be away from my family too long."

"Perhaps I can go with you." Maame said.

Everyone turned to her with shocked faces.

Maame showed a secret smile. "Perhaps we can find a place where there is no slavery, and bring all our family to live there."

Kwamina chuckled. "Did Folayan get her sense of adventure from Maame more than Papa?"

Laughter filled the room.

Emissah and Kwamina's familes left. Folayan went to her room. In the rays of starlight, her gold banded box caught her eye—each part of it a reflection of her family's journeys. Each part a reminder of her history, and the unknown. She walked around it, then sat down on the back side. She shifted position to see the light casting from the sky through the adiho window, and let her thoughts loose to travel on the moonbeams.

*Papa did not say no.*

*If he will take Maame, will he take me, too?*

*Will my husband go …?*

# CHAPTER 18

# The Kente Weaver

*Her uncle is a kente weaver, but he has no sons.*
*Kofi asked to go learn from him so the trade*
*would not die out of their family.*

*Slavery is not only what people around the world have lived with for*
*thousands of years, but it is a way debts are paid, loss is restored, and*
*order is kept.*

### April 1795, Kormantse Village

*F*olayan added something new to the trunk at least once a week.
Often, she'd pull the clothes out, hold them up to herself, refold
them and put them away.

Today, after that routine, she stood examining herself. During the
year, the shape of a woman emerged. She had a bosom at last.

And it had been a long time since Maame clicked her tongue at the
way Folayan walked. Since she was a child, the taut "reminder" beads she
had worn around her knees, and now-narrow waist had done their job.
She did not stand lock-kneed or sway-backed.

No longer so skinny she might be mistaken for a boy, she was now
slender with curves, standing tall and straight, with her beautiful behind

full and round. Serwaa had told her, "A man wants to feel his wife's padded softness, not bones."

She heard Papa and Maame in the adiho. He asked if all Folayan's clothing had been sewn. Maame told him all but the kente.

Papa said, "I have earned enough from the salt to buy her kente, but I was waiting."

"For what?" asked Maame. "It is nearing harvest time. We must go to the town many miles north east of us to buy one."

"I did not want to leave the village to buy it."

Maame replied, "You know we have no kente weavers."

"We have one now."

Folayan rushed into the courtyard.

"What!" exclaimed Maame. "Who? Who?"

"You sound like the *patu*."

"I am not a bird." She swatted Papa's arm. "Who?"

"Yooku's fourth son, Kofi."

Folayan stiffened. Adwoa had told her he was away learning a new trade, but had not said he was back.

"Yooku's wife comes from that town," said Papa. "Her uncle is a kente weaver, but he has no sons. Kofi asked to go learn from him so the trade would not die out of their family. Yooku says Kofi is saving his earnings to build a house of his own soon."

"He is ambitious." Then Maame asked, "A good fisherman, too?"

Papa nodded. "We shall see tomorrow if he is as good with his loom as he is with the net."

"Which age group is he in?"

"Between Kwesi and Ekow I think?"

*Between Akonor and Ekow, Papa*, Folayan's mind implored.

Since Folayan started painting her own calabash dishes, Kwamina and Emissah's wives encouraged her to put several more of her pretty new designs on her calabash dishes, other people would buy them.

Now, on market days, Folayan spent her time making dishes to sell. She began as soon as it was light enough to see, after the women left. On these days, she seldom took time to eat, always intent, working, wishing she could hold the sun in one place.

One market day, Folayan paused, brush in mid-air, thinking she heard her name. She went to the door.

"Folayan!" Serwaa's voice was high and anxious. Folayan hurried toward the voice. Three neighbors came out to help. They met Serwaa and another market woman, with Maame hobbling in the middle of them. All made their arms a lift and carried Maame into her bedroom.

They braced Maame down onto the pallet. Folayan asked, "What happened?"

"My ankle." Massaging it, Maame cried out. "Ohhh."

Serwaa explained. "She tripped. It is twisted."

While Folayan examined the swelling leg, Maame said, "I heard something crack in the bush. My stomach felt it. You sure you did not hear it, Serwaa?"

"The only thing I heard was your yelp when you fell." Impatience edged Serwaa's voice as if she did not want Maame to ask her again.

"I did hear something. When I looked toward the sound, I went down on a rock."

"An animal," Serwaa said.

The group agreed suggesting elephants, cattle, or monkeys.

"Whatever it was—" Maame shifted her body, and her voice grew determined, "—it was different." *Like my dream. The sounds I hear from the bush are different. After Papa, not Maame.* She thanked the neighbors for their help, and said to Serwaa and the other market woman, "I know you must go. The crowd will come to buy soon."

Serwaa nodded. The neighbors turned to leave. One of them said, "I am on my way to the market, but my grandmother is home. She will make a poultice to keep the swelling down and check on you today."

"Thank you," Serwaa said. She hesitated. "I need Folayan's help at the market."

Maame looked at Folayan with uncertainty.

"She is long past old enough. She has seen almost sixteen afenhyia. Do not think about it, just let her go."

Folayan stood speechless. A flick of Maame's hand commanded her out of the room. Folayan put away her gourds and tools. Whatever Maame's decision, Folayan had mixed feelings. Part of her did not want to forego her painting, the other part was eager to go with Serwaa.

Adwoa's maame was a market woman, too. Adwoa went right after Folayan's bout with the ants. Folayan never understood why Maame had not taken her. Serwaa often prodded Maame to take her, but that was one point on which Maame would not give in. She waited in the adiho, near Maame's door,

Having raised Papa, Serwaa sometimes took liberty to speak to him about the ache she felt when her own man spent time in the other wife's house. A ping stung Folayan's stomach. Would Kofi want a second wife? She did not see herself wanting to share him.

Folayan recalled a day when the women were eating breakfast cooked at the fields. Maame had said to Serwaa, "But a man may have as many wives as he is wealthy enough to support. When you tell my Kwantunyi these things, does he not get angry?"

"Yes. He does," Serwaa said. "I tell him one man can make only one woman truly happy. He tells me I have forgotten my place, and to hush, else I will have no home."

Serwaa must have seen sixty afenhyia now, and once she got a thought in her head, right or wrong, there was no changing her.

The other market women had stepped out into the courtyard with Folayan while the two reasoned together. In the bedroom, Serwaa's voice rose. "No, I told you! If I did hear something, what can you do?

Three hundred afenhyia and still they have not gone away! I do not believe they will ever go. And we will not go. This is our home."

Folayan asked, "Why will they not go away?"

"Who?" The voice of a neighbor market woman came from the table by the tree.

Folayan walked to the table. "The slave catchers and traders," Folayan fretted. "Why can we not just have a peaceful life?"

The woman tried to explain. "Think of it this way. Slavery is not only what people around the world have lived with for thousands of years, but it is a way debts are paid, loss is restored, and order is kept. How do we decide what happens when a murderer kills a person he planned to kill? How do we punish him?"

Folayan answered, "With instant death."

"Ah yes, but a man who accidentally kills another can pay restitution by becoming a slave. Why?"

"So by working for the victim's family, he can provide for their care by replacing the wealth he took from them."

The other woman said, "A thief becomes a slave to work off the cost of what he stole. This is the slavery we know, and the slavery our ancestors dealt in for many generations. And there were only a few slaves, not like the hundreds who have done no wrong, and have no restitution to pay. It was not complicated before the strangers started coming into our land, tearing apart our families and villages. Kidnapping us."

Folayan shuddered.

The voices in the sleeping room ebbed. Folayan could not hear Maame's muffled words, and she felt uneasy about Serwaa's: *Who would not go? Why should anyone consider leaving home? What did she mean?*

Finally, Serwaa's voice came strong again. Decisive.

"The food withers. I need Folayan's help. She will be safe."

Serwaa pulled the curtain back and came out. She crooked her finger at Folayan. "We must hurry."

# CHAPTER 19

# Gua Do: At the Market

*"They will go play now, but I'll be working,*
*finishing a very special kente cloth."*
*He flashed a smile and her heart tripped.*

**April 1795, Kormantse Beach**

Serwaa pointed to a basket for Folayan to carry and swung the remaining one onto her own head and strode from the house. Folayan hurried after, trying not to let on that she had been eavesdropping. But finally appeased her curiosity, but not enough.

She expected a strong rebuff, but she risked it. " Serwaa, is Maame afraid of something? What did she hear in the bush?"

Folayan's recurring bad dream had come to her mind while Serwaa was convincing Maame, and now again. For a long while, Serwaa did not answer.

*Will she reprimand me and tell me to go back?*

Instead, Serwaa expelled a long breath. "Slavers."

"Slavers! Why would slavers come here? We have started no war and our people are thrifty and hard working. Why do they not just leave us alone?"

Serwaa sighed, stopped and turned to face her. "I told your Maame she should not have shielded you so much. She put you in harm's way by not telling you what is happening. I suppose I may as well tell you now, for you will keep asking questions once you have seen the market."

She motioned for Folayan to come walk beside her on the narrow forest trail. "When my grandfather was a child, the slavers became dissatisfied with the few law-breakers and debtors our people sold as slaves."

"Debtors. Like Fatima's father?" Folayan said, thinking about how if it was not for Afua's persistent demeaning, she would not remember Fatima was any different from the rest of them. All had the same chores and skills to learn.

"Yes, they wanted more and more to take across the water to a big island. Slave traders made alliances with unscrupulous nsafo traitors who led them into the interior. They instigated tribal conflicts and bartered for the captured warriors. More kwesi broni forts keep being built, though we stand against them. Since then, no matter how much we resist, more slave ships keep coming. Our people have suffered great losses. We must remember what Grandfather said, 'We have to watch, and pray, but keep on living. This is our home.'"

Folayan's heart pounded hard, her head full of questions. Since she was a child, Folayan had dreamed of going to the marketplace. Now she was getting her wish. She should be happy, excited. Yet she could not forget the fear in her Maame's muffled voice, the refusal in Serwaa's brusque answers. And she could not quell the quivering in the back of her stomach.

When she arrived with Serwaa at the market, Folayan saw the others had set their market items down on Maame and Serwaa's space and had been trying to watch over them while doing their own bartering. Serwaa greeted them with thanks and moved into her place, fierce in making up time.

It was fun at the market. There was much excitement with all the people, items for sale and noise. While she tried to follow Serwaa's instructions, Folayan's gaze wandered in awe. Folayan soaked up all the sights, smells, sounds, people, Fantis she had never seen before mingling with soldiers, kwesi broni soldiers who lived over there and took the path by the palm grove. The path that went up the other hill.

Papa came by. Serwaa told him about Maame. He helped sort the largest of his fresh fish, left some with Serwaa and took the rest home. No doubt Serwaa would sell all she had. Folayan reached into the basket for more cassava and black-eyed peas. She arranged them in attractive peaks on the mat. Listening to Serwaa with a customer, Folayan wondered if she could ever barter like that.

A woman was admiring the shiny, deep purple garden eggs, so large she had to hold one plant with both hands. She asked the price, and when Folayan told her, she bought five.

*I asked too little.*

The woman paid with cowry sea shells. After Folayan tucked them away, the shadow of Fort Kormantin caught her gaze. Looking up, she felt so small seeing it from down on the beach at the bottom of the hill.

She studied the huge gray structure, seeing around the side and part of the back. It sat. Watching. Silent. As if waiting for something.

A deep mellow voice startled her.

"Well, hello. W*o ho te sen.*"

Folayan turned to stare into a broad, sepia chest. Her eyes traveled up to Kofi's handsome face.

"*Me ho ye*, very well," she responded, with a flustered smile. They inquired about every member of the other's family. Finally, Folayan asked, "How long have you been standing there?"

"Long enough to wonder what could capture you so deep in thought."

She glanced over at Serwaa, who was haggling with a man from another village about one of Folayan's bowls she'd painted in her white lace design. His wife had asked him especially for it. Serwaa sold them all the last Market Day.

"I was thinking about the fort," Folayan said.

Kofi looked up at it and was thoughtful for a moment. "What causes you to be at the market today? This is your first time, yes?"

Though she had mentioned in the greeting a bit about her mother, now she told him more.

"Can I be of any help?"

"No. Thank you, though." She smiled at him again. "How long have you been at the market today?"

"Since early this morning after fishing. We have sold all our fish now, and I—"

"How are you today, Miss Folayan?" Abeeku, one of Kofi's fishing mates eyeing her with appreciation, interrupted Kofi.

A second friend, Jojo, came up on Kofi's other side. "So you are a market woman now."

With his eyebrow raised, Abeeku went on, "I did not realize you have grown so beautiful."

Folayan blushed.

Kofi said, "I can see it is time for us to go. Good-bye, Folayan." He put his arms on his friends' shoulders and steered them away.

"Adzenkye, Folayan." Abeeku threw his good-bye over his shoulder with a cheeky smile.

Jo-jo waved. "I will look for you at Onyamedua, the end of the week."

Abeeku grinned sideways at her. "Forget about these two. Save a place for me."

"Adzenkye." She laughed.

Kofi turned back. "They will go play now, but I will be working, finishing a very special kente cloth." He flashed a smile and her heart tripped.

She watched them stride in rhythm toward their boat. She compared theirs to the swagger of her brother, Akonor, and his group who'd just crossed over their Rite of Passage to manhood a few moons ago. Their strolls proclaimed, "Look at me, I am a man!"

Kofi and his friends were in the age group ahead of Akonor and their four or five years more of maturity supported their confidence. They joined three other fishing mates, grabbed up their nets, and headed home. She was glad they would not hear the drumming in her chest, yet sad because she wanted Kofi to stay.

She turned back to her work and found a decided change in the market. She saw most of the other vendor women walking up the hill. Folayan's brothers came by and stayed until Serwaa had sold much of their wares. When it was time to leave, Folayan scanned at the deserted marketplace and above to the Fort.

Maame would return next week, and she would go back to her painting. She was not sure if she would be satisfied with just that, now.

On the way up to the village, Folayan listened to her brothers' humor, but soon caught herself giggling several times at a different conversation. She rehearsed the young men's flirtations, wondering if they could be attracted to her, or were they just teasing? The idea that Kofi might have real interest made her pulse jump. She recalled the day that Papa and Maame had gone to see Kofi about making the kente.

Adwoa had been there and related the entire conversation to Folayan that evening at the square. She told how pleased Kofi was about learning to weave the kente cloth and the chance to show his work. The last time Folayan visited her friend, she had seen Kofi's loom placed beside a wall three rooms long outside his parent's house. His taut, even work impressed her.

Her parents had listened politely as Kofi explained what Papa had already told his family concerning the young man's training. "Although," Adwoa said, "there were some things he mentioned that your Papa raised his eyebrows to and said, 'Is that so?'"

Adwoa giggled. "Kofi sounded like a proud old man sharing his wisdom with youngsters when he spoke about the kente designs and all the different weave patterns." She struck a pompous pose like that of an overbearing teacher, her voice going deep to imitate her brother.

"Each design has a different meaning. Certain patterns can be worn only by royalty. Unlike the Ashanti who will use up to five different colors on one kente, Fanti prefer two color kentes, black and white, or blue and white. We decorate ourselves with abundant gold jewelry."

The two of them laughed together at the picture Adwoa presented.

"But they were kind and listened to everything Kofi had to say. Then your Papa showed him your Kwantunyi pattern, which included something Adwoa was forbidden to reveal. Kofi promised to finish it in time for your celebration."

Folayan blushed, knowing that each time she wore the garment, she would remember Kofi's hands had caressed every thread that surrounded her.

Two days following her first market day, after the week's work was completed, meals eaten, and baths taken. People ambled toward the ancient tree in the town square to enjoy the start of the rest day.

Adwoa came and sat beside Folayan. They talked about Adwoa's approaching wedding—and speculated about Folayan's. Depending on when Papa earned all the funds he desired, Folayan's Rite of Passage should take place maybe four or five months later, after the Bakatue.

The conversation ended when four young men joined them: Jojo, Abeeku, Kofi, and Kwaku—Adwoa's betrothed.

During the evening, out of the corner of her eye, Folayan observed Kofi noticing her.

# CHAPTER 20

# War Cry

*The priest placed his hands over the chicken's head
and wrung it around and around until its neck cracked.
The body ripped from it, and flew across the yard.*

*The bellowing, banshee chant echoed after them.*

**May 1795, Kormantse Village**

Over the next three weekends, the group of young people met at sunset. Instead of talking in their regular space on the other side of the tree, Kofi's unmarried fishing companions attended Folayan's age mates, engaging in playful banter, as well as Akan proverbs and other thought-provoking topics.

On this Friday morning, Folayan heard a knock at the door. She opened it to see Fatima with a basket.

"Instead of meeting Afua at her house, she wants you to go to the Onyamedua tree at noon, if your work is done, and bring a basket this size."

All eight of the age mates met on time, wanting to know, "What are we going to do with these baskets and why is Fatima's so much bigger?"

"Wait and see. You will like it," Afua said. "We will follow Fatima to the first surprise."

Teasing and giggling about their rites of passage and impending marriages, they followed Fatima until they reached the edge of the woods.

Afua stopped and waved them into a circle around her. "I know there are only a few kyen kyen trees in our village. My father gave me permission to take you to his grove and cut bark from our trees. Fatima has learned to make cloth. I thought it would be wonderful for her to make cloth for us to sew dresses to wear when we are married women."

Fatima's eyes grew wide.

Abena said, "You want Fatima to make cloth for all of us? When would she have time to do that?"

Folayan's eyes lit up. "I would like to learn how to make the kyen kyen cloth,"

"Yes. Yes. That is what I meant," Afua said.

Folayan looked at her askance, then at the others' doubting faces. *Afua never agreed so quickly. What else does she want?*

Afua continued, "Fatima will guide us to the trees now."

When they arrived and stood looking up at a large kyen kyen tree, Afua took the lid off Fatima's basket and lifted out a machete. Everybody stepped back, some three times.

Afua handed the machete to Fatima, who showed them how to make careful cuts and pull the bark off the tree in large pieces. Folayan waited for her turn. *I need my own machete from my box.*

When everyone had enough in their baskets, Fatima put one of the strips on a tree stump, and pounded it until it could drape over her wrist.

"This one is now soft enough to sew into longer sections to make wide cloth," Fatima said.

Afua said, "We will pound our bark at my house. Let's go."

They walked some distance before Adwoa said, "This is not the way to your house. Where are we going?"

"Before you get to my house, I have a second part of the surprise." She hurried to a space about 400 feet away. At the sound of their voices, small birds sped off into the sky. Folayan looked up into the trees. A skin-headed vulture sat hidden in the shadows.

Soon Folayan spied the shrine. One of several tucked on the outskirts of the akura. Folayan noticed one corner of the thatch roof was somewhat frayed, but it was clean all around the entrance and sides like village homes. She did not trust Afua's smile. As they neared the building, her unease increased and she looked around for the best way to escape.

Afua stopped at the door. The shrine looked like a house. It had an open air adiho. In addition, it connected to a rear garden with a skimpy wall of bushes around it.

Folayan was cautious. She had never been to the shrine without her parents.

Abena asked, "Now what?"

Afua explained. "We will all be women soon. Adwoa and Yaa are about to be married. And Abena, you just ended your forty days. Ekua will begin hers next week."

Fifteen-year-old Folayan smiled, happy for them and wished it was her time. Maame told Serwaa that Papa had earned more than enough money, but wanted it to be so special that suitors would send their knockings the first week after her fortieth day.

Afua had her celebration two months ago, and five weeks for Amba. They were still waiting for knockings. Afua didn't mention that. Folayan glanced at her.

"Oh, and Folayan's coming of age will be in a few months, probably," Afua added.

"And Fatima," Folayan inserted. "She is with me."

"I thought it would be a good thing—" Afua ignored her as she continued, "—for us to offer sacrifice to the obosom for prosperous husbands and many healthy children. Especially girls, yes, girls, for us all. And we can do it together. We do not have to be alone."

Afua's voice twinged. Folayan had never thought of coming to the shrine alone. She shuddered.

Did my parents come to the shrine to pray for that? As much as she wanted to fulfill her family's need, she did not want to go into the shrine to gain favor of spirits that might be demons.

Adwoa said, "We do not have to do this at all. At the end of our forty days, our parents will petition Onyankopon for those things for us at the Onyamedua."

"But what if it is not enough?"

Folayan saw Afua's eyebrow pinch and heard the catch in her throat. All of the girls stared at Afua. Folayan had never seen her cry. No. She is not crying?

Afua said quickly, "The dresses we started making today, we can design them all the same and once we are all married, we will show everybody that we have been through everything together. We are much stronger together than apart."

Together is better than alone, is it not? Folayan wanted the blessing Afua spoke of, but not if she had to go in there with those spirits and hand-carved gods to get it.

She looked at her friends, one shaking her head with Adwoa, three nodding agreement with Afua, and Fatima trying not to be seen.

Adwoa said, "I am not going in there."

Afua said, "You already have a man, Adwoa. Are you saying you will not even go in and pray for us?"

Adwoa looked trapped. She did not answer.

"Come, let us all go in now." Afua grabbed Yaa's hand and guided them into the adiho.

After a moment, Abena asked, "Where is Adwoa?"

"Oh. Wait here for me." Afua returned to the entry.

Folayan hung back at the end of the line, watching.

Afua said, "We need you, Adwoa, to make it stronger. Come with us. It will be fine."

Folayan hesitated. *Papa said unity is important, but not when your stomach tells you something is wrong.*

Just as she decided to join Adwoa, Afua nudged her forward. Folayan cast a plaintive look back at Adwoa, who remained outside.

Fatima lingered at the door. "You said I do not need the prayers. Can I stay right here?"

"No. I may need your help," Afua said.

She led them through the back door into the garden graveyard.

Folayan's skin prickled. Her elbow grazed a human head on a stake. She jerked away and cried out. Her heart started beating against her chest. She did not want the others to know how hard this was. Walking almost on tip-toe, marking each step, her heart cried out, Wait. Wait. She looked back, staying close to the line.

The first and last time she had been here, she held her Maame's hand and kept her eyes squeezed shut. After that, her parents left her at home with one of her brothers.

*Why did we not wait outside with Adwoa? Are the others more worried about getting the right husband, or not wanting to deal with Afua if they refused?*

*Adwoa is wise, but like Afua said, her father has already accepted Kwaku's knocking.*

With all her might, she hoped Kofi would send her a knocking, but all these other girls were older than her. Even though Kofi had been smiling at her at Onyamedua, one of her age mates might catch his eye before her time.

Abena said, "Why is it that every time I have been here, the feeling is always the same?"

"I know," said Ekua. "A surprise. Hmph! Afua sure did it to us this time. Ach!" She stepped over a broken bone.

Amba complained. "I never expected to spend my day like this. It stinks out here."

Folayan came face to face with a human skeleton and screamed. She then saw several others hung in different places. She could not look anywhere without seeing one. She wanted to close her eyes, but was scared of falling on something awful.

Chicken heads and cooked foods had been placed below the skeletons.

When the girls were halfway into the garden, Folayan froze, aghast. Suddenly, a fetish priest emerged out of the dark corner.

Wanting to turn back, yet afraid of separating from the pack of age mates, Folayan watched him come toward them, carrying a basket. Her heart pounded like a djembe drum.

Folayan panicked, but could not move past him with the closed basket in his arms.

A few feet away, Yaa patted her hip, urging Folayan to come stand next to her. She lurched to Yaa's side and closed her eyes tight.

When she peeked to see if he was gone, he was nearer than before, but standing still—too close with his painted black masked face, matted locks, and unearthly silence. Folayan sniffed to hold her breath, waiting for an odor, but there was none.

Afua went to the priest. What she said to him, Folayan could not hear. He set the basket on the ground in front of Afua. It had the same design as the basket with the machete and Afua's bark strips.

Folayan heard the chicken clucking. *How long has Afua been planning to bring us to the shrine, and how did she know we would come?*

Afua opened the lid, reached in, grabbed the chicken by the neck, and pulled it out.

It flapped its wings. Like it knew what was about to happen, it squirmed and squawked. The priest took it from Afua.

Queasiness stirred Folayan's stomach. She looked off. Now, idols of wood and stone merged into her view. They lurked in shadows as well as out in the open. Tall, squat, round, small and large: nine, no eleven ... fourteen ... she stopped counting.

The priest showed Afua a fire pit of three good-sized round stones in a circle. Folayan gasped at the human skulls fitted into the spaces between them.

Folayan looked to the door of the adiho. She wanted to leave. She spied other pits here and there.

The wide-eyed girls followed Afua and huddled together.

Afua told Fatima to start the fire in the skull-rimmed pit. The priest placed his hands over the chicken's head and wrung it around and around until its neck cracked. The body ripped from it, and flew across the yard.

They squealed, screamed, and whimpered, watching it flip and jump all over. The plump body bumped over gourds of food splattering blood in its wild erratic course.

They all shrieked as it knocked one of the skeletons off its pole, bones breaking, scattering on the ground.

When the chicken landed at the clustered girls' feet, flinging blood onto three of them, they screamed and bolted away. Folayan ran toward the door.

That is when she heard the sound of water. The other girls looked around, hesitating. There was no river in their village. People had to go a small distance outside for bathing at the Etsi lagoon or down in the ocean.

No stream in the garden, but now this strange sound of running water. Where was it coming from?

Did Afua not hear it? The priest took a knife from under his garment. He gutted the bird and pulled its organs out.

Afua told each of them to take one of the parts. She put hers on the fire and commanded her age mates to do the same.

No one moved.

Afua gave them a frustrated glare, then began to pray without them.

Folayan inched closer to the door, half listening, but stopped when Afua said, "He is mine. I know that is why I am still waiting for his knocking. I was born for him," she whispered. "We two on the same day."

On the same day? Who is she talking about? Which young man is Afua's age? Folayan sucked in breath. Afua—born on Friday. Kofi? Something crashed inside Folayan.

But there are other Kofis. Is she talking about one of the married Kofis? There is one among Akonor's age mates, too. Who else?

"Oh, no." Admitting there was only one it could be, Folayan moaned and turned to leave.

Anger edged in Afua's voice. She rose from her knees. "Why did you not offer the sacrifice with me?"

Firelight flickered on her face. She stood over the burning pit. "Come here, and get these offerings." She glared at them, pointing her finger at each one.

Yaa walked toward Folayan.

"You said you were going to do this with me," Afua screamed. "All of you come over here and finish it. Come here now!"

"Afua, this is something you wanted." Yaa beckoned the others to her. "Not us. Please stop trying to force us."

Afua put her hands over her ears. "Do it! Do it!" she yelled. "I will not forget this. I will never forget!" Desperate, she looked around, searching for something. She started throwing chicken parts at them.

Two girls tore past Folayan. The chicken heart hit one of them in the back. A gizzard flew along Folayan's ear. The liver splatted on the wall by the door.

They rushed through the doorway into the adiho. Then they heard it. A chill sprinted up Folayan's back.

A war cry—but it was not Afua.

Her voice howled, "You better not leave! Come back here!"

*To hear a war song in a shrine means your life is in danger.*

Folayan's stomach wrenched. Wet with perspiration everywhere on her body except her throat, she kept swallowing to stop the dryness from strangling her.

"I will kill you. I will kill you!" Afua shrieked.

A skull crashed into the adiho. It hit Folayan's heel.

She jerked away so fast she lost her balance and fell. The more she tried to pull herself up from her awkward sprawl, the more frantic and incapacitated she became. The other girls were scrambling to gather up their baskets.

Adwoa sprang from outside to help Folayan.

The harsh, insistent song grew louder and higher, and more frightening.

Adwoa pulled Folayan up and they dashed through the doorway and onto the road.

"Do not leave me," Fatima called to them, trying to lift to her shoulder the large basket she had brought to the kyen kyen trees. It was heavy with bark and the machete. As they went back toward the door to help her, she ran out of the building with both arms hugging the basket to her belly.

The bellowing, banshee chant echoed after them.

Fatima tried again to raise her basket. With one hand by herself. Folayan reached up to brace Fatima's. Adwoa helped support Folayan's basket. Outside, the others ran singly and by twos.

*Is Afua still in the shrine?*

If they were running to their houses, Folayan didn't want to go to her house in case her family was on their way to the tree.

Their families expected them to be at Afua's house all afternoon, and to meet them at the ancient Onyamedua tree by dusk. She decided to go straight to the place in the village where she could feel safe.

# CHAPTER 21

# City of Refuge

*Folayan sank into her thoughts, reliving the awful event,
tracing her gullibility, and vowing to never let anyone else
draw her into something she did not want to do.*

*All of us have been taught to recite a long roll of our ancestors' names,
but did they worship any different gods than you? How about your parents,
or your brothers? Sisters? Does anyone travel to festivals to worship gods
we've never heard of?"*

**May 1795, Kormantse Village**

Soon it became evident to Folayan that she and her age mates all
had one mind, getting to the Onyamedua.

Folayan thought there was nowhere else she wanted to be right
now. It was to her a place of peace and protection.

When the girls arrived at the tree, no one else was there. Barely
talking, they sat and waited for the crowd to come. Folayan sank into her
thoughts, reliving the awful event, tracing her gullibility, and vowing to
never let anyone else draw her into something she did not want to do.

Ekua said, "We must go. Afua is coming."

"I see some other people not far behind her." Abena's hand shaded the sun from her eyes.

"She looks wild-eyed and puffed up with madness." Amba stood up.

"She will not dishonor herself in front of others." Yaa waved Amba back down.

Like kingfishers lined in a row, they sat ready to fly away in a flash.

Afua charged up to them and stopped ten feet away with her hands on her hips. *No blood on her fingers? She must have stopped to wash them.*

"There it is! Why did you take it?" Afua rushed upon Fatima, snatched the basket, flung the lid aside and pulled out the machete.

They all screamed, jumped up in different directions and put a safe distance between them.

Coming closer, she brandished it, threatening.

"You forgot where you sleep." She moved with menace toward Fatima. "And who you work for. Whose food you eat."

Folayan saw Abeeku approaching behind Afua. When he was near enough, he grabbed her wrist. Jojo came up on her side and restained her while Abeeku removed the machete and put it out of sight.

When they let Afua go, she kicked at Jojo.

They attempted to calm her. She kept trying to run at her age mates. When she quieted, the young men released her, but stayed right beside her. She stood, chest heaving, out of breath.

Folayan stared at her. She had never seen Afua like this. In an instant, Afua could present herself an able, poised representative of the chieftain, but her snide, vengeful acts were underhanded irritants, difficult to challenge. She used words. She did not need violence. Afua skillfully hurt people with her tongue. *When did she become like this?*

Folayan's mind chanted, *No! No!* while Abeeku brought the machete and put it in the basket. Jojo held Afua's arm, but she broke loose. With balled fist, she darted to Fatima, giving her a fierce blow on the head.

She wound up with all her might to strike her again, as though it was meant for the whole group, but Fatima dodged. Afua had swung with such force, she doubled over, lost her balance, and thudded to the ground.

The age mates gathered around Fatima, comforting her.

Jojo caught Afua by both wrists, but kept her feet away from him.

"Let me go!" she demanded.

"I would gladly let you go, for when I do, you will get what you deserve."

"Do you realize who you are talking to?"

"I have not forgotten. Do you realize what you are doing to yourself?"

"What do you mean?"

"Our laws say a slaveholder who harms a slave will receive the same treatment. Is that what you want, Afua?"

Folayan saw her clenched teeth, through parted lips, but she stopped fighting.

Folayan looked around. A handful of people had settled under the tree. How long they'd been there or if they witnessed the incident, she did not know. She was glad her family had not arrived.

Folayan elbowed Adwoa, who surveyed the scene and shook her head.

"I am sad for Afua and embarrassed for us," Adwoa whispered. "As her age mates, we are deemed to be of the same feather."

A few minutes later, when Kofi came with the rest of his family, he greeted his friends and the young women. They acknowledged him, then sank into silence.

He studied their faces. "What happened?"

No one spoke. He stood before his sister. "Adwoa?"

She squirmed.

"Adwoa."

She sighed. "It started at the shrine. I did not go in. The others will have to tell you the rest."

He asked questions.

Afua accused all eight of her friends of causing the problem.

The young women tried to explain their part. Afua kept interrupting. Kofi said, "One at a time. Afua, you speak first."

She told her story, beginning with how she took two weeks planning to have such a special day for them. "And they betrayed me!" she screamed at her age mates. "And then left me there alone!"

Folayan searched the faces of shocked onlookers. She asked, "Can we go sit over there in that clearing? Our parents can still see us."

The three males sat opposite the females. Abeeku placed Afua between Jojo and himself, but Jojo went to the other side of Abeeku. Afua scooted closer to Kofi.

Folayan gazed at her, getting upset, until she observed Afua's demeanor. *She must be thinking they pity her, but she showed herself to be a brawling woman. Serwaa said no man wants that.*

Afua sat looking up at Kofi, ignoring the other two. She pouted and acted like a wounded egret.

Kofi called on each girl to give her account.

When it was Folayan's turn, she said, "I was scared from the beginning. I only went in because …" She paused, unwilling to announce that she wanted him to marry her. She turned her head. "Uhm … I just should not have gone in, and when the war song began, I got out of there."

Abeeku tried to shift the conversation. He teased them all. They relaxed.

Then Jojo said, "What about you, Fatima? What did you think about everything?"

Fatima looked at Afua, and shook her head.

Abeeku mumbled something.

Afua chuckled.

Kofi snapped the tip off a dry twig and flicked it away from him. "The shrine is nothing to laugh about."

"No. It is not." Abeeku shifted position. "I only wondered what is the difference in the shrine and this place. Scared of the shrine, but happy to be here. If it is all about spirits, is it not true that this tree is one big spirit that we worship?"

"We do not worship this tree. It is a place where Onyankopon— God Almighty, Tweduampon, visits with us."

The corners of Abeeku's mouth stretched downward. "Still, how is that different?"

Kofi explained. "The tree is a place where people meet to find safe haven. A place for protection, peace, and counseling. It is our city of refuge."

"What is that—city of refuge? What are you making up?"

"The kwesi broni preacher has a Book that tells about a people whose God told them to set up cities of refuge where they could escape anyone bent on revenge."

*A book? I wonder if it is like the books the Timbuktu merchants read to my brothers and Papa?*

Kofi paused and looked at each one in the group. He said slowly, "Our tree is like that. It is God's tree. The tree is not God—it is our meeting place. No one is allowed to harm you at the Onyamedua."

Every eye turned on Afua.

She sat up, straight-backed. "What about the oto? The women will soon come put the cloth down around the base of the tree and spread the yam and egg on it. Doesn't that mean we are worshipping the tree?"

Jojo said, "The oto is for the ancestors."

"Do they eat it—or do the spirits?" Amba ventured.

"Nobody. It is set out there to remember and honor the ancestors' lives. By the end of the week, it dries up unless an animal comes along and eats it," Kofi said flatly.

Gasps and whispers rippled through the row of females.

"Be careful, Kofi," Abeeku warned.

"Fear, Abeeku? Why should we let fear rule us? We are trapped in fright because there is much we do not know."

"I know if you go too far, no father will give you his daughter to marry. And you will be childless."

Kofi looked beyond Afua at Abeeku, then pointed to the young women. "Is there anything else you wonder about?"

Yaa said, "What is the difference in ancestors, ancestral gods, and the spirits? What shrieked at us in the shrine?"

Kofi said, "When I went away to learn kente weaving, I met many people and discovered much about other villages. Since then, I have had my own questions, but I do not want to just tell you what I think."

"Good!" snorted Abeeku. "Because I fear your thoughts can get us into trouble."

Kofi laughed with everybody. "I suggest we ask our families some questions. Who thinks we should do that?"

There were several nods.

"Is anybody afraid to do it?" No one answered Kofi. "The way to get rid of fright is to understand where it comes from. There are two kinds of fear. Respect or fright. To be wise and respectful is not the same as being afraid."

"What will we ask them?" Abena spoke up.

"About our ancestors' journey to this place. All of us have been taught to recite a long roll of our ancestors' names, but did they worship any different gods than you? How about your parents, or your brothers? Sisters? Does anyone travel to festivals to worship gods we have never heard of?" He paused.

All eyes followed his gaze to Folayan.

"Folayan is an artist. Maybe she will draw us a picture of what we find out." He smiled at her.

*Unh! He is quite pleasant to look at. Handsome. Yes. Hmm.* Folayan's face felt warm. Hiding her grin behind her hand, she could not resist assessing everyone's expression. He asked her to draw a picture. Of course, she would. Smiling, she nodded and looked down to calm her pounding heart.

"This is what we can do. Find small, thumb-sized stones for each god. Bring your collection back here next Friday."

"Can we ask the people who are already here at the tree now, as well as other villagers?" Ekua said.

"Yes. I think we will be surprised by what we find out."

"Another surprise?" Folayan grimaced and whispered to Adwoa, "I do not know if I am ready for that."

"Me neither."

# CHAPTER 22

# *Too Close to Strangers*

*And if he did not watch out,
before he even cast his net—the most valuable catch of all
would end up in one of his companions' net.*

**May 1795, Kormantse Village**

While she walked home in the dark with her family, worries about the war cry invaded Folayan's musings about Kofi. She did not linger in the adiho, except to ask Papa if she could look at his maps. She selected the oldest scroll.

Pulling the curtain aside, she heard her aunt's steady, even breathing. Asleep already.

The long day of contrasts rolled through her head.

Into the dark room, through the adiho window, a white beam shone onto her Kwantunyi box.

Folayan crawled to it. She took out the fabrics and stacked them neatly beside her knee. Then one by one, in the patch of moon light, she

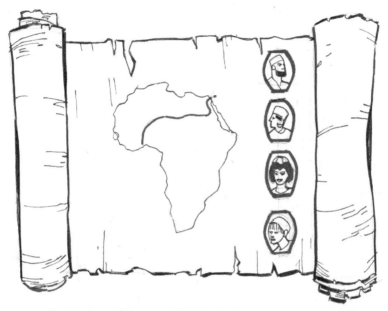

examined gifts that had waited for her to be born. Now she dreamed of using them when she'd be a hostess in the home she'd share with her husband.

Papa said the items in his box spoke 1200 years of family history. He told her that she must one day add something to that box herself. Something of significance. *But what?*

She unrolled the scroll and studied the ancient map by the bright moonlight. *Will my husband lead me to some adventurous place? Who will he be? A good man like Papa? Will he be Kofi? How many children will I have?*

Folayan yawned, rolled the scroll and set it on her shelf.

After putting her other things carefully back into her box, she lay down, but her thoughts would not calm. Those heroes and heroines of her past kept traveling through her brain. It seemed they knew so much about life. She envied the knowledge and understanding of her ancestors.

The next morning, she explained about yesterday. Papa answered her questions about their ancestors, deities, spirits, and traditions.

"When I go up to Kumasi, even today they continue ceremonies of sacrifice the great leader Moses guided the people of the Most High to do."

Papa said, "The Africans have practiced these rituals since long before Christ was born."

She waited for her father to explain. When he did not, she asked, "Christ. Jesus. Why are you and my brothers talking so much about Him when you never did before—before this last journey to Timbuktu?" *I want to know about Him, but they all speak in riddles.*

She looked at both parents. No one explained. Serwaa got up and left the room with no words, but her shoulders drooped humph.

Usually Folayan would not venture further into space that body language hindered.

Papa leaned forward. "When I get the Books—I mean the Old Testament, the Gospels, and the Psalms—or even a full Bible, I will be happy to learn as much as I can. I plan to see what matches our traditions. Until then, your mother knows more about the Christians than I do."

Folayan shifted around with a questioning eyebrow. *What will Maame say?*

"Kwamina, Kwesi, and Akonor, you spoke of Jesus when you were talking about the king's dream, and that other king who became a Christian. What was his name?

Kwamina answered, "Constantine."

"Yes, him, Constantine. Do the Christians have many gods, too?

Maame said, "No, they only have The Most High who is one God—in three persons: the Father, the Son, and the Holy Spirit. These three have many different names and responsibilities." She winced, shifting her injured ankled on the pilloe in front of her.Folayan frowned.

Maame said, "It is no different from us. What is the name we call the Most High?

Folayan pursed her lip. "Onyankopon Tweduampon Kwame."

"See. Three names one God," Maame said, "The I am that I am? He is now and forever was and always will be. There is no God before Him or greater than Him." Folayan looked to her Papa, who remained silent.

Maame continued. "The preacher spoke even another name: 'One like God' another name for the Son. He says it is the Christ, 'the Chosen One,' and that He came to our earth to be a man for a while to help us see how to walk in His shoes, so people who want to can go to live with the Most High in his house in the sky."

Folayan repeated the words until the picture fixed in her head, then she asked, "Why do I know so little about this Christ?"

Maame spoke. "Through the years Kwamina has often asked me questions and I answer them. These are not new ideas, our people who came from Kush and before that, Kmt, and before that, Canaan, they knew about the promised Savior."

Folayan and every one in the room listened intently. *How could this be that Maame knew so much, and kept it inside her for so long?*

"Maame, my brothers talked about the king's dream they spoke of a Savior, but I want to know more. What else did our ancestors know about Him?"

"They knew about the wilderness tabernacle with its continued promise that a Savior would come someday and be sacrificed to put an end to sin. They knew He came as a baby and kept the promise given long ago to our first ancestors, Adam and Eve."

"How did they know?" Folayan searched into her mother's eyes.

"Well, they knew because God set in place reminders, so we would spend time with Him, never forget Him, and know how much He loves us. The first reminder comes at nnason, the end of every sixth day, when the day of rest begins. Do we still do that?"

"Yes. We do." Folayan said, "But not everybody."

"We do not follow everybody. We remember and do what God told us to do. Not what men tell us to do."

Folayan glanced at her mother, who seemed wistful. She touched her arm, "Maame? What is the matter?"

Maame looked down at Folayan's hand, then put hers on top of it. "Sometimes I think about the fort over there, and the intruders' presence. Little by little we are changing, doing more of their ways. Forgetting our own."

They were silent for a moment.

Folayan asked, "Are there any more of God's reminders?"

"God made some ways for our ancestors to celebrate every few moons during the year. The festivals helped them remember how God was leading, taking care of them, and keeping His promises."

"What kind of festivals?"

"One is called Passover," Maame responded.

"I know about Passover," Papa said. "It was for us to remember that God rescued them from slavery in Kmt."

"Do we do that?" asked Folayan.

Maame, stopped and stared at her, "What do you think we are doing when we put the blood on the door posts and over the top of the door frame?"

Folayan felt sheepish, "Oh I thought … I did not know that … you mean that came out of the Bible?"

Maame's face softened, "Yes, Folayan. We have a number of customs that our ancestors practiced long before we left Canaan and followed the Nile River down to the land of Kush. And although our ancestors practiced the rituals that reminded them of the Most High and the Promise, they also started copying rituals of their neighbors. And they forgot much that they had known from the beginning."

Frustration rose inside Folayan. "But what about me? You knew all these things. Did you not think I would want to know, too?"

"Not everyone wants to talk about Him. Fanti people know much more about Christian ideas because they associate more with the kwesi bronis. As a young wife, I learned to wait until I was asked to speak about these things."

Papa looked straight at Maame. "Though the Fantis have great knowledge and skills, I believe they come too close to the strangers. I do not trust as easily as the Fanti do."

Folayan thought about differences between her mother's Fanti people and her Papa's, the Etsi. But right now they seemed too uncomfortable; she would ask more about them later. She looked around for some way to relieve the tension. In this last year, it seemed as if her home that was usually so peaceful, bubbled every so often with tension—*tension that starts with me.*

She held the map out and studied it, wishing she had one of her own. "It never meant so much until you told me all those places I did not know."

Her finger traced the longest road. *That is it! My first gift to my box.* "Papa, may I paint a picture of this before I give it back to you?"

He smiled broadly. "Certainly."

Kwamina cleared his throat.

Papa glanced at him, then said, "Can you make some pictures for your brothers, too?"

"Of course," she said. "But I need more cloth."

They offered to buy some at market, but she said, "No, it will take me longer, but I will find a way."

She hugged Papa and hurried to her room. In the corner, she spied the basket with the kyen kyen bark.

*I can make picture cloth from this. I do not want a dress like Afua's anyway, and I never will go in that shrine again.*

While other family members went out to spend the last couple hours of the Rest Day with friends at the tree, Folayan stayed with her Papa, fixing details in her mind.

By Wednesday evening, after working at the market, Folayan finished painting the ancient tree and background. Friday morning, Adwoa dropped by.

Adwoa said, "Over the last weeks we have talked mostly about me and my wedding plans. Today, you tell me how your Coming of Age is progressing."

Folayan chuckled and crooked her finger. "Follow me." It thrilled her each time she stepped into her room with her gold-banded box sitting there.

Adwoa exclaimed, "Oh! It is beautiful." She pointed to the gleaming ebony lid, the silver, gold, and brass. Your papa loves you so much."

Folayan said, "Papa tried for a long time to find one like his. And though I may only travel across the village to the home of the man I marry, it is my Kwantunyi box."

Folayan opened the box. Atop the fabrics, lay a painted woodcut. "Remember this?" She reached for the portrait.

"I certainly do. I see my Maame's everyday on the wall. Sometimes I study the one you gave me at my celebration." She pointed. "See how happy we are. That was so nice of you to do that for our mothers—and me!"

They opened the fabrics, then refolded them while tallking, giggling, planning. "It is wonderful, is it not?" Adwoa said, "Soon we both will marry and start our own families."

Folayan said, "You mean soon *you* will marry, but things happen for me at a turtle's pace."

"I do not know about that. Remember, my womanhood came almost a full afenhyia before my celebration. Then it has been six moons and all the reports have not come back on Kwaku." Adwoa looked away.

Folayan reached for her hand. "The conduct testimonies will all praise him, like yours did. You and I know that."

"Thank you, Folayan. It is so hard waiting. Oh, I meant to tell you, Kofi's been asking questions about you, ever since he noticed you on your first market day. He missed you last Saturday, too, when you did not come worship with us at all. I teased him."

Folayan tried to cover her grin.

Adwoa laughed. "I reminded him about the very long net all of them use together to bring in the big catch. It has its purpose. But each of his companions has a personal net, and they are casting them out."

Folayan imagined her friend counseling her brother, and what his facial expression might have been like.

Adwoa added, "I told him he was so interested in the time and place for fishing and weaving, he did not take time to look for a wife."

Folayan held her breath, while Adwoa continued speaking. "And if he did not watch out, before he even cast out his net—the most valuable catch of all would end up in one of his companion's nets."

Adwoa raised her eyebrows with a knowing smile.

Folayan giggled. "What did he say?"

"He said nothing, but got a determined look on his face."

Folayan's hope soared.

"Have you collected many stones?" Adwoa asked. "Yaa has thirty-two. Every time I count, Kofi brings in more. So I gave up. We will see tonight."

"I only have eleven."

"Where's your painting?"

Folayan took it down off the shelf.

"Oh. That is nice. You can even see the gnarly bark on the trunk. I really like it. Kofi will be pleased, too," Adwoa said. "Can we take it to show him now?"

# CHAPTER 23

# A Pile of Stones

*Kofi pulled out another stone and named a different god,*
*and his dread. Again nothing happened to him.*
*He did it three more times.*

*Some left three stones, others ten, seventeen—deities from the land, sea,*
*and wind for every process of life.*

**May 1795, Kormantse Village**

O f the many times Folayan had raced to Adwoa's house, Kofi had never been the object of her visit. Or, at least Folayan hoped she'd managed to keep her feelings hidden enough that he did not guess how much she liked him.

"This is excellent." He glanced at her as he studied the painting. His finger traced the path leading to the Onyame dua tree, the little cove to the side where their friends nestled, and the tall bush behind them, all graced by the golden-red sunset sky. She only had to fill in the people.

"You do very nice work, Folayan." Kofi carefully handed it back to her.

As he did, his fingertips brushed hers, and she gasped. A surprising tingling seemed to pass between them.

Adwoa chuckled. "Both of you caught your breath."

He grinned. "I admit it." He touched his sister's arm. "Hmm. Nothing."

Laughing, Adwoa swatted him.

Embarrased, Folayan could only smile and look away.

But she felt his gaze on her until he spoke, "Adwoa said you started the picture, but I never expected so much."

"Yes." She smiled up at him. "What is the main thing you want painted?"

"The pile of stones."

"Oh?" Folayan forced herself to meet his eyes in playful challenge. She stifled a giggle. Standing there so close to him, she could feel his breath, and she realized what she really wanted to paint was … him. Her chest tightened and her blood rushed. Her face felt warm—hot.

Folayan sighed with some relief when Adwoa's eldest brother opened the door and spoke from the entryway.

"Kofi?"

"Yes?" Kofi and Adwoa went to the short wide hall.

"What is this I am hearing? Oh, hello, Folayan." After the proper greetings, he nudged Kofi. "You have got the whole village astir. Everybody is talking about ancestors and gods."

Kofi laughed. "It is all because of them." He pointed.

"What?" Adwoa blinked.

"Their age mates went to the shrine and came away with troubling questions. I thought I would try to help. That is all."

His brother did not to accept his explanation. "Abeeku is worried the priests and elders will be upset. With you."

Kofi's smile vanished. "I do not understand. Are they angry? We only mean to discuss beliefs we have been taught our whole lives, and well, what we think of those things."

His brother shook his head. "I believe it is because of your meetings with that milk-skinned Sunday man." He moved in front of Kofi, eye to eye. "What is that preacher telling you?"

"No need to worry. Trust me," Kofi said. "We must go to the tree now." He picked up a small basket.

Folayan said, "I need to get my stones and painting tools."

On the way, Adwoa asked, "Kofi I am worried about this pile of stones. Why do you want to stir things up with so many people?"

Folayan studied his face, reminding her of how Papa thought deeply before speaking sometimes.

Kofi answered, "I have experienced some things that terrified me and made me feel helpless. And ... yes, I have been talking to the preacher. I believe now that the Most High does not want to frighten us—the devils do. They want to keep us from knowing how much God loves us. He wants the praise and honor due only to Him.

"I want the stone pile so we can see with our eyes how many ways our attention is broken up and given to things that did not create us. We speak the words, 'The Most High—Creator of all people and things.' But are they just words? What do we care more about—Him or the idols? I am not saying people must stop whatever they are doing, that is their choice. I am just answering questions you girls asked after you fled from the shrine.

"Since it came up, I feel now is the time—might be the only time to have a good look at it. I have decided to change my own ways. If people become angry with me for calling attention to it, and if I have to leave this village to make this change in my life. I will."

Folayan caught her breath. Adwoa took her hand and said, "Kofi, is it not enough just to do it? Why do you want a painting?"

"I have learned that God will judge all people to see if they want to live with Him forever. Each person's life actions are written in a book so they can see for themselves their own choices. That banshee scream you all heard in the shrine was real. I want Folayan to paint this day when we choose who we will serve. The picture will remind us. Anyone who asks can count the stones for themselves. Each stone is a free choice."

As they walked, Folayan decided that he could have kept his concerns to himself, but he cared about others, and he was so brave, and she liked him more than ever before.

Folayan had tried all week to pretend and push away her apprehension, but her turmoil about the spirits and the war cry mounted. *Did we do something we will forever regret?*

She did not know if she could steady the paint brushes in her hand. Nearing the tree of peace and safety, she halted.

"Folayan, what is wrong?" Kofi asked. His brow knit and his eyes searched her face for an answer.

She told them, "It is the shrine. Adwoa, you did not go in, but I did. Now I fear someone is going to die because of me!"

"Why do you feel that way, Folayan?"

"The banshee screams. I do not know ... I just ... I had bad feelings before we went in."

Kofi moved to her with arms open, but Adwoa stopped him, and embraced Folayan in his place.

He sucked in a breath, and released it slowly. "It is for this reason we must do what we are doing tonight. Pray for me. Pray to Onyankopon, the Almighty I am that I am. Today is Memeneda, the day He chooses to meet with us. He will help us speak for Him."

Behind them, excited chattering surged.

"Kofi! The village hero." Abeeku walked up, slapped him on the back, and drew him forward.

Folayan situated to see the group and Kofi easily.

Folayan watched her age mates settle in a half circle. Not only Jojo and Abeeku, but also their other seven fishing companions, as well as their wives, joined them. Adwoa's betrothed came and sat beside her.

Jojo lit a fire in front of the half-circle.

Abeeku said, "Let us move to the other side of the fire, so that our backs are to those people surrounding the tree."

"No. We want to see the faces of the group of you, as the speakers stand to the side and talk to all of us." Folayan recognized the voice of the chieftain's linguist. She prayed.

Folayan didn't see the chieftain, but Abeeku's grin disappeared. The knot bobbled in his throat.

"Let us begin."

Kofi first gave proper honor to the Most High God, to the omahene, the elders, and the priests.

"I acknowledge our shrine. As in one house, family members may each submit to different gods, I value our teachings that allow each villager to choose whom they will serve. No one is forced to worship against his will.

"I have come to think that there is more to know."

Someone from under the tree asked, "Is that what the kwesi broni told you?"

"These are my grandfather's words. However, I have noticed the Dutch preacher respects our merchants. He is different from the other Portuguese and British priests who have lived around here since before my grandfather started fishing, but still know only a handful of our words. The preacher speaks Fanti well."

Kofi continued. "The old kwesi broni asked me about fishing and told me he is a fisher of men. I thought he meant slave catcher. So, each time I planned my escape, and talked to him only if he was alone, knowing I can overpower him.

"I asked him why he kept trying to get me to talk to him. He said he wanted to be my friend."

"Friend?" Abeeku snorted.

"From that time my grandfather counseled me to never trust the friendship of the kwesi broni. One day, I watched the preacher warily, he was coughing a great amount. He is not well. He says he has important things to tell me. He believes he will die soon."

Sketching Kofi's serious face, Folayan paused. Her mother felt kindly toward the preacher, too.

*But how much time does Kofi spend with …?*

"I feel that I need to hear what he has to say. The first time we talked, he told me God is Love." Kofi mostly faced the small group. Folayan noticed his struggle to keep from glancing at the people at the tree, also.

"Whenever he speaks about the Love of God, I feel that I want to know more. I now understand that it was Love that caused Him to create our world."

Kofi spoke deliberately. "He says the Creator, Onyankopon, includes the Father, the Holy Spirit, and the Fisherman who came to live on this earth. The Fisherman is God's Son. The kwesi broni celebrate his birth on the day they call Christmas."

Folayan let her hands rest, and listened, and pondered. *Son of God? The Fisherman?*

"He says some of our Akan practices are like the ways of this great Fisherman. He asked me who taught us those ways.

"He has a Book listing those ancient customs about women's time of the moon and  taboos. It says a widow should marry her husband's brother if he is not married so she will not be left alone."

*Is that the same book my brother told us about?*

"We do the same!" Folayan heard other women chattering in surprise that another people far away had the same customs as they did.

"I told him that we have known the ways of Onyankopon many generations. I asked why his people say we have no history or knowledge except that which they bring us." He looked at Folayan and continued.

She nodded encouragement, "He said they are not interested in knowing these things about us, and neither do they know what to ask, but there are some important things they can tell us."

"Did you ask what kind of things?" the linguist asked.

"Yes. I did." Kofi hesitated. "He said we do not know that our idols and gods, the *obosom,* are enemies of Onyankopon. They steal honor that belongs only to Him."

"Enough! Stop." His brother spurted, startling Folayan. She prayed for Kofi to be calm, and clear.

"I thought so, too, so I told my grandfather about things the preacher said about the obosom. From a tiny boy, I've been afraid of making one of them angry, like the god of the harvest. We worship him at the Bakatue. I was always afraid of starvation."

Kofi beckoned for two of his nephews to sit by him. He said, "What are your instructions?"

The first boy said, "To count each stone as people put it into the pile."

"And you?" Kofi asked the other.

The second pointed at the first boy, "To count also, so he cannot hear me. We will have two records."

"Yes, in the face of two witnesses, we establish the truthful testimony."

Kofi reached into his basket and pulled out a stone. He placed it on the ground. "I do not want to be afraid of the god of harvest anymore."

Folayan's hand began to shake. *How did he dare say that? He is a brave man.* She prayed for his protection and waited. Nothing happened. *But—he did not speak against the god, he only said he did not want to be afraid.*

Kofi pulled out another stone and named a different god, and his dread. Again nothing happened to him. He did it three more times.

She could not hear the crickets for the drumming in her ears. She scanned her motionless age mates in the firelight.

"Before I tell you the advice Grandfather gave me, I want my friends to share what they learned this week." He reached for his sister's hand and helped her up. "Adwoa, pull out a stone, and tell us the obosom it represents."

Adwoa said, "I am thinking of the god of war. I am so scared my brothers will go and be captured. I do not want to be afraid anymore."

Adwoa added more stones to the pile. Then Yaa stood up and added hers. The list of punishments and terrors lengthened and the pile grew. Before long, people from under the tree were adding their rocks.

"Death."

"Impotency."

"Sickness."

This and that and other incurables.

"Leprosy."

"Barrenness."

Kofi turned to Folayan and held out his hand. She hesitated, shaking her head. He nodded, and smiled tenderly. "Come Folayan. Do not be afraid. Stand right here by me."

She looked around to see her family, all of them sitting together. Her Maame, too, giving honor to the Creator. She refused to miss this opening of the Rest Day with village friends, even when her sons had to lift her up and carry her in their arms to the meeting place.

*What would she say if I cast a stone into the pile? Papa? Serwaa? My brothers?*

But Folayan wanted to be free. With her heart pounding fast, her mouth dry, Folayan left her canvas and joined Kofi, who reminded them all to speak loud enough.

She began. "I … we heard the war cry in the shrine. I am afraid of someone dying. I do not want my Papa to be killed by a snake. I do not want to die or anyone else to die. I do not want to be afraid." One by one she spoke about her other pebbles, and put all her stones on the pile that had grown as high as her hip.

Folayan went back to finish the painting. Some left three stones, others ten, seventeen—deities from the land, sea, and wind. Some for every process of life.

Then Kofi asked the boys who'd been counting, "How many stones do we have? Tell Folayan only."

One boy whispered it in Folayan's ear.

Then Kofi told the second boy. "Speak loudly and tell them how many you counted."

He shouted, "One thousand and eight!"

Folayan nodded. "They totaled the same, 1008."

Kofi said, "More than 1000 gods."

He paused and looked deliberately around the crowd. "How do we serve them? If we give the fetish gods our time—how much is left to serve the Most High? Should we give Him the scraps?"

Kofi had remained the whole time beside the pile, encouraging each person who wanted to add their stones.

Folayan watched them come to the pile, drop stones and walk away. Were they feeling like her? She tested her feelings ... almost free from fear. It was a decision. No dance, no drums, no phenomena. A simple decision to not be afraid. *But is it more than that?*

Kofi walked to the edge of the crowd and helped an elder up. "I asked my Grandfather Nana to come help me tell his story. Some of you know my brothers and I apprenticed to him in a trade that would have made us very wealthy. His images were not blocky or rough, but smooth and fine detailed like the ones from Benin."

"That is right!" people in the audience verified Kofi's statement.

"From age seven, I worked with him making all kinds of idols, small and large. When I was sixteen, he began making a four-foot carving. Not to sell. He called it his personal god, his masterpiece. He made me promise to keep a secret, but he is here today to tell you about it himself."

The old man leaned on his staff, and cleared his throat. His hoarse voice sailed into the hushed crowd.

"Six years ago, I made a hard choice. Then as now, Kofi came and found me.

"That day I huddled in a corner. He sat on the floor beside me and waited for me to speak. He was afraid, but still he waited. Finally, I told him—I destroyed it. My masterpiece. I burned it and buried the ashes."

A hundred gasps swelled into a single hollow of caught breath.

Nana told about how he got started making idols and earned a good living until the day came that changed him.

"I had a rough time of it, but I know now that the Onyankopon, the Most High God is forgiving, the obosom are not. We all know the proverb:

If Tweduampon has a stone to throw,

it takes him a long time to throw it.

The lesser gods throw stones quickly.

Folayan followed the turning of the gray-headed carver as he peered out at the crowd beyond the flickering fire light.

"I am still here." His voice creaked. "I was not torn apart as I feared."

Murmurings spread throughout the listeners.

"I have kept silent for all this time, and told no one except this man." He reached up and patted Kofi's shoulder. "But if any of you come to visit me, I will tell you why I made the choice and what happened to me."

Kofi took one step forward beside him. He looked at the small group, and at the wide audience. In a clear and loud tone, he said, "The Most High God does not try to make you be afraid."

The old man looked up, his face full of pride for his grandson. Kofi smiled and embraced him.

It warmed Folayan's heart. *I really like him,* she admitted. *And I want to hear the rest of his grandfather's secret ... but I cannot go alone. Who will go with me?*

# CHAPTER 24

# To Wash Away

*She had waited each day for some kind of doom
to afflict her family ... and prayed to the Creator
to wash away her anxiety and for protection.*

**May 1795, Kormantse Village**

Wooden bowls of various sizes stacked up in four lines on one wall of Kofi's grandfather's adiho.

It took several days, but Folayan was here with Maame, the first in their family to speak of the stones. Her mother had volunteered to come to Grandfather Nana's with her. She used a staff to help lighten the weight on her foot.

Early that morning, Folayan had shaped soap balls for her family, and brought a set of ten to Kofi's grandfather. Beside the soaps, three gourds sat on his table—the only hint of a woman's touch. They reminded Folayan she had attended his only wife's funeral six years ago.

"Are you Adwoa's age mate who painted these gourds?" He picked up the smallest one. "My wife loved them."

"Yes. I did." Folayan grinned. "Thank you."

"I thought so when I saw you the other night painting."

Maame chuckled. "Every so often your wife would stop by my space and ask about my little artist."

He smiled. "Thank you again for coming to attend to her during her sickness. You did your best to help her. I saw how hard you tried and how hurt you were when she could not recover."

Folayan looked aside. She worried about Maame and Serwaa when women asked for help beyond child birthing. They knew much about discovering the causes of discomfort and the herbs to help them, but she wanted them to be careful not to attract so much attention. *Please, Maame, remember the fetish priest's jealousy of the healing arts.*

"The ague surprised me, taking her so fast." Maame shook her head, brows taut in remorse.

He nodded. "The relentless chills and fever were just too much for her old body to withstand the malaria this time."

Folayan muttered, "Why is there so much suffering? *And fear?*"

Neither one answered her. Just like at home, for the last four days since the meeting at the tree, no one in her house mentioned the "counting of the gods." She dare not bring it up, but all eyes showed questioning.

She had waited each day for some kind of doom to afflict her family and when she lay down to sleep at night, she released a sigh of relief, and prayed to the Creator to wash away her anxiety and for protection.

*I am glad Maame and Serwaa accompanied me today. But if they will not listen to me either, what use is it to ask the question I most want answered? Will somebody please tell me how to stop being afraid of the obosom?*

Maame leaned down and rubbed her ankle, then changed the subject. "You have not married another?"

"No. My nieces keep me well fed." He patted his stomach. "I work in my garden, and do my carving. I have customers for my bowls—and visitors. I am content."

A voice called at the door, "Agoo, Nana?"

"Amee!" Grandfather smiled, to Folayan's dismay and joy, "It is Kofi. I told him I was having visitors today."

Kofi entered and after greetings, he placed a seat between Nana and Folayan. *Can he hear my heart drumming?*

Maame went to examine the bowls. "So pretty." She measured from her elbow to finger tips across the mouth of a bowl, then picked up a different one. Folayan stood to go look at the table with varied small items: hair combs, spoons, musical instruments.

Kofi joined her, "Is there a carved item that you seek?"

She reached for a mirror with and adinkra carved on the back. "My Maame has one set inside a Sankofa, but I do not see any thing like—"

Kofi held up his hand, "Let me look in this room here." He came back out, his bright smile made her flutter inside. "Is this like what you want?"

"Oh, yes, the one Maame has is about the size of her open hand. It would take me many paintings to earn enough cowries to pay for this. And how would I hold it up?"

Grandfather said, "It is for hanging on the wall."

Kofi shifted it, "Here let me hold it up so, you can see yourself."

Folayan, gasped, and clasped her hand over her mouth

Kofi asked, "What is the matter?"

"Oh, I ....just... have not seen myself for a long time."

Kofi chuckled, "You did not realize what a beautiful woman you have become?"

Serwaa and Grandfather laughed and commented in agreement. Maame smiled and glanced at Kofi. Twice.

Folayan lowered her eyes, blushing. "Thank you. You can put it away now. It is something for me to work hard for."

Maame said, "I have seen these from my space at the Wednesday market, but when I finish selling my wares, you have disappeared."

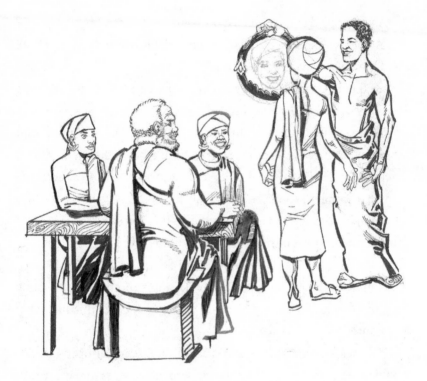

"I deliver them, and my daughter sells them for me."

"Adwoa's mother?" Folayan asked.

He nodded. "They are often sold by midday and after shopping, I usually meet with the preacher."

Maame said, "From the fort—the sun day man?"

Folayan looked up at her. *The soldiers, their priests, are not they all sun day men?*

"Yes. He speaks of you sometimes."

"What?" Maame asked. "Me?"

"He tells me about some of your conversations." Grandfather Nana rubbed his chin. "He and I sit near a palm tree and eat together. He speaks of you as one would babble on about his daughter."

*The kwesi broni? Maame like a daughter?* Folayan raised her eyebrows before Maame said, "He did tell me once that he had no children."

"Hmm ... Grandfather rubbed his chin, and tapped Kofi's chair. " I am sure Folayan has some big questions for me."

Kofi shifted to see her better. "Go right ahead. Ask. I am only here to be with him."

Folayan looked at Maame, then Serwaa, and swallowed, "Please tell us more about your 'choice'?"

"Ah, yes. My masterpiece." He paused, looked up through the adiho opening, and chewed—what? Not kola nut, his mouth was not black. Folayan could not tell.

"It was a hard time for me after my wife ... my thoughts refused to collect in one place. I sometimes fell apart right here in the house by myself. One day Kofi found me huddled in a corner. He sat on the floor beside me, silent. Finally, I told him—I destroyed it. I burned it and buried the ashes."

"The st-, the statue?" Folayan stuttered. Her reaction surprised her, as when she heard him say it before. But seeing the carved eating tools, bowls, and seats, she pictured what specific detail he must have designed on the idol.

"I saw fright flood Kofi. He did not want to leave me, and I knew he was scared to bring me with him to his parent's house. He asked if I was afraid. I was paralyzed with fright, but I said, 'I am still breathing. Come morning we will see.'"

Folayan's insides matched her mother's astonished face. *He waited all night—expecting to die at the hands of the gods.* She asked, "What caused you to destroy it?"

"As I shaped the wood, I thought about how I had gone out, found the perfect tree, cut it down. I brought the log back and shaped my god out of it. For an instant I wondered who was the god—it or me?

"Then, I heard a voice say, 'Choose.' Just like that. Twice, it said, 'Choose.'" He wiped his forehead.

Folayan held her breath.

His fingers ploughed rows through his hair, leaving a crown of white wool. He whispered, "I will never forget how Kofi stood there gazing at me asking 'Choose? Did you not tell me the gods gave you the skills to make them? Choose what?'

"I had betrayed him. I could not stand myself or bear to look at him. I told him to go home and come back when he was a man. On his way out, Kofi gripped the door handle, stopped and looked back at me. He wiped his face, and stood tall, yet his eyes revealed his pain."

Folayan pictured Kofi, a youth, his eyes wide. She spoke tenderly, "You must have been hurting very much, too."

"I was in turmoil. I did not know what terrors awaited me. If I was going to be attacked that night? If I would wake up at all? If my family would come and find my body ripped into pieces? Whatever was going to happen, Kofi had to know the truth. If I never saw him again, he had to know my choice."

Maame asked, "To burn the idol or to send Kofi away?"

"To change my ways. I explained to Kofi that the obosom—the lesser gods—did not give me any skills. The Most High gave me the skills—and I used them against Him."

"Against Him?" Folayan frowned. "How?"

"With these." He held up his crippled fingers. "I robbed God of the honor that belongs only to the Almighty."

Confused, Folayan opened her hands. "What do you mean you robbed Him?"

"He made us. He made this world. Our ancestors called Him Creator, the I am that I am, but we still put our own desires in place of His. We take the honor that belongs to Him and give it to idols."

Folayan nibbled her thumbnail. *Stealing from the Creator.*

Grandfather Nana sat with his hands clasped between his knees. "I did not want to be alone. So, I made a statue to keep me company. I put my trust in a chunk of wood."

Maame opened her mouth, shut it, then reached for her bowl. *Is Maame angry?*

The old man coughed. "I told myself all the idols I constructed had the powers like the Most High—just less. I convinced myself that it was good to do that. Then I went further. I took pride in my talents and carved idols for other people and trained my grandsons to do the same. And I had my wife selling—." He broke off talking.

The low moan muffled in his throat. Maame shifted on her seat. Folayan stayed stock still until he spoke with a tremor in his voice.

"But God … knew me and brought me out of my stupor. Now, I will only worship the Most High."

Maame settled down. Her hand went to her heart, her eyes revealed a seeking. "How did you come to that place? What did Kofi say?"

"Stories rose up in my mind. Kofi listened. I told him every one that I remembered about men, women, children—friends, struck with catastrophe, convinced it was because they had angered the obosom. They got so sick from fear, they died. Some of them still clutching idols—idols I had made."

Folayan winced and swallowed tears.

"I had been carving my masterpiece to please the god I was most afraid of. Always scared he was going to give me an incurable disease. Something that might grow inside me, that I felt helpless to fight. An invisible enemy."

Maame's hand still gripped her chest.

"And worse than anything—would my children suffer because I had offended the obosom?"

Folayan's breath caught. *Offend? Offend?*

She looked at him. "The obosom become offended by the smallest things, but you chopped and burned. And there were no screeching howls. You are sitting here in front of us, alive and in your right mind. And you are not afraid?"

"No. No, I am no longer afraid."

*Why?* Folayan leaned forward. "Why did they not choke you until pus pushed from your eyes? Why did they not tear you to pieces?"

He shuddered and stared at her, his brow pinched. He took a moment to respond. "I have asked myself similar things many times." He paused. "I believe it is because they have no power over the Most High who protects me. They did not tell me to choose. He did."

Folayan sat back. *No power.* Now she stared, her thoughts jumbling. *The Most High has feelings. He cares about us—me. He wants me to care about Him ... and show that I appreciate the things He does for me. Have I been praying to lesser gods who ... have no power at all?*

She walked to the stacks of bowls and back, wringing her hands. *This is what Kofi meant. This is why he was not afraid to speak so boldly in front of the chief, and the priests, and the people.*

*But God ... sees us ignoring Him.*

She groaned in awe. "A thousand gods, idols, and demons we give our worship to." *And yet, the Creator allows us to live.*

Her heart pained for the Most High ... and for this remorseful old man.

With his head in his hands, he lamented. "I became a hermit until one day at the market, one of the obroni—the preacher spoke to me. Two years later, I told him about my invisible enemy. He said, 'All through the Book,' that he called a Bible, 'the Creator has put encouragements. Every time we met after that he woud remind me of one of them by bringing me small paper written in Twi.'"

*The Bible!* Stunned, Folayan asked, "The preacher can write in our Akan language?"

"Yes, he can. Many words. I teach him the word in our language and he writes how it sounds and teaches me how to read it."

Folayan watched, wide-eyed, as Kofi's grandfather reached for the mid-sized gourd, and pulled out several messages. He read, "'Fear not,' 'Do not be afraid,' 'God has not given us the spirit of fear, but of power and of love, and of a sound mind.'"

He shuffled through the papers, then held up another. "This is one the Fisherman said. 'We have been rescued from our enemies so we can serve God without fear.'"

Folayan whispered, "The Fisherman from the sky?"

Grandfather Nana nodded. "I am no longer afraid that the obosom are angry about something I did, and I do not know what I did. Upset about it this day, not upset about it at another time."

He sighed and stopped speaking.

"Why do you sigh?" Folayan worried.

"I sigh … I sigh because of relief. I know the Most High does not change. My whole chest is empty of tightness. I have peace. I am amazed at how kind and caring the Creator is. That is why I sigh. The preacher's Book has lists of things God wants us to do and not to do— to keep us safe from evil."

"What?" Maame breathed out.

"Yes. Simple lists with explanations and no worry—It tells us how to please Him and be happy."

Folayan twisted to look at the gourd with the messages from God's Book. "It has lists to help us be happy? What if people do not want to do what the lists say?"

"If we reject the Most High, and want other gods, He still protects us for a time, until we persist and insist on going our own way and leave His protection. He will not force us to stay with Him, but it brings Him joy when people choose to return to His care."

Folayan recognized Kofi's smile on the old man's face. It warmed her heart. She smiled and said, softly, "Your grandson is much like you."

"I am grateful Kofi came back to me this year, after learning to weave kente cloth—a man now with questions of his own about the obosom, and how the Most High God of my ancestors answered my prayers."

*Yes. I, too, am grateful.*

Maame's eyebrow tweaked upward. Folayan stood. "Your story has given me courage."

He rose from his seat. "When you young people counted the stones, you gave me courage. You showed me how far we have gone astray from the heritage our ancestors brought from the other side of the Nile Valley and the Great Desert."

"They had already started worshipping other gods before then," said Maame.

"Yes, but not a thousand! Surely not."

"You are right." Maame embraced her bowl, and accepted his hand to help her up. "We all have choices to make."

He and Kofi walked them to the door. Nana said, "Remember stones can represent different things. Some may stand for hopes and skills and knowledge of who you are. Do not be afraid to go after those."

Folayan paused to ponder his words. *I could write them on Papa's parchment.* Then she looked him in the eyes and asked, "Grandfather Nana, would you teach me to read the little scrolls in your gourd?"

He blinked. "Well … I could do that. Yes, I will."

She turned to her mother. "Who will come with me?"

Serwaa shook her head. Folayan glanced at Kofi. Who smiled. Folayan looked away blushing.

Silent in surprise for a moment, then with half a nod, Maame said, "I can do that. And bring messages the preacher gave to me. Next Thursday we will come."

All five laughed.

"Next Thursday," he said.

# CHAPTER 25

# *Speechless*

*I cannot help myself. I want to be near you,
to hold you, to share myself and my whole life
with you forever."*

**June 1795, Kormantse Village**

It was soon clear that Maame's injury was more than just a twist. Her ankle took many weeks to heal and when it did, Maame limped just a little ever after.

During the time she was healing, Serwaa claimed she could not do all the market work alone, she had to have Folayan with her.

Kofi and his friends came to say hello during each market day and Folayan began to look forward to loading up her basket and making the walk down to the shore. At Adwoa's wedding, Kofi walked beside Folayan.

To her joy, he told her, with a grin, that their two families would help each other bring in the crops during the next few weeks. She wondered if he had anything to do with her father's choice of whom to work with this year. But then, their fathers being fishing companions, their two families had shared harvest time several years in the past.

When the harvest began, Kofi came to her house early each day. On the last afternoon, when they had finished the women's fields and the men's, and headed home, Kofi seemed anxious. "May I sit with you tonight at the square?" he asked.

Wide eyed, she looked up at him and nodded.

Throughout the evening meal preparations and baths, Folayan wondered what he had to say. It seemed like everyone moved like snails while getting ready to go. When the family arrived at the square, Kofi came to meet them.

He spoke to her mother. "Before we sit down, may your daughter walk over here with me for a while?"

Folayan looked at her mother who gave permission and said to Folayan, "You know to stay in our sight."

"Yes, Maame."

They strolled a short distance, then Kofi explained that he was making good progress on her kente and three more people had arranged for him to make cloths. Soon he would have enough money to start his house in about six moons. "I need an extra-long adiho to fit my loom so I can work inside."

Folayan thought that was a good idea, but thought about the adiho being open to the sky. She said, "How will you protect the weaving from rain?"

"I have made a covering with posts and moveable thatched mats of millet stalks to go over it."

"Ohhhh." She looked at him with admiration.

He grinned and pulled a branch toward him and ran his fingers up and down a straight portion of it. He broke it off at a knotted part. Folayan noted that it would make a handy prod or stirring stick.

After peeling away a few leaves, he used it to draw the four lines of his adiho in the soil. He added two rooms outside the back line. "Do you think that is good?" He seemed relieved when she agreed, then he revealed more plans and asked her thoughts.

"Questions! You are so full of questions," she exclaimed when he'd just asked her three in a row and was starting another before she could answer the first. He had been plying her with questions each day, while they walked to and from the fields, but this night she felt overwhelmed. She wasn't sure if this strange feeling came from so many questions or the fact that she sometimes had trouble thinking straight when he was near.

"Oh, I am sorry. I will slow down. It is just that I have so much I want to know about you, and want you to know about me. I ... in these last few weeks, there is something happening to me. It is driving me to you as never to anyone before."

He paused and glanced at her, pulled another leaf off the stem. She listened, waiting.

He cleared his throat, making way, it seemed, for words he had rehearsed. Yet, he was being careful not to stumble over them.

"You are so beautiful and the way you look at me with that twinkle in your eyes and the little smile and dimple in your cheek causes me to feel strange inside." He lifted her chin with his finger.

"Sometimes I feel powerful. Sometimes weak. Maybe it is the womanly dignity in the way you stand, something about you makes me think I cannot refuse your slightest request."

Folayan was speechless. She just looked at him, so tall and lean and deep brown. Though his face was narrow with a strong jaw, he was muscular. His black eyes could be piercing, but most of the time, they shone with laughter. His smile, though absent now, often flashed quick, lighting up his whole face, and her whole soul. She felt breathless, thinking about him, looking at him, hearing his words.

"It frightens me so much," he continued, "that some days I have even said to myself I will not speak to you tomorrow. I will stay away.

"But when tomorrow comes, you are in my mind. I cannot help myself. I want to be near you, to hold you, to share myself and my whole life with you forever."

He looked off as if he could not believe he was so blunt in telling her so much. When he turned back, he searched deep into her eyes and said, "I hope with all my soul you feel the same way about me."

Then he asked her about the knocking.

He waited a long moment for her to speak. When she did not, he dropped the stem, turned on his heel and left.

She watched him go, leaving the words she wanted to say hanging all jumbled in her throat.

# CHAPTER 26

# Bakatue

*Huge walls, in places white, yet dingy with black-green splotches.*
*At the top were rectangular lookout holes. Long black,*
*round iron tubes rested on the rims, like at Fort Amsterdam.*
*Serwaa said they called them cannons.*

**End of June 1795, Edina, Gold Coast**

Since Folayan last spoke to Kofi, three more of her age mates held their Rite of Passage celebrations. Abena's ended right before Adwoa's wedding.

The Bakatue would begin in one week. Akonor and Kwesi helped the men of Edina and others construct the dam and the seawater surged into the huge fish-filled lagoon. Then they built a bridge alongside a wide strip of sandy beach that divided the lagoon and the sea.

People streamed from their villages, sometimes with several full baskets on top of baskets balanced on their heads. Others had stacks of individual items—wares of the same kind to sell. Often the loads were three times as tall as the person bearing them. With graceful, perfect posture they bore their neat, packed clothing, food stuffs, and goods to sell or use for themselves during the week. Some piled their items on top of oxen, donkeys, horses, or camels. A few had their animals pulling a wagon. Wealth, poverty, no matter: all headed for the Edina Bakatue.

The villages of lofty Kormantse and Abandze below counted in the family of Cape Coast and El Mina castles. If the villagers walked the Cape Coast way, they would arrive at the trader's town of Edina in fewer than two hours. Visiting with each other made the trip pleasurable.

On the days that religious ceremonies allowed shoppinng, Serwaa, Maame, and Folayan were on the other side of the merchant's mats. There was much excitement with many different items for sale.

While she tried to follow Serwaa's instructions, Folayan's gaze wandered in awe. People from many villages mingled with the kwesi broni who lived in the El Mina castle, or the town they built surrounding the homes of Africans near the Benya Lagoon.

Folayan had heard others in her family speak of the fair-skinned Sunday men and women. She had seen soldiers at Fort Kormantin which the kwesi broni here called Fort Amsterdam. She knew the old preacher who always asked about Maame.

But she had seen none of their women. And she had not known they would look like this with their long black or brown or yellow hair, and skin almost colorless. Some were more pink or rusty-colored, but all bore the same affliction of the strange skin paleness, milky whey.

She studied the skin of their faces, hands, arms, necks and breasts half-showing out from open squares lined with trims of tiny folds or lace like hers that Papa brought from his expeditions.

Unlike Fanti women's garments in three pieces, these kwesi broni women wore two pieces, similar to a short etam that hung loose over their arms, and a one piece dress. The top half with the open bosom appeared to be sewn at the waist to their big puffy bottoms that scraped the ground.

And the words they spoke.

Serwaa understood some of it. "Dutch," she said, "and before them were the Danish. The Portuguese have been here the longest." Serwaa pointed to some settlers. The men in long robes were priests and preachers. Most of the others were soldiers who guarded the castle. El Mina.

Folayan stared at the giant mass of white stone blocks, standing a few hundred yards to the east of them. In all the times she had visited her grandmother and Maame's extended family, she had ever been fascinated with the great building.

Bright white as the sun glinted off of it, ominous in its massiveness, and mysterious in its stillness, as the rolling waves splashed against it. Fort Kormantin—rather, Amsterdam—large though it was, seemed so small and drab gray in comparison.

In all her games with Adwoa, with their four-foot-long miniature Elminas, they had tried to recreate those giant walls that came together in giant round rooms that went from the ground, up higher than the walls; huge walls, in places white, yet dingy with black-green splotches. At the top were rectangular lookout holes. Long black, round iron tubes rested on the rims, like at Fort Amsterdam. Serwaa said they called them cannons.

"My cousins have seen them shoot out fire and smoke at ships flying strange flags that come too close to the shallow waters," Folayan told Adwoa when she returned from her first family trip to visit Maame's relatives near Edina.

But when Adwoa saw it for herself, she said, "It is much different to imagine a thing from someone else's eyes, and then see from your own."

Each time they had come to Edina, Folayan wanted to play El Mina games less and less. By this time, she did not like the castle. It seemed cold, impersonal, frightening. And it smelled bad. She asked Serwaa, "What do you think goes on in there? Is it the same as in Fort Kormantin?"

Serwaa said, "Do not worry your head. Look, see how the kwesi broni smile. They are nice. You see that other woman over there, wearing the blue *kaba* and skirt and green-flowered *etam*?"

"Yes."

"She is married to one of the *kwesi broni*. That little boy is their son."

Folayan stared at the tanned child, the color of a *tweapea* chewing stick, and at his Fanti mother who was mahogany-colored like her.

Folayan considered the white castle again. She did not like it, and said so.

"Do not look at it, then," said Serwaa. "Just make sure you stay here with the women near me. Whether here or at the rest of the lagoon, you must not wander off alone."

The castle jutted out almost to the sea. Folayan squinted across the water. Papa and her brothers fished here in this part of the sea in their boats only when they came to the Bakatue.

Papa had told stories of fishermen who sailed all the way across the sea to a far, far land and traded their goods. They said brown people lived near the shores of that land. They also met people who looked like them and spoke some Akan words.

They said those people had been captured from here and sold as slaves. In the new land that they were taken to, they escaped, and kept living there near the sea, but hid their homes in the bush. The place they talked about had a river. A long, long river called ...? It started like her name: *Fola, no Ama, Ama—something*. She would ask Papa.

Other people they met there were lighter brown, with straight hair like the kwesi broni. She hoped Papa would never wish to go across the sea to trade, like those other Africans. It was frightening enough to think that her brothers might sometimes sail around this castle with slave ships so often in its waters.

She stretched, but could not see any of the large fishing canoes out here in the water. She scanned the shore, and at last spied twelve canoes clustered together a quarter of a mile away from the market, in the opposite direction of the castle.

One of the main events was a solemn net-casting ceremony that symbolized the start of the new fishing season, and the catch was offered to the lesser deities that the people of the area worshipped. The fishing and boat races were favorites. With her family and friends, Folayan rooted for her brothers and other Kormantse villagers who competed in all the lagoon merriment

It was mid-week when Papa came looking for her at the crafts area where she spent a couple days painting. He told her, "I know a man who wants to see your wares. How many have you completed?"

She showed him the four she had left. She had brought ten cored and dried gourds to the festival, hoping to learn new techniques and gain customers. He sat down beside her, examining them. After some *ummms* and *ahhs*, he said, "Your work is so different from the common calabashes. But that is because you are like your Papa." He chuckled. "I very much like this one with the sea's white waves around the bottom. You make me proud, daughter."

"Thank you." Folayan tucked her head to the side and smiled. "I have been watching the pottery makers. I would like to learn to do that. Do you think I can, Papa?"

"I think you will succeed at whatever you set your mind to do."

"I will do it then. I should learn much in the days we have left."

"Yes, but Maame is concerned that you are spending too much time over here. You know she will not get up to go visit anyone, for watching out for you."

Folayan cupped her hand over her eyebrow to see where her mother sat in direct view of the craft area.

"Do not spend all your time here hiding from your friends," he said.

"All right. I will see what I can learn in two hours a day. Do my friends think I am hiding?" *Does Kofi?*

Papa shrugged. "They have asked me your whereabouts several times. And your brothers have been getting questions about you from a number of young men."

"Me?" asked Folayan.

"Why should my most beautiful, talented, industrious daughter be surprised?"

"Your only daughter."

"Ah yes. And my eyes have witnesses. Those young men agree."

She giggled.

He looked around the artist center. "Where is Akonor? He is supposed to be here with you."

"He was over there wrestling earlier." Folayan pointed toward a crowd cheering the contenders, in the sand, who were strong-arming and flipping each other high alongside the lagoon. When she spied Akonor on the sidelines jumping with shouts of elation for his agemate, she turned back, "Papa, I wanted to   ask you about a story you told us." She reminded him of the details.

His brow furrowed as if reaching back into his mind. He said "Oh, you mean the *Rio Amazonas*. Yes, the *marones* hid back in the forest from the captors. Sometimes, they were also called Cormantees."

"Like our village? How do you know about them, the marones?"

"Actually, I learned it at one of the Bakatues many years ago. Old fishermen told of journeys past. The Portuguese soldiers also spoke of it. Those words are Portuguese—amazonas and marones and rio. Rio means river. The marones fought like Ashanti to keep from being made slaves again." Papa looked again toward Akonor.

"You said the marones speak some Akan words—our words. Yes?" Folayan retrieved his attention. "And the Cormantees?"

"Yes. They say they were treated cruelly in that new land and rebelled together. They attack any intruders. They have stayed free there."

Folayan pondered the power of determination and unity.

Papa said, "But the fishermen are traders like me, who were not slaves. From the old times they have sailed back and forth across the sea to buy and sell goods, not people."

"How did the Portuguese learn about them?"

"Exploring. Trying to gain wealth. Sailors tell that when they arrived at the land of the Rio Amazonas, the people who lived there near the beach had handiworks just like the ones the sailors saw in Africa. The people described the black traders that came every once in a while, bringing them tools from across the big water."

"Oooh," Folayan said. She sat in thought until he waved her on to finish a bowl. With that done, she paused and blurted, "Papa. You will not go across the sea so far away like them, will you?"

He studied her and looked toward the left a small distance from them. His wife sat able to view Folayan working among the crafters. Maame relaxed, laughing and talking with her relatives who lived on the outskirts of Edina.

Then he stood and patted Folayan's shoulder. "I could not go so far away without your mother and you and my sons and all my grandchildren. No, six months overland journey is enough. That sea out there holds too many unknowns for me."

She looked up at him, relieved. "Thank you, Papa."

He lingered beside her for a moment, gazing out at the ocean, before saying, "I must go fetch Okwamu, he wants to see your calabashes."

Folayan watched him blend into the people. A glance to the right brought her village friends in focus. She decided she would finish the remaining gourds quickly and not come to the craft center for the last half of the week.

⊕⟶⚞

For the most part, Folayan enjoyed the music, stories, dances, food, and the visitors from so many other villages. The women paraded joyfully in their garments and most beautiful head wraps. By custom, the queens and wives of the paramount chieftains used more cloth, and wore on their heads the highest, widest, most elaborate *dukus*.

Folayan studied them, noting that those who impressed her most always had calm expressions. When people came to them, they were greeted with genuine smiles. The royal women were knowledgeable about many topics. They listened intently when someone else was speaking.

Folayan recalled her second Bakatue when she was nine, and throughout the years, she had been in awe of these gracious women. Now, she was one moon away from sixteen and almost a woman herself.

With that bit of extra courage, she was comfortable enough to join in the circles of women who spoke with them and tucked away the observations in her heart. She tried to apply what she learned to gracefully deal with the unpleasant parts of the festival.

During the Bakatue, Folayan received a good share of attention from young men from other villages. Occasionally, Adwoa or another friend would send her knowing glances when this happened, but Folayan was too confused about Kofi and the sudden withdrawal of his company to be more than polite to the friendly strangers who surrounded her.

Many times when the young men were attentive to her, Serwaa described them, "like a flock of birds to a patch of spilt corn," Abeeku or Jojo or both would join the group. They would laugh and talk.

The bond between the three of them was easy to see and the other fellows soon left her with her two sentries shielding her from their advances. She wished for Kofi's attention instead. So while grateful for her friends, Folayan felt guilty, for she could not help stealing glances at Kofi who was often in view, just always at a distance.

Afua was also always around, now clearly a woman. She had a pretty face, innocent-looking wide-eyes, and knew well how to be charming. Not lost on Folayan was how she frequented Kofi's side, sometimes offering him food or drink, or offering comfort with shy, sideways glances.

Kofi did not come near Folayan the entire festival. *Did he mean those things he said? Does he think I do not care for him? Why could I not have told him I feel the same way? All I had do was just tell him.*

She noticed Papa watching her with Abeeku and smiling. Abeeku had a habit of making himself stand out in a group.

*I hope he does not think I am interested in Abeeku.* Alarmed, she wanted to leave the festival right then.

At the end of the week, when everything concluded, and everyone once more settled into their normal routine, the women at Papa's house relaxed together with their sewing, talking about what a grand time it had been. Folayan felt happy it was over.

They talked about all the people who had come and gone, who did what, and with whom. Kwesi's wife reminded everyone of how attentive Jojo and Abeeku had been to Folayan. Her gleeful sisters-in-law listed what they thought about each man's attributes.

"Abeeku makes Folayan laugh. He would be good for her," Kwesi's wife said.

Ekow's wife countered with, "What of Jojo? He is very strong and has four brothers and four sisters. He would certainly give her daughters. Or perhaps Okwamu. He followed her all morning the first day of the festival. He is very wealthy."

"That old foo- ... uh sly fox!" Serwaa exclaimed. All the young women sat, eyes wide, startled by such language as that. But Serwaa was older than Okwamu. She said it and did not blink as she continued her opposition. "He cannot even remember the names of his other five wives. He has no need of Folayan. She needs a young man who thinks his own thoughts, who is serious about life's challenges."

"Oho!" Kwesi's wife laughed. "And what of you, Folayan? Do you agree with the kind of man your Serwaa has determined for you?"

Before Folayan could speak, Ekow's wife shook her head. "Better to ask if her Papa will agree."

Folayan considered a moment. "I think he would. Those are good qualities in a husband. Still, I also want someone full of laughter, but not silly."

She paused, pondering her aunt's sway on her. "Silly" was another word her people believed one should call no one, but she told herself she'd used it as a trait to avoid.

"I want someone who is ambitious, and does not have to wait for his age mates before he will do anything new. One who is kind and caring of other people, but also holds the respect of the rest of the clan because he can solve problems without hurting people. I want him to be—"

Folayan sighed, glancing at her mother. "I want a man who will always cherish me like Papa does Maame."

"You want someone special, sister," Kwesi's wife said with a teasing grin. "I thought I received the last man like that when I married your brother."

Folayan shook her head, smiling just a little. "Not the last."

"Ah, well, let us hope this special man is quick enough to send his knocking first," Ekow's wife said. "It would be a sad thing should Papa have to accept someone else not so special."

Folayan caught her breath as the truth of those words hit her. By their customs, if a man or his family had no bad reports, her Papa was almost required to accept the first suitor to send a gift. Her whole future depended on whose hand knocked at her father's door first.

"Humph!" Serwaa's bold snort broke Folayan's thoughts. "What happened to Kofi? I have not seen him around here since we brought in the harvest."

With everyone looking at her in sudden silence, embarrassed Folayan blinked wide several times and teared up.

"I do not know, Serwaa. Please. May I be excused?" She jumped up and rushed to her room.

Folayan sat cross-legged on her pallet, looking down at her hands in her lap when Serwaa came to sit beside her. Folayan could not look at her for fear the tears would start again.

"I did not mean to say anything that would hurt you, girl. It is just that I think Kofi would be a good man for you. For a time, it seemed Kofi thought the same. What happened?"

It took a while, but Folayan got out the story of Kofi's strange confession, her silence, and his ensuing distance. As she ended the story, she felt like a little girl again, trying to explain why she had hurt her brother.

"And now I do not know if he still feels the same about me."

Serwaa put her arms around Folayan. "Listen. I have been watching him, and those other two. Jojo just wants you. Abeeku probably would like to marry you, but he is the kind who wants the best prize to show off, and will be wealthy and have several wives. Kofi loves you and will have no room in his heart for anyone else."

For an instant, an image from the Bakatue imposed itself upon Folayan's mind. Once more, Afua had been speaking with Kofi. They were saying goodbye, for she saw Kofi speak, then step away. Afua's reply was a nod and a demure smile.

The moment Kofi turned, Afua sent Folayan a sideways glance—and there was nothing demure in the smirk that curled her lips.

Folayan sighed. "I hope you are right, Serwaa."

# CHAPTER 27

# *Forty Days*

*It was the custom for girls to spend their examination weeks
in the house of the clan chieftain's family. To have the community
leaders witness for a girl's maturity and purity
was one of the greatest honors.*

**July 1796, Kormantse Village**

Folayan continued to go to market until her seclusion time. Maame
and Serwaa had made the arrangements moons before when
Papa decided on the date. Still, Folayan woke that first morning with
fluttering in her belly.

Maame came into her room with the gift of a new comb of carved
ebony wood and helped her with her hair. They chose what she would
wear, and when Folayan was dressed, Maame kissed her forehead and
held her tight. Then Maame let out a deep breath.

Even though Maame turned her head aside, Folayan saw water in
her eyes. Maame wiped them with the back of her hand and smiled.
"It is time to go," she said.

*Is she not happy for me?* Seeing her mother's shame for the tears,
Folayan only returned her smile and reached for her hand. Maame

still walked with a limp, yet always held her head high. Folayan did the same.

They strolled to the clan family house where Folayan would spend the next forty days being tested and taught. She tried to keep at bay certain misgivings. It was the custom for girls to spend their examination weeks in the house of the clan chieftain's family. To have the community leaders witness for a girl's maturity and purity was one of the greatest honors.

Still, this was Afua's family. Her father's grandmother would be Folayan's teacher and judge. Folayan could not imagine Afua having reported many good things about her to them. How much influence would Afua's whisperings have on the Nanabesia's disposition?

On their arrival, the clan leader's wife welcomed them. After the greetings and family inquiries, Maame returned home.

Afua was not present and the people of the house seemed sincere in their congratulations as they welcomed Folayan and placed her in the official care of the clan leader's grandmother, Nanabesia. The old woman's eyes sparkled with pleasure and Folayan's fears fell away.

"Ama Kwantunyi, the Traveler's girl-child, born on the seventh day." Her bony hands grasped both of Folayan's. "So you have come of age. And you have grown up as pretty as your Maame. It seems like it was no more than a moon ago your papa lifted you up at your naming day ceremony." She pointed a crinkled finger. "I remember he gave you a Yoruba name. Tell me again what it means."

"Folayan means 'one who walks in dignity.'"

"Ah yes." She laughed. "Come over here girl, and let us see how well you do that."

So began Folayan's lessons. It was a time of examining what her Maame had taught her and learning more things she still needed to know. She slept the whole six weeks at the house with Nanabesia schooling her in the ways of a dutiful wife, of a nurturing mother, and of a thoughtful hostess.

During the lessons, beauticians pampered Folayan. Her Papa had hired the best in the village and some from Abandze. The women readied her clothes for the day, bathed her body, then massaged her all over with perfumed oils. They clipped her nails, primed her scalp.

Early in the first week, Maame and Serwaa walked over to Nanabesia's house. They stayed watching as the hairdresser shaved Folayan's head. Folayan grimaced inside as she felt the knife slicing her hair away. Folayan forced her face still, determined to show no emotion. *Can I truly be a good wife? Will I bring honor to my family? Will Kofi come to my celebration? Will he think I am pretty? Will any of the young men think so? Will they want me for a wife? Or will only older men want to marry me?* She twitched.

The beautician bent down "Did I stick you?"

"No." Folayan looked up at her. "Well, a bit."

She glanced at her Maame sitting with Serwaa; both looking pretty in long wraps covering one shoulder and draping to their ankles. As clumps of her hair dropped to the floor, she studied the beautiful dukus tied in extravagant folds on their heads. Folayan wore one of her new dresses from her trunk. Nanabesia, older than Serwaa, looked grand in a lovely flowing green and white kente. Folayan wondered if Kofi had made it.

Kofi. He was still weaving hers. The last time they walked back from harvesting their fields he told her, "I like the picture you painted for my mother. It has made her happy."

"Thank you." Her heart sang.

She missed the talks and laughter they shared every day.

Since their last meeting at the Onyamedua, not a day had passed that she did not rehearse something he said and did during those six weeks of harvest time. So many details, the smallest details, the slightest nuances in his voice, and facial expressions, all loomed large for her now.

Captive in the beauticians' hands, she retraced her journey with Kofi once more.

During that harvest time, she had worked all day long, waiting for that hour to walk beyond his house up to hers. Folayan enjoyed just listening to his deep, pleasant voice, watching him speak so fervently about his dreams, and ambitions. Observing his shy manner, she admired how he was a leader among his age mates. She was pleased with his determination to achieve his goals.

"Why are you building a house when you are so young?" she had asked.

"I want to efficiently use my time. I will weave in my adiho. It will be as long as two and a half sleeping rooms. I will build that soon." He drew a long rectangle. "Then I will add the roofed rooms to the outside of the adiho wall as I need them. I will start with the sleeping room for me and my wife and first child."

Even now, her insides fluttered when she recalled how their eyes locked when he said that. His smile playful. His eyes searching. She chewed the thought—*his wife will not sleep at her father's house, or his father's, or in her own in a ring of houses for several wives.* He planned to be a man of means, but his wife would sleep with him.

She exhaled.

Kofi continued, "And I will pay for it from the kentes I make. I want to sell my kentes …"

"… in faraway places." They said it together. And laughed.

Kofi told her, "The next time your papa goes on a journey, I want to send kentes with him."

Her youngest brother, Akonor, had teased her often, saying it didn't matter that her name was also Kwantunyi, she would marry and have many babies, but go nowhere.

"I always hoped I could go on a journey with Papa," she said, testing Kofi. *Traveling. Is that a thing Kofi's wife would not do?*

Kofi talked with his long fingers; strong, yet tender hands, sending thrills rushing through her when he grabbed her hand. "If you were my wife, we could go with him one day. You are a market woman; together we will sell many kentes and calabashes." He chuckled, eyes bright at the possibility.

That was her hope until the day she made the mistake. She must have rehearsed it every day since he left her standing there speechless. Now, she relived it once more, examining again every detail:

"Folayan," he had said, too many weeks ago. "I care for you and want to share my life with you." Peeling leaves away from the bough, his voice had softened. "It gets harder each day to leave you at your house." He then blurted, "Will you accept my knocking if I send one?"

She blinked catching her breath. So surprised at his abrupt expression, she hesitated.

Before she answered, he dropped the leafy stem, turned on his heel and hurried away from her, disappearing into the shadows.

That night her fretted sleep kept repeating the scene and sent her early the next morning to the spot where he'd left her. She wanted to find the rod he'd used to draw his house. There it lay, still green with three leaves intact on the tip, their edges curling atop yellowed grass. He must have been so nervous attempting to ask her the question she had dreamed of hearing for years.

Folayan picked up the forearm-length stem. She took it home. Among her painted gourds, she selected a tall one and poured water into it, then the stem. After several days she added in soil around the branch and prayed that it would take root.

Weeks later, she took the planted bough with tiny new leaves to Adwoa's new home. With wide eyes, she explained to her best friend her dilemma. "Please give this to Kofi and tell him I want what he wants."

Now, Folayan glanced over at her Maame's intent gaze at the hair-dresser. Serwaa talked with Nanabesia. Folayan glimpsed the clumps of her hair around her on the floor. Not wanting to see them, she closed her eyes and imagined Kofi again.

So many weeks had passed. Still he had not come. Today she sat wincing as the knife pinched her scalp. She'd seen him and Afua at the Bakatue. She'd caught him observing her with Abeeku and Jojo and the other young men trying to talk to her.

Folayan needed to know if Kofi had changed his mind and, if so, to hear it from his own mouth. Other men would come to her cele-bration and see that she was a woman now. She longed to answer him face to face then.

The beautician's deft knife finished tiny strokes down to her neck. Tears welled up from deep and spilled out of Folayan. She did not say a word, sniffing, struggling to stifle the flow.

The beautician noticed. "Did I hurt you?" she said again. "There is no blood. Girl, what is the matter?" She smoothed the bottom two-thirds of Folayan's head with shea butter tinted with fragrance.

A servant brought a cloth for Folayan to wipe her wet face. Her worry about Kofi coupled with anticipation of becoming a woman and the uncertainty of what attended that wavered in her.

Yet, Folayan could not stop sobbing. She looked to her mother, longing for her to come to her so she could put her head on her shoul-der, and hear her soothing words. and hide inside her arms. Though her mother stayed put, Folayan noticed Maame's hands which could not stop wringing.

Then Serwaa took Maame out the door. Folayan felt like her strength left with them, but she could not let the chieftain's grand-mother think she was not ready. Her Papa had spent so much from cowie shells, salt and gold, thinking she was ready. Her sisters-in-law said she was ready. Folayan kept swallowing to squelch the sobs. She repeated to herself, "It will be all right. Everything will be all right."

Nanabesia let Folayan cry until she was dry.

When the ladies had swept the floor, wrapped up and given her the cut hair, they left. Nanabesia motioned her to come close. "Tell me your name again, child, the different name. What does it mean?"

Folayan looked down. She wanted to be called woman instead of child. She pushed out, "One who walks in dignity."

"Good." Nanabesia's long, forefinger lifted Folayan's chin. "You know it. Now live it."

"Yes, I will. Thank you. I will." Folayan smoothed her hand around her scalp—fresh and new, like a newborn baby, her future. She was happy to reach the top of her head, all shaved from her ears down to the nape of her neck. They had left a thick wooly crown—her history. She could leave it like that, or braid it. She knew the beauticians would make it pretty for her celebration. But she had to get past Nanabesia first.

Each day when the ritual ended, she felt like a floral bouquet, shaped and trimmed and fragrant. Her skin was soft; her hair was wonderful. She felt so pretty. Each night, she lay in bed, her mind rehearsing what she had learned.

"When a man comes to your house to see your husband who is not at home," Nanabesia had asked, "what will you do?

"As with all visitors, I invite him in, offer him a seat, and give him a drink of water, then I ask what his mission is."

"Why do you not turn him away?"

"If he has come on simple business, it is courtesy. However, if he is being pursued and has come to my husband for help, it is a refuge that may save his life."

"Good. You have learned well. There is just one more thing for us to talk about."

Even in the dark, Folayan blushed at the memory of the discussion that came next.

Nanabesia had not been shy as she revealed the arts of the marriage privilege. Beginning with instructions in cleanliness, she opened to Folayan secrets of gifting unceasing delight to her husband.

Folayan snuggled down under her covers. She fell asleep pondering: *This condition called marriage—so many responsibilities, so much to know. What will it be like to be a grown—really grown woman with Kofi as my husband?*

# CHAPTER 28

# Rite of Passage

*Things they watched me do and say, even as a babe,
things I forgot, mischievous things I did, and ways I helped them.
Predictions they made through the years about how I would grow up
to be, and that I will make some fortunate husband a fine wife.*

I hand you a two-edged blade. A princess is one born with a great responsibility, and talent to execute that responsibility in leading her people to better lives.

"When you have joy, share with as many as you can. When sorrow comes, use it to teach others to cope and grow.

"Contention will always exist between the world and my Afua until she finds her own wisdom. Hold fast to yours, child, and she will have no power over you."

**July 1796, Kormantse**

By the end of the fifth week, Folayan had survived the things she'd been most nervous about: the hair cutting, the sitting outside of the house several hours on two days displaying evidence she was equipped to breastfeed a baby, and most of all, the demonstration to Nanabesia of daily life skills she'd need to perform in the house, field, market, village, and in raising her children and bringing honor to her husband and their families.

She had worn her old clothes through the testing weeks. Now, as the sixth and final week began, she could wear the pretty clothing Papa had provided: seven garments in all, enough for each day of the festival. He had great confidence in her. Customarily, a father would give two or three dresses to his daughter to take into marriage, and let the husband-to-be provide two or more garments as part of the dowry. Thus, he freed the aspiring husband to add to the dowry something else of greater worth.

Papa had signaled that his daughter was of prodigious value to him. She had proven her right to be famous as villagers came to acknowledge her crossing.

◦────

Papa and Maame returned to the chief's house with food for the early guests. They sat for a few moments with Folayan. As they left her side, Papa said, "I am proud. You will make a fine wife."

*Will Kofi think so? Will he even come?* She needed to talk to Adwoa. For the time being, though, she must show Nanabesia and the rest of the village she was a woman, mature and dignified.

Folayan smiled in wonder and offered genuine thanks as the first visitors came in bearing gifts. By the fourth day, presents were stacked on the sides of the full trunk Papa bought for her. Those who had not brought gifts would return with them on the last evening, when all the relatives and friends would gather.

Some of her visitors talked of the weather, farming, or about being a market woman. Others spoke about what it takes to keep a house and raise a family. Then there were proverbs and folk stories about Anansi, the spider. Others gave her life lessons through tales of princesses and princes and mystical moments of young maidens and men who loved them and the villains who complicated their lives. All of them gave advice providing studies on hard work, thriftiness, cleanliness, persistence, orderly government, courtesy, getting along with others in the village and life values that brought happiness, wealth, and satisfaction.

All of them praised Folayan's beauty.

Young women chatted with her, some in the age group before hers, some of whom she had visited during their own celebrations. They chatted and giggled about marriage, informing her, and each other, about the young men now looking for wives.

Those who had not had their festival yet asked about things the old grandmother had taught her. To peers, Folayan was gracious and answered their questions properly. To the younger ones not part of her companion group, she said, "For the rest of what I have learned, you will have to wait until your time comes. Perhaps I will come then and teach you."

By the end of the third day, nine suitors had spent significant time in conversation with her and her Papa. Several were from Kormantse, and some, to her surprise, came from different villages. They had heard from drum talk that this was her Rite of Passage Week. Others had tried to get to know her at the Bakatue, but Abeeku and Jojo obstructed them.

Whenever there were no guests, Folayan talked with Nanabesia or relaxed deep into her own thoughts.

*This is so different from how I felt at other Rite of Passage ceremonies. As a guest, I was just there for the festivity, thinking how pretty the honored girl looked, and about the gifts, and when my time arrived, would any suitors come for me?*

*I saw people in ones, twos, and small groups sit with her and share wisdoms about life, and I thought the girls were so composed and gracious.*

*And me planning how I would sit and speak, hnh … but I did not know … about the tumult of emotions that accompany this final crossing into adulthood.*

*One moment I am embarrassed, the next, I hold back tears, or I laugh. What is happening inside me? It is like the swelling sea rolls in waves of astonishment and gratitude, as I hear what people know about me.*

*Things they watched me do and say, even as a babe, things I forgot, mischievous things I did, and ways I helped them. Predictions they made through the years about how I would grow up to be, and that I will make some fortunate husband a fine wife.*

*Here I am, alone, though I hear people whispering throughout the house. I wish I could fly to my house and crawl again into my Serwaa's arms and she can hold me tight, and tell me how much she loves me, and that I am precious to her. And then she will teach me something new. Something to surprise Nanabesia with, as I have so many times these forty days. And I always smiled, and said, "My Serwaa taught me." Will she say I am too big now to be cuddled?*

*Here I sit on Papa's egua, his throne—a whole week being presented to the village as a woman—accomplished and marriageable. Am I ready?*

On the evening of the fifth day, the ladies of Folayan's age group came to visit. It was late; only two of the suitors lingered to talk with Folayan's parents, affording the girls private time to talk amongst themselves.

Adwoa arrived with her husband and when he went to speak with the host family, she joined her friends. They instructed Folayan in wifely expectations, now that they had all had their coming of age ceremonies— all except Fatima.

At the mention of her name, Folayan realized she had not been among them this week. "Where is Fatima?" she asked.

"I told her not to come," Afua spit out.

"What? Why would you tell her that?" Folayan asked.

"Because I no longer associate with her."

Amidst the murmurings, Folayan leaned forward. "What happened now, Afua?" Anything could set off Afua. The smallest thing.

"I do not associate with slaves," Afua responded.

"Slaves? What are you talking about?"

"She is a slave." The corners of Afua's mouth wrinkled. "My uncle purchased her in Kumasi years ago. Now, since she has worked off her father's debt, she thinks she will be treated the same as us. I do not care if my aunt did ask her to stay with the family. I do not care if she has forgotten where she came from. I will never forget."

Folayan frowned at Afua. *I never think about that until she spits it out of nowhere. Why does she keep stirring?*

Adwoa spoke. "If I remember right, she came to our akura when you were seven. Most of us were five or six years old. Except Folayan— she was four. We showed no difference then. Why should we start now? Are you saying we should ignore Fatima? Stop speaking to her, working beside her, sitting under Onyamedua and laughing with her?"

Afua smirked. "If I do anything, it will be to laugh at her."

"And why, Afua?" Adwoa demanded. "What do you want? Shall she suddenly leave us and go to her birth district? We are her village now. You may want her out of your sight, but I do not. If something happened and your family had to sell you to work off a debt, would you not want to be treated as you had been when you were free? Fatima has committed no crime."

Folayan's stomach tightened. She wanted to send Afua away, but had to be polite.

"It does not matter," Afua insisted. "It is not me. It is her. I do not want her around me. The next thing you know, she will try to marry one of our eligible young men—maybe Abeeku or Jojo or …"

"That is allowable in our clan, Afua," Adwoa said.

The other girls agreed, saying that Fatima had always been their friend. If she married into the village, each one would accept her into their own family. Folayan heard these remarks, but her heart was listening to something else.

She finished Afua's last sentence in her mind—surely she had been about to add Kofi's name. Folayan was not happy with the attention Afua had been giving to Kofi in the last few months. Although Kofi seemed not to respond, Afua always positioned herself close to him or to provide some small service whenever Folayan was near. All done to irritate her, Folayan was sure, by the glances of triumph or disdain the other girl always sent her way. Just the kind of disdain with which she now dismissed their defense of Fatima.

Folayan could see that Adwoa's anger matched the rising ire in her chest.

Folayan spoke while marveling at how the words leapt from her tongue. "Well, I suppose it is understandable. Some people might be afraid that a former slave could catch a husband from our village when they could not."

Afua glared at her. "You be careful how you talk to me."

Folayan stared back the same challenge. Her palm burned with the desire to slap Afua, but Papa's words echoed in her head, *Fools take the easy path to strike and destroy, the wise take courage to think and build.*

"I said, you better be careful, Folayan." Afua approached, goading her.

Suddenly, another voice inserted. "You be careful, Afua, or someone might decide to tell you what they really think of you, o daughter of the chieftain's *fourth* wife."

Stunned, all turned to stare at the tiny, creased woman leaning on her staff behind Folayan. None had noticed Nanabesia's silent approach.

Through the years, Afua had made much of her position as the chieftain's daughter.

But Folayan had heard long ago, the noise of "the plump pig" who wandered the village burping, that between the three surviving wives of the chieftain's previous five, Afua's father rarely visited her mother's house, preferring to spend most of his time with his favorite, and older wife.

So hot was the anger blazing in Afua's eyes, for a moment Folayan thought the girl might strike the old woman. Then Afua gathered herself and offered a conciliatory smile.

"You are right, Grandmother, all this excitement over a slave. We should not let ourselves be bothered."

"I am right. Fatima is no longer a slave, so you no longer have the burden of controlling her. She is free to be a friend and equal to any in the village and you will not concern yourself with the problem again," Nanabesia said.

Afua was stone—her body rigid, lips taut. Folayan watched the battle in her eyes. Folayan also perceived that none of the others dared look at Afua, except Adwoa.

Finally, a brittle smile crackled Afua's lips.

"As you wish, my grandmother." She bowed her head. "Folayan, congratulations and a restful night." She turned and left.

The movement broke the thread of tension and Folayan took a deep breath. Her friends, too, regained mobility and quickly bid her good evening, except Adwoa.

Nanabesia marched forward to sit on the stool next to Folayan. A quick glance around showed Folayan that all her other guests had gone and the chieftain's family had withdrawn to their rooms.

Folayan sank to her seat, horrified to think that anyone else may have overheard her confrontation with Afua. Folayan saw how easily all the prettiness and pride and perfection of her glorious celebration might come crashing down with just a breath of gossip.

She could be marked as a brawling woman and lose respect in the community. No matter Kofi's desires toward her, his parents would not allow a union with such a woman.

Her shame deepened as Nanabesia sighed and shook her head. "I do not understand this anger my granddaughter carries."

Folayan stared at the woman, amazed. *Where was the wrath she was sure she had earned for that moment of lost self-control? Was she not to be censored and the clan mother's sponsorship withdrawn?* Folayan could not believe what she saw in the woman's faraway gaze. There was no anger toward her, nor even for Afua—yet her eyes remained sad.

"All love and guidance Afua has rejected with arrogance and disdain. Her entire life, that child has honed the use of sideways looks and sly words into cruel weapons." Nanabesia's expression was tender when she turned to Folayan. "But she was not the only one who has grown up learning the power of words, yes? It is clear you have learned more than just stories from your father. You have taken his wisdom, too."

"Nanabesia. I used cruel words with Afua."

"In defense of the helpless," Nanabesia said. Folayan looked down where the woman's gnarled right hand covered hers. The left hand's cool, wrinkled fingers curled into Folayan's palm that moments before had burned with a desire for vengeance.

"Yes, strong words, but not cruel. Your father named you well, Folayan. Dignity is a kente of strength to wrap you tight and you spread it wide for another who had none."

Sadness rose in Nanabesia's eyes.

"Contention will always exist between the world and my Afua until she finds her own wisdom. Hold fast to yours, child, and she will have no power over you."

Nanabesia rose and left her. Folayan and Adwoa watched the elegant woman exit.

Then Folayan turned to Adwoa and took her hand. Kwaku, her husband came and stood by them. She said, "I must be going."

"Yes." Folayan nodded.

Adwoa was at the door, stopped, and came back. "By the way, has Kofi come to see you yet?"

Folayan's stomach jolted. She whispered, "No."

Adwoa said, "Oh. I see I have stayed silent too long."

The blue hwaani hwaani light filtered pale through the darkness, breaking into the final day of Folayan's last week of seclusion.

"Folayan? Folayan?"

Folayan looked over at Nanabesia's bed. It was empty.

"Come in." Folayan pulled the cover up to her neck. The door opened and Nanabesia entered with someone behind her.

"Maame," Folayan exclaimed with a wide smile.

Maame smiled back. "Get up, young woman. We must go to the Onyamedua. We are waiting in the adiho."

Folayan lifted off her bed cover, stood up, washed herself, dressed, and followed Maame. *Young woman.* She smiled.

"Good morning." She grinned at Serwaa and Papa. They smiled back at her.

"Nanabesia tells me you have done excellently," said Papa.

Folayan hugged Nanabesia. "Thank you for all you have taught me."

Nanabesia nodded. "You have given me joy. Many will come to you to teach them and you will serve them well."

Folayan glanced back at Papa. He grinned at her.

The four of them walked toward the great, gnarled tree. Maame carried the oto, the offering of yam and eggs. Serwaa had the palm wine. When they arrived, they spread a white cloth on the ground around the tree. Maame and Serwaa then mixed the wine into the yam and eggs and spread them onto the cloth. Papa poured the libation honoring the ancestors.

He looked to the sky and praised the Most High God.

"Thank You, Onyankopon Kwame, for allowing my child, my only girl child, to come of age. Soon she will marry. I pray that you will bless her womb and fill it with girls. For our clan, Twaduampon, for our clan."

Folayan watched her Papa. Joy filled her to know that he was so proud and pleased with her. Humbled by the seriousness in his eyes, she knew what was at stake. Folayan looked at Serwaa, who had no children. She thought about her brothers. Though five in number, that meant nothing, for the line did not pass through them. The future or extinction of their family was bound in her. Silently, she prayed that her first child would be a girl.

As they walked away from the Onyamedua, Folayan deliberately slowed her pace, talking about different things she'd been tested on and how Maame had taught her this, Serwaa that.

As usual, Papa's long strides carried him soon to the Ofram tree, he paused and looked back at them. He pointed as if he was going on ahead. Folayan and Maame waved him on. Now, Folayan could talk to them about something over which she had struggled.

*How can I ask Maame if I may wear something different than expected for the last day of my celebration.* She blurted it out.

Maame's eyes widened, "My kente? You want to wear my kente. Oh daughter, none of them is new. You have these pretty new garments. Your Papa has gone to such expense."

Folayan said, "The kentes are silk, they have been well kept. You seldom wear them. I have thought about this for three weeks. Papa gets to travel, tell the stories, he is my hero, and for my ayefro, I will wear the kente he paid Kofi to make. And tonight I will wear some of the golden combs he brought back through the years, but I want something from you, too. I want people to see you in me."

Maame looked back and forth from Folayan to Serwaa. "He has dreamed of this day for so long."

Folayan tried again, "Have you dreamed too, Maame? You always look so beautiful in your kentes, wearing your grand duku with so much cloth you look just like a queen. From a little girl, at every festival I was always so proud of you. I would tell people not from our village, 'That beautiful one there, she is my Maame.' I always wished that one day I will look like you." Folayan walked a few steps ahead. Then she turned. "Besides that, you have three kentes. Please, may I wear one of them?"

Finally, Serwaa said, "She is your only girl child. Let us go home and get them and decide."

Maame laughed. "But you will not wear a duku tonight, with as much money as your Papa has paid the beauticians for that Abysinnia."

Folayan threw her arms around her Maame. "Meda wase. Meda wase. But will you please choose for me, the one that has the most meaning for you. One that you can tell me about after I am married, and I can tell my own girl child one day."

She walked back to Nanabesia's house with a heart full of excitement. By the time she reached the house, the weight of her responsibility had returned.

At the clan house, the bathers and groomers were waiting.

They had begun the beauty ritual when Maame and Serwaa arrived with the royal blue kente woven with with red, green, and gold companion threads. As she held the folded garment in her arms, tight to her chest, both women stood back smiling at her.

Serwaa said, "You are glowing."

Maame dabbed at her eyes, "I am not crying. It is joy overflowing from my heart and thanksgiving to Onyankopon for answering my prayers. I pled with him for a girl child, He blessed me doubly with you."

They only stayed a few minutes, then hurried home. Maame and Serwaa and her sisters-in-law would spend the day completing the cooking for the evening guests which would be the greatest number for all the week.

On this day, the hairdressers did something special. They brushed Folayan's new growth up into the unshaven section above her ears, blending it smooth and straight, rounding all into a mound of waves, high, like a crown, black and shiny, in the hairstyle they called Abysinnia. Last, they laced it with golden combs Papa had brought her from Timbuktu.

Several hours later, pampered, fragrant, and feeling flawlessly beautiful, she waited in the largest roof-covered room before the ceremony began.

Her brothers and their wives were the first to arrive with mounds and mounds of food. Then parents and Serwaa arrived. Papa and Serwaa greeted her and went to help with the food arrangements.

Papa, then Maame hugged her and slipped a small oval pouch into her hand. "For this final day of your Examination, it has a short and long gold cords to wear at you neck or on your wrist."

The size of the circle made when  thumb and forefinger  touch at the tips, the pouch was lovely. One side was  woven in the same colors as in her dress. The other side was black with gold thread coiled in the shape of a sankofa bird. Around the rim a triple ring of gold thread secured the sides together."

"Kente cloth matching the dress. I have never seen you wear it before?"

"No it was made especially for you. Before bringing you the dress today, Serwaa suggested we go to Kofi's house asking if he had threads the colors of the garment we had chosen. He stopped his work to help us make it. When he wondered why you were not wearing the kente he made for you, we told him you wanted to wear it when you are a bride."

Folayan's heart was beating fast. she tried to calm her wild thoughts and speak evenly, "It is like a tiny gold-banded box. What is inside it?"

"Something you must give back to me until an appointed time, but look."

Folayan peeked, " Oh! Meda wase, Maame! Meda wase. I will wear it here." She placed her hand over her heart.

A beautician carefully guided it over her elaborate hairstyle and around her neck.

"Beautiful." A servant approached Maame said, "I am being summoned. "I talk with you again later. I am so proud of you."

Folayan drew in a deep breath and released a slow exhale. She looked around this room; it was three times as large as those in regular homes. Kofi's would not be this long. How much smaller, she wondered? She shook the thought away.

Folayan so hoped he would come. But if he did not, she promised herself that her world would not be stuck in the emotion of a man who refused to forgive. She would set her sights on Papa's next journey with Maame and whichever brothers he chose. Maame. She would not be one to sit and wait and worry for a knocking. Folayan tilted her head, swallowed, and pushed that intrusive thought out, too. It would come when Onyankopon Kwame willed it.

The beauticians had dressed her in her Maame's kente and draped regal blue, white, and gold fine twine into her hair. When she was ready, grandmother Nanabesia led her into the clan house courtyard. Folayan glided across the floor and sat down with care.

She settled onto her father's ancestral stool. The groomers secured the kente around her and draped the additional length of fabric to the floor. The last groomer placed the ntama so that it graced one shoulder and flowed into the rest of the cloth, which surrounded her feet like a wide cloud.

Drawing upon the memory of the queens, regal yet gracious, she held the center of the room. Nanabesia sat near the door to greet the well-wishers; witnesses who would see Folayan and carry the word that she had become a true woman.

Folayan looked at the seats placed in front of her and awaited her first guest. Her heart drummed in her ears.

"Look there!" Folayan followed Nanabesia's command and gaze. "You are those three blended into one. Your father and aunt's wise forehead, their clear, wide, yet deep-thinking eyes, and the same, exact nose. Your mother's high cheek bones, chin, and welcoming smile."

Folayan studied them, while her teacher continued, "You have your aunt's confidence and determination, your mother's beauty and gracefulness, your father's quest for knowledge and regal bearing. He walks like a king, and you—

"You are a princess," whispered Nanabesia.

"Oh, pardon, Nanabesia, but I am just Folayan."

"Is not your father the chieftain's second counselor in many matters of government and trade?"

"Yes."

"Do you think that position comes without honor?"

"Yes, I mean no, but—"

"Because you are the only daughter of Kwantunyi, I have watched you grow. I took you through a full examination, as I have many young women. Few deserve distinction. To some it comes by birth, to others by gift. I hand you a two-edged blade. A princess is one born with a great responsibility, and talent to execute that responsibility in leading her people to better lives.

"When you have joy, share with as many as you can. When sorrow comes, use it to teach others to cope and grow. When you gain knowledge, knead it into the minds of all in the village. Often, you will feel lost, but you must lead the way to a safe place. According to what you have been handed, more is expected."

In silence, she studied her young charge.

Folayan glanced down at her hands. The elder saw something special in her. Would she be able to measure up to Nanabesia's faith? She realized that the first step was a decision to try.

Bringing that memory of the queens into clarity, Folayan took a deep breath to expand her rib cage. She lifted her neck to the fullest length, pressed her shoulders down. Her chin was up, tilted ever so slightly. In that moment she knew Maame had been right all along the years. Her dignity made her a queen.

Nanabesia's eyes twinkled.

The drums began to talk and sing. Dancers moved across the floor. People praised her and added last bits of advice. Folayan remained gracious, but kept scanning the room.

Guests came in waves. Some still bringing gifts. It seemed that there were five times more people, then she realized many had also come earlier in the week. Some suitors here to study her again before the knockings began. The people who lingered to converse with her now had not sat with her on other days. At one point she saw Afua go by and had to push back a surge of fear. She pressed the nugget inside the pouch tight to her bosom and breathed deeply until her peace returned.

While she listened to a recently widowed older man, she was surprised to see Adwoa come up behind him. Adwoa remained respectful and quiet for a time, but when the man kept talking, she mouthed the words, "Kofi is coming."

Folayan's heart zigzagged. She forced herself to maintain a direct and pleasant expression, but she did not hear another word the man said. When Kofi entered, Folayan's mouth went dry. Something fluttered behind her stomach.

Kofi came to her, his face somber, his eyes urgent. Folayan lost all pretense of hearing her current visitor seated before her. Her full attention centered on the young man who stood behind the older. The widower looked up at Kofi and back to her, then said, "I will speak with you again, Folayan."

She smiled. "Yes." Pointing to the tables, she invited him to dine from the wonderful platters.

Kofi moved closer to her, but did not sit down. "Congratulations," he said.

It had been nearly four moons since she had heard his voice. Her breath came short. Her words squeezed through her constricted throat. "Meda wase. Thank you."

"You look beautiful. As I knew you would."

"It is my mother's kente cloth. I wait anxiously to wear the one you made for me." She would have dropped her eyes in a demure fashion, but could not take her gaze from his face. The flutter inside became a hard, sharp ache.

"I am sure you will make me proud of my work." He stood staring at her and she drank in the nearness of him. His eye told her he had more to say. His mouth remained closed. Then Abeeku stepped up behind Kofi.

"Is this man keeping you from your other guests? Move on, Kofi." He put his arm around Kofi's shoulder, teasing. "Let a man who wants to get a wife have this space."

Abeeku struck a thoughtful pose, then spoke with a sly smile. "I wonder how many men have already prepared their knocking?"

Abeeku, whose joking ways often made Folayan laugh, could not do to her heart what Kofi's smile did now. At this moment, she would have done anything to be blessed with that small wonder rather than watch the seriousness darken in Kofi's eyes at his friend's words.

"I wonder, as well." Kofi looked at her, questioning.

A slow light emerged in Folayan's head. She realized that, although she knew how she felt about Kofi, he had seen her being kind and laughing with Abeeku and Jojo, just like with him. He had a stout reason to be unsure that her affection for him was any different than for his age mates.

The silence grew. Both stood before her.

"Well," Kofi sighed. "I suppose I should be going." He clasped her hand. "Whoever becomes your husband will be blessed." He turned to go.

She blinked, surprised. She half-rose from her seat. "Kofi!"

He stopped and pivoted back. People nearby looked at them.

She coaxed the words out. "At the square ... I ... Me too!"

Uncertainty bolted from Kofi's eyes. He nodded acceptance. His chest rose and expelled a gust of breath. He straightened, appearing to tower over all others present. He flashed a smile that ignited a flame of joy in her heart. It was an impressive, confident man who went to greet her parents and Serwaa.

Folayan promised that once she was back in the room they shared, she would get every sentence out of Serwaa. She chuckled, knowing Serwaa's inevitable teasing was the price she'd have to pay for *each word*. She settled back into her seat and realized Abeeku was still there. She tried to calm her pulse and steady her breath.

"Now, what were you saying?"

Abeeku studied her.

"I was not saying anything," he said. "I was thinking about how many knockings might be sent to your house in the next few weeks.

Thinking I might even send one." He looked at her and now it was the man of laughter who was serious. "Do you think your father would accept it?"

"Abeeku." Folayan lowered her eyes. "You know that a girl never knows what her father will do."

"But what about you, would you accept it?"

"Excuse me, Folayan, I brought you some food." Adwoa stood there with a small calabash. "Abeeku, are you wooing my friend?"

"I hope so." He laughed. "But I believe I must try another method." His gaze flicked to where Kofi talked with Folayan's parents, then back to the bowl Adwoa held. "Mmmmm, fou fou and herring. I will have some. Folayan, I will see you soon. Good evening, Adwoa."

He sauntered toward the tables, but when Kofi walked away, Abeeku went to speak with her parents.

From the door, Kofi waved at her. She waved back and watched until he was gone. She clicked her tongue at her friend. "You know you interrupted a very important conversation."

Adwoa shrugged, but could not hold back a mischievous grin. "I could not help myself. I have spent too much of my life getting you out of prickly situations. How can I stop now?"

"My friend, thank you." Folayan smiled, hugged her cheek to cheek and whispered, "He came, Adwoa. He came."

"Yes. He did." Adwoa held her bowl out, being careful of Folayan's kente cloth. "Do you want some of this kenkey now?"

Folayan said, "Yes, but I dare not." Adwoa pinched off a piece of each item and fed them to Folayan discreetly.

While Adwoa went to put the bowl away, Folayan noticed that Abeeku had said something that caused her father to turn sideways to keep his laugh within.

When Adwoa returned, Folayan said, "A pot is about to boil over.""

A burst of laughter from that area beckoned Folayan and Adwoa to watch the hilarity. Abeeku bent from his own wit.

Folayan said, "Abeeku has a special place in my Papa's heart."

They continued to watch the men. Folayan's mother moved to attend to some ladies.

"Does Abeeku seem different to you?" Folayan asked.

"I think so. Much more confident, for about a week, since his father was installed as the chief's linguist."

"Oh. Oh, yes. Nanabesia told me."

Adwoa said, "Folayan, my husband is ready to go. May you be blessed with many knockings and accept only my brother's." She chuckled.

"Do you think he will send one?"

"I very much think he will."

Abeeku did not leave her Papa, even when three other men tried to hold conversation with him. Folayan watched him until the widower came back.

"Miss Folayan." He smiled grandly. "May I have some of your time now?"

"Certainly."

He commented on how pretty she was and asked her several questions. She glanced at her father. Abeeku had disappeared.

Folayan decided it was time for her to ask a question or two. "How many wives do you have, sir?"

He looked surprised. "Only ... not one, at the present time."

She said sweetly, "And how many do you plan to have?"

He was speechless. His chin wobbled up and down. Then he smiled at her. "If I had a wife as beautiful and industrious as you, I would want only one."

She smiled, told him she was sorry about the loss of his first wife and let him talk on about himself.

Her thoughts remained erratic with worry about the knocking. She was ready for the forty days to be finished. Her brothers relieved the man of his attention to her and congratulated their sister with hugs. Papa was next, and then Maame.

She reached out for Folayan, lightly caressing her forehead and cheek.

Folayan sighed into the comfort of her mother's warm embrace and whisper. "It is almost done, my ch—daughter. Almost done."

# CHAPTER 29

# The Knocking

*From one moment to the next, her brother had become free
to do as he pleased—to travel with Papa or go off on his own.
However, for his final rite of passage into manhood, he must prove
himself worthy of a wife and responsible, skilled, hardworking,
and honorable enough to bring new life into this world.*

**August 1796, Kormantse**

The next morning Folayan was grateful for a peaceful night's
sleep. Excitement thrilled her. Her family arrived at dawn
with substantial gifts of thankfulness for Nanabesia and the chieftan.
They also removed her things from the clan house back to her parents'
home. All her brothers and the wives came and made several trips.
Serwaa had remained behind to speak with Nanabesia.

After the other women arranged all the new presents in her room,
they made sure there was space for her trunk, the last item the men
would bring.

While Maame and Kwesi's wife prepared the plates for the men,
Folayan helped Ekow's wife, fill several dishes from the celebration
for her ill mother, and went with her to take the food. Folayan's cheeks

ached from smiling so much all week and because now, in this house full of women, she stood equal to them all.

The thought tingled through her that at any moment a knocking could be sent to her house. When her father returned bringing the gold-banded box and his throne she had sat on receiving guests, he would remain in the house for several days to receive the first envoys.

Papa had said often that he did not expect to wait past this evening before the first offer was made. Folayan recalled the determination in that last glance Kofi sent her.

The women's chatter startled into silence as the entry door slammed open. Serwaa rushed in and secured the door. She advanced into the adi-ho, head wrap askew, eyes wide, breasts heaving great breaths.

"Serwaa? What has happened? Are you ill?" Maame, at her side now, offered her arm.

"No," Serwaa shook her head, despair in her gaze. "They are coming! Abeeku's people bring his knocking."

"No, no." Folayan gasped. "It is too early, Kofi has not yet come."

"Are you certain they are for Abeeku?" Maame asked.

Serwaa nodded as she gulped the cup of water Kwesi's wife brought her. "I recognized his father's brother. Abeeku is with them," she said, wiping her lips. "I left the clan house just as Kwabena and the others returned for the trunk and stool. I came upon Abeeku's party from behind."

"Did they see you?"

"No. I do not think so. I darted behind houses and ran."

A loud, firm knock sounded at the entry door. Folayan's heart twisted. Maame whispered, "Abeeku, first?"

Folayan shook her head and grabbed her mother's hand. Her voice was hoarse, low with fear. "Oh, Maame, please. It is not Kofi."

Maame hesitated. She was her husband's intermediary until he returned. She must welcome all guests, offer hospitality, accept messages, petitions, and gifts in his name. Not to do so could bring shame on their entire house.

Maame looked around the circle of women. Her decision would bear upon all their lives. At the last she turned to Serwaa, the eldest of them all.

"What shall I do?"

In an instant, Serwaa's face and eyes firmed with resolve. "We do nothing. This is Kwabena's decision."

She brought her finger up before her mouth. Then she grasped Maame's hand. One by one, they linked hands and stood shoulder to shoulder. Twice more, those outside signaled for entrance, then all was quiet.

The women stood so for a long while. Folayan scarcely breathed, though her heart was beating so hard she was certain their visitors could hear, and would know they were being ignored. Sweat beaded her face, a slow trickle ran down the small of her back. It had been a long time with no sound, but they dared not move. Had their visitors gone? Perhaps they were camped outside the house waiting for someone to return? Folayan saw the same question in each woman's eyes.

Ekow's wife gasped as a thumping blow hit against the door, followed by sounds of muffled surprise. Folayan recognized Akonor's voice. There was nothing else to do. Their circle dissolved and Maame hurried to open the door.

Papa and her brothers staggered in with their burdens, wondering why the women didn't open the door quickly. Folayan showed her four grunting brothers where to put her laden trunk. Kwamina put the egua in place for Papa to sit on. Then Serwaa, Folayan and her sisters-in-law settled her brothers with food and drink. Papa looked surprised, then concerned, when Maame did not serve him, but touched his arm and looked toward their room.

"We must talk, husband."

The other women withdrew to the cooking spaces, where Folayan could not force a single bite of food past her lips. Nor could she bear to sit in her room and hear her parents talking about her dilemma.

If Abeeku had not gone away, she would have been required to stay put in her room while they made a petition for her, then come out to Papa's summons and greet the guests. Since Abeeku had left, she dared not be in the house when anyone else came. She would not dishonor her Papa by refusing to come out, but ... if she was not there?

She grabbed a work basket and said to the women, "We will need more sponges soon. I will go gather plantains."

Before anyone spoke, Folayan hurried out the kitchen door, past the stone bukyia with glowing hot red stones, around the house, away from the village. She knew not where she ran until she found herself on the cliff, scanning the wide expanse of valley and mountains. She sank to the ground, releasing a groan of frustration. She lay curled in a ball while her tears wet the grass and dust beneath her head.

Shadows of the pawpaw trees slipped away, leaving her in the harsh noon sunlight before she was self-possessed enough to sit up and wipe her face. She stood and sought the simple relief of shade. Folayan sighed and stared out over the sea.

So much had changed in the last afenhyia. She was a woman now, about to be married, perhaps. Akonor was a man and would soon take his second trip as such with Papa beyond those mountains. She shook her head. A whole year had passed since Papa presented Akonor with a beautiful carved dagger that his son could use in performing his adult responsibilities. Such a simple thing to carry such importance.

From one moment to the next, her brother had become free to do as he pleased—to travel with Papa or go off on his own. However, for his final rite of passage into manhood, he must prove himself worthy of a wife and responsible, skilled, hardworking, and honorable enough to bring new life into this world.

Papa would still find a wife for him in two or three years, but Akonor could give him much information on who he would like Papa to choose.

However, she was moving from the authority of one man to another and she did not even have a say as to with whom she would share that future.

She picked up a flat pebble and sailed it out into the air. "I suppose Akonor was right," she spoke softly. "I will never go on a journey with Papa." The finality of that hung in the air. Unwilling to accept such a lowering thought, she grabbed it back with desperate hope. "Unless he invites me and my new husband."

She held her breath, not willing to let her thought loose past that plain word—*husband*. So much of her future happiness depended on one man's decision and the simple timing of a visit. The possibilities overwhelmed her, and she covered her face with her hands.

"Oh, Kofi! Please! Do not send it too late."

# CHAPTER 30

# A Good Name

*Fear rammed Folayan's belly. Something strange glimmered in
Afua's sidelong glance and Folayan knew she was in danger.*

**August 1796, Kormantse**

Too restless to sit any more, Folayan walked. Gaining the road,
she nearly ran into Afua before she realized anyone was near.
She apologized, but Afua stood back, looking strangely at her.

"Are you unwell, Folayan? Did you fall?"

"No. I ... I ... am fine," Folayan stuttered. Then with a shock she
realized how she must look. Grass and leaves clung to her wrinkled
clothes. Her skin felt hot and eyes puffy. She set herself straight. "I was
just taking time for myself. I guess I fell asleep."

Afua's words were quiet, natural. "Were you alone? Where is Abeeku?"

"Abeeku?" Folayan glanced around, feeling guilty, then she looked
directly at Afua. *Could she know what had happened at her house this
morning?* "I have not seen Abeeku at all today. Why do you ask?"

Afua shrugged. "It is widely known that Abeeku intends to send a knocking. And he is your partner in the marriage game."

"Was, Afua." *With time enough for the Bakatue and my seclusion.* "The game has been over for many weeks."

"Not for all," Afua said, a tiny curl at her lips. "Many lasting bonds can be built from a game."

Folayan looked hard at her companion. There was something not right in the way Afua observed her. Folayan could not remember the girl ever seeming so calm, so reserved, almost separate from all around them. Perhaps she was still angered by the reprimand she had received from Nanabesia.

A blade of dry grass fell from above Folayan's ear. Hoping Afua didn't see, she resisted patting in search for more, but couldn't stop herself, while trying not to disturb her Abysinia. It seemed to be still intact and mostly debris-free.

Folayan took steps on the road. "Well, there was nothing lasting built for me. It was a game in celebration of Adwoa and it is finished. Now, I must go. I have promised to gather plantains."

Afua turned and headed toward the village main.

Not to make herself a liar, Folayan took a shortcut through the bush. Two hours later, when her shoulder ached under the weight of her full basket, she still was not ready to return home, so she sought advice from her best friend.

She'd raised her hand to knock at the door of Adwoa's mother-in-law's house when she saw someone turn the corner and approach. Adwoa opened the door and her welcoming smile was a sweet relief to Folayan's weary heart.

"I have been gathering plantains all afternoon and thought you might have use for some."

"Ah, with Kwaku's appetite, I will always welcome a gift of food." Adwoa welcomed her inside her new husband's house with a warm hug, but grumbled in Folayan's ear.

"Afua is right behind you. I hope she is not coming here." But before she could close the door, Afua called out from the road.

"Wo ho te sen, Adwoa."

"Mehoye," Adwoa responded. Turning to Folayan, she said, "Go sit down and I will bring you a drink of water."

"That will be nice, thank you," Afua said, breezing through the entry into the adiho and settling onto a stool across the way. She looked directly at Folayan, a sneer on her mouth. "You still look worn out. Sit down and we will all have a good visit."

Adwoa and Folayan exchanged a look of amazement. With a prim tightening of her lips, Adwoa closed the door and escorted Folayan to a seat, but remained standing.

"How can I help you, Afua?"

"Oh, I was just passing this way and thought I would visit your new home since I have not done so. Are Kwaku's parents not at home?"

"They have gone out."

Folayan waited for Adwoa to express appreciation for Afua's visit or offer some refreshment, but silence ensued.

Afua spoke. "I went by to see your parents today."

"Is that so?" Adwoa asked.

"Yes." Afua shrugged. She sent Folayan a pleasant smile and spoke to her. "Ever since Kofi and I were paired at Adwoa's Kings and Queens game, her parents and I have gotten to know each other quite well."

⊙━━━☒

Folayan remembered that awful day the unmarried girls and boys played "Pick-your-lover" which would establish couples for "Kings and Queens." She had taken part only because Adwoa assured her that Kofi would play if she did.

She was certain something had been arranged when the boys and girls lined up facing each other for the pairing dance and she and Kofi were matched, up until the last moment when Afua slipped into line ahead of her. Then Folayan had ended up paired with Abeeku.

Often with their parents' approval, after the game ended, partners continued the pairing beyond the normal month and a half, thus experiencing every responsibility of marriage together, except the marriage bed.

For Folayan, it had been an unrelenting six weeks, struggling to rein in her jealousy and fear. Folayan's eyes kept finding Kofi and Afua whenever she saw them out in the village. Even though Abeeku had taken her chin in hand and turned her face back to him several times, he still sent her a knocking.

Now the flush of emotion in her was too confusing. She needed to talk to Adwoa, but Afua looked like she planned to stay for a long while. Folayan refused to react to Afua's words, she would not give her that satisfaction. Still, she could not stay here with this woman.

Folayan stood up. "Adwoa, I must be going."

Adwoa's disappointment marked her face. As she walked with Folayan to the door she whispered, "Please do not leave me here with her alone."

In the entry, they heard footsteps approaching the door and Adwoa's husband. Kwaku entered. He delivered cheerful greetings and inquiries about Folayan's family then asked, "Where are you going?"

Before she could answer, Kofi stepped into the house. His eyes revealed joyful surprise. He flashed his bright smile as he greeted her. She returned a delighted response as her aching heart relaxed.

In the adiho, Afua, who could not be seen from the entry, called out, "Kofi?"

Kofi looked at his sister and mouthed the name, "Afua?" He grimaced at Adwoa's nod. His hands rose to signify that he could not be bothered with her today. He turned to leave.

"Kofi."

Afua stood in the entry. Her soft, solicitous smile matched her voice. "Kofi, what a surprise to see you here. Come sit down in the seat next to me."

Afua took his hand and pulled him behind her. With his other hand, Kofi grabbed Folayan's wrist and held tight. She let him lead her back into the adiho. Afua sat and patted the single stool beside her.

Kofi did not let go of Folayan's hand. "No, Afua. I will sit over here. Adwoa, you may take that seat."

Afua giggled. "Do not be silly, Kofi, a wife should sit next to her husband. Adwoa must sit with Kwaku and you will sit with me. Another seat can be brought for Folayan—if she truly intends to stay out in public."

Fear rammed Folayan's belly. Something strange glimmered in Afua's sidelong glance and Folayan knew she was in danger.

Adwoa, however, had had enough.

"What are you talking about, Afua? Why are you still playing the King's and Queens game? It is done. For many weeks it has been done."

Afua ignored her. Folayan heard the forced brightness in her next words.

"Kofi, your parents say they can give you money for me to buy and cook your food whenever you ask. They are always very welcoming when I visit them."

Kofi moved to stand directly before her. "Afua, I do not need or want them to give me money. The game is over. It was over before it started. I know you remember the questions you asked me, and I had the same answer each time—Folayan. Folayan. Folayan. And this morning I sent her my knocking."

Folayan sucked in breath and swallowed hard.

"There, you see!" Adwoa exclaimed. "How much more clear can it be that my brother wants nothing from you, Afua? He will never marry you. He has sent his knocking to Folayan."

Afua was cheerful. "He can withdraw it. No one will think badly of him if the rumor is proved true."

There was a moment of shocked silence. Then Kofi's teeth ground in exasperation, and his breath hitched. "What rumor?" He walked to the other side of the room. His jaw clenched.

Afua rose. Her eyes wide, her voice hardly a whisper. "The rumor—" she glanced at Folayan and swallowed, "—that Folayan and Abeeku's game may have gone too far."

Folayan trembled. Her knees gave way.

Adwoa was suddenly there to guide her down onto a stool.

Kofi turned around, his head down, his palms braced against the wall. Kwaku went to him and gripped Kofi's left shoulder.

"What have you done, Afua?" Adwoa demanded. "There is no such rumor unless you started it."

Folayan's heart beat painfully. She was speechless with despair.

Adwoa apparently had much to say, for she advanced on Afua. Hands on her hips, she stood nearly nose to nose with their age mate.

"You will not bring this deceit into our house, Afua. We are no longer children. Back then, you said or did anything you could to get what you wanted. However, it might have hurt other people did not matter—it was always just a selfish game about you."

Kwaku called his wife.

Adwoa stepped back to his side, but kept talking. "I am tired of it. We are grown now and you will not get away with that hatefulness any more. No more games, Afua. You will not bring shame to Folayan. Kofi is not going to marry you. He loves Folayan!"

Folayan prayed that her friend's words were true. If the fury in Kofi's face meant anything, they were. Or was it because he believed what Afua said about her?

She clung to the curved edges of her stool; her hands went cold, numb. "Kofi," she whispered.

He turned her way, and looked into her frightened eyes. As she searched his, she saw the crinkle at their corners. His face softened, too. Tension flushed out of her body.

She sighed.

The adiho seemed full of light and Folayan's heart beat with strange, deep strength, but Kofi had not said anything else. She stood up, knowing exactly what needed to be done.

"I must return home, Adwoa. This rumor may have already reached my father. I must go and explain it to him."

Afua looked up at Kofi. Her expression mixed bravado and nervousness. "You see, Kofi, she goes to confess. After that, nothing will stand between us."

"Oh!" Adwoa rounded on Afua in exasperation.

"No, Adwoa, let it be," Folayan cautioned her friend. "What Afua is saying about me is untrue. I remain untouched by any man. My father will know what to do."

She was certain by the strange glitter in Afua's eyes that something there was not right. Further talk would solve nothing. Folayan turned for the door.

"Wait, Folayan," Kofi commanded. "I am coming with you. I will speak with your father as well."

"Yes, yes!" Afua pushed forward to take Kofi's arm. "You must go and withdraw your knocking at once."

All was silent and Folayan saw understanding dawn in her friends, watching Afua's too-eager smile, her fevered eyes and desperate clutching of Kofi. Adwoa stepped forward.

Adwoa said, "That is a plan. Kwaku, you should go with them as chaperone. Afua and I will wait here." When Afua would have argued, Adwoa gently linked her arm. "Afua, do you really think it is wise to be seen with Folayan? Her scandal might brush off onto you. Stay with me and we will make food for when the men return."

Afua protested, but Kofi, staring straight ahead, said quietly, "It is true. I have not yet eaten."

Afua could not push them out the door fast enough.

Along the way, they stopped at Kofi's home. Yooku and his wife confirmed that Afua had come by that afternoon, asking if they had heard some news concerning Folayan and Abeeku.

After explanations and discussions, it was believed the rumor was something Afua had started just that afternoon. When Kofi made it clear he would speak with Folayan's parents, they agreed to accompany them.

Yooku was somber as he sat across from Folayan's father, and then said, "We must speak with Abeeku, but, if this lie was begun only today, perhaps we can settle it between our families."

All agreed but that hope disappeared moments later when Emissah came in, agitated, having just learned of the gossip. He calmed when he heard the truth.

Folayan and Maame stood inside the entry. Waiting for Akonor before going to the elders' homes, the men chatted outside. Yooku said, "Three times over here in one day. That has not happened since we were boys, Kwabena, before we started fishing."

"Yes," Papa sighed. "But Yooku, three times? You came to bring the knocking, and for this problem."

"No." Yooku shook his head. He went to the nearby tree, and pulled a cloth off the branch. "We were here with Kofi before the blue light faded. We hung this folded kente ntama for you."

Keeping the door ajar, Folayan listened. Her mouth dried.

"We left before hwaani hwaani light. All of us," said Kwamina.

"We must have just missed you," Yooku said.

Maame gripped Folayan's hand.

"Abeeku's grandfather asked if he was the first one," Papa said. "I told him yes."

A silent moment passed before Papa said, "Let us go to the elders."

# Water and Wine

*But she had to wait. They all had waited for the council day,
judgment day, when sentences were passed. On this day,
she was to stand before the chieftain at the Onyamedua.
Folayan decided that all eyes would be on her. Different from
at her Coming of Age celebration, this day could end in shame,
her future denied her, or reclaimed with the dignity of
her name being preserved.*

*Afua did not appear to understand how her rumor mirrored idle
thoughts of her mind with the desires that filled her own heart. She did
not seem to understand that it was not a light matter.*

**August 1796, Kormantse**

*P*apa and his sons did not return until morning. He said nothing,
except, "Daughter, do not leave this house until the elders call us
to the judgment."

For two days, Kofi's parents and hers traced the trail of the rumor.

Folayan walked around the house, the women not talking. But for
the children's antics, the misery would have been unbearable. To keep

away thoughts of her instant fall from celebration to shame, Folayan washed the walls, swept, and polished the floors with *ntwuma* dust—three times in the three days since the rumor began. Wherever one's eye lingered, the burnished gleam of the floor reflected sky light, but could not dispel Folayan's fretting.

*But I have to wait. We have all waited for the council day, judgment day, when sentences were passed. On this day, I must stand before the chieftain at the Onyamedua. All eyes will be on me. This is different from my Coming of Age celebration. This day can end in shame, my future denied me, or reclaimed with the dignity of my name being preserved.*

Folayan tossed on her bed wrestling with her covers for hours before morning light filtered into the room. She had stewed over Afua's lies. What must people be saying about her? Would her good name be fixed in disgrace for the rest of her life? This was council day. She had not thought about her appearance for judgement day, had not cared.

She searched her gold-banded box for a garment. Her hands paused on a dress Ekow's wife made for her—green with tiny black print squares. She had worn it on the second day of her celebration week. She spied the cloth below it—her Zebra hide. She smoothed her hands over it. A bubble surged up to her throat. More than anything she wanted to know why it happened to him.

Serwaa lay on her pallet watching, then pulling the covers up over her shoulders, she sat up.

Folayan hugged her aunt and gave morning greetings, "Mema wo akye."

Serwaa responded, then dressed while Folayan still tried to choose.

Folayan thought about wearing the zebra hide as an ntama over her shoulder, but decided that she would not wear his hide as a garment. She would fold it neatly over her forearm as a reminder to all that Zebra had no reason to wander off by himself. He knew the way and had always come home on his own.

Serwaa went to her own trunk. She pulled out fabric that Folayan had never seen before. She placed it in Folayan's hands. "I too have a garment for you. It was not finished when your Papa gave you your gold-banded box. So, I planned to save it and give it to you on the day you marry."

"Serwaa, it is so beautiful. Almost like Maame's kente that I wore for my Coming of Age celebration." As Folayan unfolded it, the light cast gleams on the purple, gold, blue and white woven kente, touches of red, and … it had narrow zebra patterned lengths woven here and there through it.

Hesitant to ask, Folayan whispered, "Who made it?"

"Kofi." Serwaa smiled. "I went to him after he brought your wedding kente to your father."

"How did he have the time?"

"He worked many hours by torchlight. I thought silk would wear better and be easier to weave into the cloth and stronger rather than hand stitching the hide strips to the cloth. And beside that …."

Folayan nodded. Her heart felt so full. She lifted the cloth to her face and rubbed a zebra strip on her cheek. Woven. Silk. Serwaa knew having her friend's skin so close might make her sad sometimes.

"Daughter. Would you do something for me today?"

"Anything I can do, you know I will. What is it Serwaa?"

"Wear this dress to the Council. It speaks of your value to your family and to the village. It reminds them that the matter of your zebra has not been solved. Just as someone treated him wrongly and caused his death, you are being wrongly accused." Her voice was strong and she stood straight-backed as she looked up into Folayan's eyes.

It seemed to Folayan that she felt strength flow from her aunt into her. "I will wear it Serwaa."

"There is one more thing. You painted pictures for your mother and for Adwoa's mother."

Folayan nodded.

"Where is mine?"

"Oh! Sorry Serwaa! I will make you one … I will start tomorrow."

"Sit down there on your Kwantunyi box."

Folayan obeyed.

Serwaa said, "I want the picture to be of you wearing this garment, sitting on this box just like you are, with the scroll of the merchant trade routes showing you are rising up with your heritage. The courage and accomplishments of your people give you strength. I want you to start it today, before we go to the council. It will give you confidence, and help you remember who you are—you are not, nor do you depend upon what other people may say."

She lifted Folayan's chin, "Who are you?"

"I am Ama Kwantunyi Folayan."

"Yes, Ama Kwantunyi Folayan—born on Onyankopon's day, daughter of the traveler, is one who walks in dignity. That is the Folayan the people will see today tall, straight, poised, and beautiful. I want my picture to show that woman and I want it to be started on the day of battle. On the day of your triumph."

Her finger guided Folayan up to standing position.

Serwaa commanded, "I will bring your first meal to you. Now, get your artist tools. You have most of the morning to draw at least the body shape. Can you do that for me?"

"I will do my best." Folayan went to her basket of supplies, and took her charcoal stick down off the shelf and went to her parent's room. Her mother only asked, "How are you feeling today?"

Tears burst from Folyan's eyes, "Oh, Maame what will I do if they believe Afua?"

"No matter what, you will walk in dignity. Give me the gold nugget pouch."

Folayan searched the shelf. "It is not here." She and Maame searched the room twice. "Maame may I look in the box?" Maame nodded, her brow furrowed, she worried.

Folayan took all the contents out stacking them neatly. No pouch on the bottom.

They heard Papa's voice entering the house. Maame whispered. "Put it all back!"

Before she could, Papa pulled the curtain aside, "Here you are. What are you doing?"

Maame would not answer.

Folayan said. "We—were trying to find the pouch."

Papa said, "Oh. I put it in here. He opened the little corner compartment. "I thought it should have its own space so it would not get lost." He put it in Folayan's hand. He beckoned Maame. She got up turning a questioning eyebrow to Folayan who chuckled and went to her room.

A few minutes later, Maame joined her, "Look at the pebble and 'Remember the gold in you.' Gold-water-truth, they will stand. Wine will rot."

Folayan laid the garment out to see the pattern while she drew. Then she sat down on her gold-banded box. Her anxiety rising, she tried to calm, by examining it soft, smooth, yet beautiful and pure. *Will Kofi think I am also? Will he take back his knocking?* She realized she had worried this way at her celebration. Abeeku had declared that he would send a knocking, but Kofi had not even come once in the whole week. *Why am I having so much trouble about being with Kofi? Is this pebble an omen? Is it good or bad? Will the council today prevent me from becoming his wife?* She breathed in deeply.

By mid-morning, Folayan had outlined her body sitting on the box as well as the pattern in the dress cloth. She used the self-portrait she had made for her mother, and her golden mirror to see her facial expression. Serwaa had said battle. She certainly did not feel that way. She felt afraid, bewildered. When the sun neared its highest point in the sky, Maame came into the bedroom.

Maame said, "Very nice. I see this one does not have the smile that my picture has."

Folayan said, "Have you seen many pictures of people smiling?"

"As I think of it, no. Perhaps that is why mine is so special to me."

"Serwaa and Adwoa told me smiling pictures are of people who are not serious about life. I am very serious today."

"Yes. Yes." She wrapped her arms around Folayan. "Be strong and of good courage. The truth will come out. Like the smile that remains in your eyes."

"I hope so Maame." Folayan realized that for the whole morning she had not fretted. Her focus had been so strong on the image. She felt somewhat relaxed. She glanced again at the charcoal line drawing. The concern in the face matched how she felt inside, but it was a small portion of what had tormented her for the last three days.

"It is time to put that away, and dress to go to the Onyamedua."

Folayan breathed in deep and exhaled. She felt better, so much better.

She dressed, tied her head in the duku. She picked up the ntama, then fingered the Zebra hide. Which one? Finally, she swallowed and hung the folded hide over her left shoulder. Pulling the doorway curtain back, she repeated to herself, "Courage."

When she entered the adiho, family members commented on how pretty she looked, and that they thought it was a good idea to remind the people of Zebra. The jitters in her stomach calmed.

At the Onyamedua, her family took their places They would be up front for all the village to watch them, too. Abeeku and Afua were already standing up there, waiting for the procession.

Folayan hesitated. She rubbed her wet hands together, swallowed hard and stepped forward. Midway, Kofi caught up "I brought our plant you rescued and nourished. I watered and trimmed it. See, it has grown strong, like our love is, and our marriage will be. I believe you."

Folayan breathed relief, as they walked to Abeeku and Afua.

Again, she saw something strange flit in Afua's eyes. Then it was gone.

"What is this, Folayan?" Afua reached to touch the ntama.

Folayan stepped back. *How could she pretend that we are friends?*

"I have not seen your zebra for a long time," Afua purred. "Where have you been keeping him?"

Folayan was astounded. She had rehearsed things Afua might say, but to feign that she did not know he was dead. Folayan sighed.

Afua came close and dared to finger it. "Oh, it is soft."

Folayan stepped back. Afua pinched the ntama and let it drop to the ground. A gasp reverberated through the crowd.

Kofi picked it up, brushed it. His touch comforted Folayan as he lay the black and white ntama back on her shoulder.

Folayan smiled and said, "Meda Wase, Kofi. Even though my Zebra is gone, I will always have my happy memories."

The music began. The attendants, councillors, and elders entered, followed by the chieftain, who sat in the center front on his egua. His sister sat on his left side, his linguist stood on his right. The leaders sat on the two side sections on both sides of the wide aisle. Nanabesia sat in the section on the right side of the aisle, in the first seat, in the front row, near the chieftain's sister. The families of the accused sat in that section also.

The entire village listened attentively.

Abeeku was first. He and his family members reported that he had been in his house all morning until he and his envoy went to Folayan's house. Then they returned home to wait for a while before going back. The second time, he gave the knocking to her father. Foyalan was not there.

When Folayan stepped up to be questioned, she made sure to stand tall. Thinking of the kandake queens, she held her head high, praying that Onyankopon would help her bring honor to her family.

Folayan told her part, answered each question in detail, and stated that she had been falsely accused. Her parents were next, then Kofi's parents, then Kofi. Finally, Afua stepped forward to tell her part.

When Afua paused, an elder asked, "Was Abeeku there?"

"I never saw Abeeku," Afua answered. Although her head was not down, she looked off to the side.

After many questions, an elder said, "Let us hear the conclusion of the whole matter. What is the water in your words, Afua?"

"The water is that I saw Folayan at about noon. She had grass in her hair. Her clothing was rumpled. She said she had fallen asleep."

"What is the wine in your words?" the elder repeated the question four times. Each time the questions made her leave off excess words and speak the core difference between the water and the wine of Afua's story.

Finally, Afua sighed and said, "Instead of speaking what she told me, I told Kofi's parents what I wanted it to be."

"You lied."

"Yes. I lied."

With a slight shake of the head, she stood taller, and bearing a haughty expression, muttered, "What does it matter?"

She spoke her reason why it seemed fit for her to do so. Afua did not appear to understand how her rumor mirrored idle thoughts of her mind with the desires that filled her own heart. She did not seem to understand that it was not a light matter. She was blind to the shame she had brought on her family, the sadness upon Nanabesia's shoulders.

"Zebra!" a voice called from the audience. "What about Zebra?" Others took up the chant.

Afua boldly turned and moved close to Folayan. Her eyes gloated. She smirked, "Where is your Zebra?"

Folayan seethed, clenched her teeth, and turned away, determined to keep her breathing even. *Remember the promise. Remember. Remember.*

A fifth elder who had asked only two questions all afternoon, spoke—according to custom—to the linguist, who spoke to the chieftain. Then with permission, the elder said, "It seems that the whispering wind is with child and desires to give birth. Is there anyone among the elders or villagers who has a word to say in this matter regarding Abeeku and Folayan—or Afua—or Zebra?"

People looked around, but the grumbling hushed.

A voice from the middle said, "I have something to say." The crowd parted to let him through. When he stood before the linguist, his voice trembled. Out of the corner of her eye, Folayan watched the chieftain lean slightly forward.

"Afua hired men to take the colt and he-goat to the forest."

Like muffled thunder, the sentence raced through the audience.

He continued, "Afua told me to take the Zebra. I protested. She would not accept my refusals. She told me she knew I was a poor man. She was angry and threatened to make up lies about me. I was afraid. My family only has me to provide for them.

He looked at Folayan, "Then Afua started talking on and on about taking your he-goat. She said, I did not have to kill it, just tie it up." I finally agreed to take the he-goat."

He addressed Papa directly. "I am so sorry. I took your he-goat. I worried many days that I would be found out."

Papa stood up, reached out and put his hand on the man's shoulder.

The man's voice started to crack. He paused a moment, "Then you came to me and said you had heard that I needed to make more money. You offered me work on your caravan. It was because of traveling with you that I have been able to build up my own goat herd. I have ten now. Please forgive me and allow me to make restitution with one of my goats.

Papa said, "There is no need of restitution. My he-goat is very alive and healthy."

"But I caused your family distress!"

Papa put both hands on the man's shoulders. "You have done enough."

Papa turned to the linguist  asked to speak to the chieftain and elders. "I can explain why I believe this man is telling the truth." With permission, Papa said, "About two weeks after Zebra was lost, my youngest son came to me and said there is another goat joined with our herd.

"I had my sons make inquiries around the village, asking if anyone had lost a goat. They learned that this man only had three goats days before, but suddenly, he only had two."

The man's face looked stricken.

But Papa continued talking to the man in a calm voice, "Your neighbors said you had celebrated no feast recently. They said you were trying to build up your herd.

"When my sons were satisfied that you were the only person the he-goat could have come from, I hired you and I watched you. For six months as we traveled, you never said anything when they purposefully mentioned Zebra, nor did you speak of having lost a goat.

"Otherwise, I saw that you were an honest, hardworking man. So, I invited you to come on a second journey."

The man opened and closed his mouth several times, trying to speak. Overcome, the man fell on his knees. "Please, please forgive me. You have been so good to me. And I caused your daughter's pet to die. I could have warned you. I ...."

Papa raised his hand. "It is enough. It is done. Go in peace."

The man stood up, and hurried from the crowd.

Folayan was incredulous; neither Papa or her brothers had said a word. Except Akonor did tell her about the goat that joined their herd. He said they were waiting for somebody to announce they were missing a goat at the Friday night meeting at Onyamedua, but no one did."

The elder asked the solemn audience. "Our custom is to hear more than one witness on a matter."

"What he is saying is true." From the left side of the crowd, another man came forward with his wife. The man said, "Afua tried to force me to do it, too, but I said no. She wanted me to get a partner to help me distract the zebra and goat with food, and take them far from the village into the bush. She was angry and threatened to say I abused her. She vowed to get somebody to help her. I went home and told my wife immediately. Then we went to the elder Opoku."

He pointed at the old man, who nodded permission to continue. "He told me we would watch and see if the culprit was found out by someone else, and then I could be a witness. We have been afraid these two years, afraid to say anything about it, lest we be accused."

Folayan heard the grumbling of the audience and knew Afua had lost all respect in their community. Whisperings simmered and spilled out, in testimonies of various hurts that Afua had caused this one or that one in the village.

She would find no husband to give her a child here. There were also murmurings of banishment. Her own actions showed that she chose not to be happy in Kormantse.

The judgment gave her two choices: leave Kormantse on her own, with opportunity to return when she had proved a changed life, or be banished forever, empty of a chance for reconciliation.

The demand was also made that Afua pay restitution for the zebra in money or land before sunset.

Folayan hoped Afua could learn to change. Still she was most relieved when Afua's mother took her daughter to live with relatives over in the little village of Anomabou.

After the judgment, Afua's fate was the only thing that was clear. However, no one could be sure who actually brought Folayan the first knocking, Kofi or Abeeku. That evening the family gathered in the adiho.

Papa said, "Daughter, pull your stool over here." When she sat down beside him, he said, "I thought I decided about your husband."

All side conversations hushed.

"It has been four days since your Rite of Passage. On your first day back with us, two knockings came to us early in the blue light and another in the afternoon before we heard the bad news. We are not sure who actually brought the first knocking, Abeeku or Kofi.

"During the celebration at the clan house several others showed strong interest in you, but they might have changed their minds because of the rumor. And those other four from different villages who have brought knockings still may withdraw just because of the stigma. Therefore, the time I thought I had for pondering has fled."

Folayan held her breath and trying to appear calm, leaned forward, chewing her thumbnail.

"A decision must be made today, but given nudging from the other women in my life I will at least ask you some questions before I announce my choice."

Folayan swallowed and sat up straight.

"One is a leader. He will prosper and therefore provide for you well and make you happy. That one is Abeeku."

"Papa!" Her eyes filled with tears. "Abeeku? But Kofi's grandmother came to Maame …" she squeaked, "… to pick a flower."

"Yes. Many weeks ago, yet I have not seen Kofi around here since then. I watch you with Abeeku. He makes you laugh. At the Bakatue …"

Folayan blurted, "Yes, with Abeeku and Jojo. They are just friends. Kofi and I laugh, too. He makes his plans happen. He is already prospering."

"At the Bakatue I saw Kofi with Afua often." Papa's voice was stern.

"Oh, no Papa. It was Afua, still playing the Kings and Queens game, sticking to him when he tried to get away from her. Kofi did not talk to me because I did not answer him when he told me how much he cared for me and asked if I would accept his knocking. I was too surprised to tell him I felt that way about him, too. He did not know."

She grabbed both of her father's hands, looked wide into his eyes, and pushed her words past her taut throat. "He is kind. And industrious. He is the one, Papa, who saved me from the ants in the ofram tree."

"Ofram tree? When was that?"

"When I was nine." She sniffed and wiped her eyes with both hands, and revealed the incident.

"Why did I not know?"

"You were on journey. I asked Maame not to tell you."

"Kofi?" Questions lingered in his voice.

She nodded. Papa looked at her for a long moment. Then at Maame and Serwaa. Their smiles approved.

He went to his room. Serwaa took him Folayan's potted plant.

No one moved or spoke a word. Folayan sat with her head down until he finally came out and sat on his egua.

"Sons," he said. "Please go to Yooku and tell him I will accept Kofi's knocking."

Folayan released a long breath. Then she went and sat on her heels beside Papa and lay her head on his knee, "Thank you."

In short time, her brothers returned home, followed by Kofi's envoy. Folayan was sent to her room until asked to come out.

Kofi's father made the official request, "I would like to pick a flower from your garden for my son, Kofi."

The ritual included her speaking her agreement in the presence of both families.

She looked at Kofi, and smiled. "Yes. Yes. I consent."

Kofi beamed. She felt his eyes follow her as she went back into her room.

The men negotiated the bride price that Kofi would bring when he claimed his wife, but first the character inquiry had to be completed.

Because attention had been drawn so recently to Folayan, villagers were quick to testify to Yooku and Papa the knowledge they had about their child's intended spouse's personality, morals intelligence, industry, courtesy, spiritual condition, respect for elders and ancestors, kindnesses and benefit to the community.

Did they have any destructive habits? Had they committed any crimes? Were they worthy of the privilege to marry anyone, and beyond themselves, was the family physically strong? Were there any diseases, cripples, or weak-minds in their family history?

The Kormantse and Edina reports came to their parents within one week—both were deemed honorable. The last hurdle was waiting for reports from distant villages. True to Akonor's prediction, Folayan had been nowhere else; however, Kofi had.

Papa did not want to delay until someone who, by chance, was travelling to this or to that place for their business and then bring back the reports. That could take months. He sent all five sons and one of Kofi's brothers out together to collect the testimonies.

On horseback, following the high road, at certain points they divided in pairs to visit villages, then rejoined each other, until they arrived at the furthest distance, the village where Kofi learned to weave kente cloth, then worked their way back on the low road. By the time they returned, they'd visited villages, interior and by the sea, all along the way, finishing with those nearest to Kormantse.

While waiting, Folayan refused to be anxious. Kofi had told her he might not visit as much as he would like. He had kentes to complete before the wedding. Adwoa hinted that he was working on his bride price.

Folayan spent time at the farm, painted sale items for the market, and relaxed with her family, for there was no doubt in her mind that Kofi would be confirmed as bright, unassuming, upright and honest in all his dealings.

Then Papa would give his blessing to prepare for the ayefro.

# CHAPTER 32

*Ayefro*

*Life had brought her many adventures and much instruction
that subdued her feisty spirit. Life had developed in her skills
and talents and turned her into a lady. Now, here she stood
with this man she had admired from afar for half her life.*

**October 1796, Kormantse**

It took Folayan's brothers five weeks to travel and return with news of Kofi's conduct and character. Papa hired the beauticians again.

The day began with Folayan lying still, taking in the silence, broken by her thoughts of life's changes, and watching the dark from behind closed lids until blue rays of light seeped into the room. She heard Serwaa stir and eventually sit up on her bed. Folayan also sat up, moved over to Serwaa's bed, snuggled beside Serwaa and rested her head on her shoulder. Serwaa slipped her arm around Folayan's waist.

"Tell me some stories," Folayan purred.

"Stories?" Serwaa chuckled. "About what?"

"Start with the day I was born and how Papa almost named me Serwaa, too."

Like when she was a very little girl, Folayan continued to request stories she'd heard many times. Serwaa complied, one after the other. Stories known by none of the people at the Rite of Passage. Stories from the eyes and heart of the old woman who was the first to see her break from the womb—the one who whispered, "Akosua, you have brought into the world ... a girl child."

Except when Folayan was with her parents, she and Serwaa had been inseparable, until she grew old enough to go off with her age mates. Finally, Serwaa told about the day Kofi's grandmother came to her asking to speak to Maame. She hinted that Kofi was looking for a wife.

"... My beautiful flower." Serwaa placed her hands on both of Folayan's shoulders and looked her in the eyes. "You have made me very, very proud. Today you are a bride. You will be a great Fanti woman."

She wrapped her arms around her niece, who likewise clung tight to her.

"Meda wase, Serwaa. Meda wase."

Upon hearing voices in the adiho, Folayan went to each sister-in-law exchanging hugs and making plans with them, and talking with each child. This was a bittersweet day in the Kwantunyi house, for though excitement was evidenced in every word and gesture, the somber realization that Folayan was leaving their home forever lay heavy in the air.

Her brothers tried to act like they were unaffected.

As her brothers' wives lived in her father's house, now she would join Kofi's household. Under most circumstances, Folayan would be coming back to this house after the wedding rites, if the groom's family had no room for her, or she'd be moving into their home with them for several years, but Kofi was remarkable. She would soon be living in her own house with him. Her status would change, as well as her responsibilities to the community.

She already had a trunk of clothes, velvet, jewels, and other items from Papa. The dowry included land that Kofi had bought for her that would pass down to her daughters.

Bathed with fragrances and pampered, her skin felt soft all over; soft like her braid loose and wavy now. She felt beautiful inside, and smelled like a grove of hibiscus flowers.

It was nearing sunset when the beauticians left. Folayan stood in the center of the adiho, her hair combed high in the royal pyramid of tekua waves that held three rows with twelve golden combs her father had brought especially for her from his travels. Her face glowed.

She stood dressed and stunning in the gold, white and black wedding kente, that Kofi, her groom had woven for her. He had intricately blended the Gye Nyame adinkra.

It was beautiful. She felt beautiful.

Once more, Folayan sat like a queen, this time in the middle of her father's adiho. Faintly, she could hear the drumming and singing of the people accompanying Kofi as he left his father's house. The music grew louder as more people joined the groom's party, winding through the akura to her Papa's home.

Voices blended with the beautiful tones of the drums—talking drums, djembes, and *donnos*. Her heart marched with the rhythm, her excitement escalated as the laughter and song and drums drew closer. When they were in front of her house, Papa went out to greet them.

Kofi's brothers entered first, each carrying a part of the bride price: for her mother, they gave a bottle of palm wine, a small bag of gold, three sheep, two goats; for the bride, two cloths of damask and taffeta for garments, and a map of a parcel of land.

The bride price was Kofi's thank-you for the gift of their daughter to be his wife. Several days earlier Maame had told her the bride price they'd settled on. Now, Folayan watched Papa's eyebrows go up with the two additional sheep and the cloths.

Kofi had exceeded the negotiated dowry, giving more than three times what was commonly given. If it were possible for her to love him more, her heart swelled to contain it. He had erased the stigma of the rumor, doused triple any embers for all the wedding party to see that Kofi believed she was a bride of great value.

With a full smile, Papa accepted the dowry.

And the drums crescendoed.

Kofi strode in and her breath leapt from her. So tall. So black. So handsome. A king, grand and glorious so handsome standing there flashing that delightful smile, adoring her.

Kofi came to her in his black and white kente and cap. Her breathing still unsteady, her heart felt so full, his kente matched hers, both of them decked in much gold. They stood together for a moment, looking at each other. She recalled how she had abruptly changed the garment for her coming of age day. Yet, here he was in matching splendor.

"How did you have time to make it?"

"I started working on mine when our families brought in the harvest together. Even though I had no answer from you, each strand was a daily prayer—and a decision to send a knocking anyway."

"How did you know Papa would accept it?"

"I did not know—if he would, or if you would—but I was determined."

The fervor in his eyes told her, that at last, this day she was his queen.

The two families sat on the seats arranged in two rows across from each other, on one side Kofi's family, on the other, the Kwantunyis. Joviality filled the room.

Then when the time had come, each of her brothers hugged her, told her how beautiful she was, gave her more words of advice, and a few to Kofi, as well.

"Kofi, I know you realize how fortunate you are to pick the most beautiful girl in the village." Emissah pronounced her words with pomp. "I expect the proper pride when you walk down the street with my sister."

"Oh, he will," Kwamina joined in. "Our Folayan will become such a great merchant woman, Kofi can just hang up his nets and weave kentes all day."

"All the better to be closer to her." Kofi laughed.

Adwoa said, "I will always remind you I was the one who got you to persuade our papa to ask if our families could bring in the harvest together last year." She looked directly at Folayan. "My plan was to give Kofi a chance to talk to you without interference."

Kofi leaned over and grasped his sister's hand. "And I will never stop thanking you."

Akonor stood, nodding as if he were a wise elder. "Folayan, you see what a good man you have found. You be a good wife and always remember your place—no stone-throwing or ant battles." He handed her a parchment scroll. "Papa and I taught you to read it. Now I am keeping the rest of my promise—a book of your own. Here are the first pages."

Maame sucked her teeth, but Folayan saw the emotion in Akonor's eyes when he came to embrace her, while she, too, blinked back tears.

Then her father stood, spoke words to the couple, and asked in everybody's hearing for the third time, "Folayan, is it your choice to marry Kofi?"

Each time she answered, "Yes."

Then Papa welcomed the joining of the two families. Everyone rose, and Papa offered praise and thanksgiving to the Most High.

After a final glance around, Folayan kissed her parents, and took Kofi's hand.

She stepped, nervous yet bright-eyed, out into the dim of evening, her last time to be in this house as a maiden. Two torch-bearers led the way. Four of her brothers lifted her ebony and gold chest to their shoulders and walked behind her. The rest of her family fell in at the rear, then the other torch-carrying age mates, drummers, and singers.

As Folayan walked she tried to sort out anxious feelings: joy, fear, hope, loss, wonder. The procession moved past different houses. She retraced events in her life. Nearing the giant ofram tree, she glanced at her youngest brother Akonor, so tall and handsome now, eighteen afenhyia, he would be married himself in three or four years, but he would not have to leave his parents' home. She smiled, recalling how he had teased her so much at age nine when she took his challenge to climb that ofram, to look for her Papa's return.

At her side now, with torch in hand, Adwoa must have been thinking the same thing. "Folayan," she said with a chuckle. "Remember when you climbed that tree and Kofi saved you?"

Folayan giggled with her. "Yes. He became my hero that day." She squeezed Kofi's hand and mused, "That was the first day I loved him."

She looked up at him, wondering what he was thinking.

Folayan reached out and touched Adwoa's hand. "Thank you, my friend, my sister. I want to hug you right now, but I am afraid the guests would march right over us."

Adwoa looked around. "There are twice as many people who have joined us since we left your house."

Folayan's eyebrows rose. She dared not look back, just concentrated on walking like the queens at the Bakatue.

The drum talk swelled. Folayan observed they were passing Nanabesia's house.

Rising taller, she repeated to herself, "Gracefully, gracefully—with dignity, only a few steps to go."

Folayan was happy to see Nanabesia join the procession, a precious honor. Folayan smiled brightly at her, and thought about things Nanabesia had taught her about husbands and wives, duties, and privileges.

Folayan flushed. Kofi was looking down at her, smiling. She became breathless—her hand fluttered to her mouth with anxiety and anticipation.

They turned the corner and came to Afua's house—empty.

"Good," Kofi grunted. "She is not here to spoil any part of this day."

Against her will, Folayan thought, *If she could, she would. I wonder how she had the nerve to come to last Wednesday market. But it is an open market, people from many villages along the shore attend it.* Afua had gone from booth to booth, as if there was no banishment upon her. Folayan recalled how she had two young men with her. *Strangers. Were they from Anomabu or somewhere else? The way she talked and giggled with one of them, it seemed as if she had found someone to marry. Could the other one be his brother or cousin?*

The joyous singing distracted Folayan. Her steps matched the drummers. All her age mates waved palm fronds, and the singers lifted their marriage songs, one round up, and then another.

Folayan glanced out of the corner of her eye. They were passing Kofi's grandfather's house. Nana had arrived at Papa's as the procession line was forming, he teased, "I heard that I missed the knockings, but perhaps you will be merciful and accept my dowry." He grinned and placed it in her hands.

"Oh!" Folayan looked up at Kofi, "The Sankofa mirror!"

He chuckled, "Too late, Grandfather. She is my wife, now."

Nana kept them laughing up to the final house, where on many days she'd played with her best friend. Kofi's arm slid around her waist, his fingers squeezed her side. He took a step. She halted and looked up into his eyes in the flickering torch light, swallowed hard several times, and mouthed, "Just a moment, please."

It seemed like it had taken half a day, but it only took from sunset to black sky for Kofi to weave through the village to her house, and now—here. She looked around at the joyous crowd who had accompanied them.

Life had brought her many adventures and much instruction that subdued her feisty spirit. She squeezed Akonor's scroll. Life had developed in her skills and talents and turned her into a lady. Now, here she stood with this man she had admired from afar for nearly half her life.

Kofi waited with her. For several seconds, she whispered the adinkra in its full two words, "Gye Nyame—Except God, nothing happens." Then she said it again, with affection in one short word. "Gye'ame ... Gye'ame" She drew in a deep breath, gifted her husband her brightest smile, and nodded.

They entered her new home.

He toured her around the interior courtyard, charming the guests in the adiho, inviting them to enjoy the food and drink. After an hour, he put his hand on her elbow, and moved through the crowd toward one of the side rooms. Her heart sped.

Before entering the room, she paused at the doorway. She glanced back and found her parents, facing each other. As if given a cue, they smiled at her, then turned back to look again into each other's eyes. Folayan peeked up to the night sky and twinkling stars. Kofi ushered her inside and pulled the curtain closed.

He stood looking at her. "You are so beautiful—and you are my bride." He drew her to him. "At last."

She could not tell if the pounding in her ears was the swelling of the drums or her heart as he cupped her face in his hands and kissed her once, then again gently, slowly, urgently.

# CHAPTER 33

# *Questions*

*When some young women went to their new homes
to establish their places with a new mother and sisters,
anxious days ensued. Sometimes it was not a good fit*

*To the villagers and to Folayan, the black-robes were part of the intruder's
castles and forts and the uneasiness which those structures raised in her
heart. Except when the black robes stopped at her stall, she avoided them*

**October 1796, Kormantse**

Light flitted into the window onto Folayan's face. She opened her
eyes and blinked into Kofi's. He lay on his side, his head resting
on his elbow. He smiled, leaned forward and kissed her softly. "Good
morning, Wife."

His features strong and handsome, she caressed his brow. His
smile made her quiver. He kissed her twice.

They dozed.

Folayan awoke the second time when she heard voices out in the
adiho. Kofi arose and reached to pull her up. Then he went to one of
the large clay pots and scooped a dipper of water out and poured it
into a medium-sized gourd for Folayan and another one for himself.

When the couple emerged from their room, Kofi's parents, two older brothers with their wives and eight- and ten-year-old daughters greeted them with beaming faces. They embraced Folayan and welcomed her again into their family.

Folayan helped prepare breakfast, which she ate with the females while Kofi ate with the males. Afterward Kofi went outside to work at his loom that stretched low, the length of fifteen arms—elbow to finger tips.

The women divided household chores. Folayan and Adwoa's niece cleaned the bukyia fire pit and the outside area. The others worked in the kitchen room and adiho. After each one cleaned her own sleeping room, Kofi's mother announced, "We have done enough here. Today, we will go to Folayan's new house. Perhaps we can finish it before the week ends."

Since Adwoa had moved to her husband's family home, Folayan had not been over here. She should have known though that Kofi's house was close to completion. How was it that Adwoa had not told her? How was it that the village ears had not heard? She realized so much had happened in the last few weeks—the knockings, Afua's rumor …

Folayan sucked in a breath of relief. Her name had been restored beyond a doubt. Both Kofi and Abeeku had testified to her virtue. For Kofi's parents' faith in her, she would be forever grateful. She believed there was no better wedding present than their respect and confidence in her.

When some young women went to their new homes to establish their places with a new mother and sisters, anxious days ensued. Sometimes it was not a good fit. *Even though things are good, will they stay that way?*

Folayan had been in and out of this house since she was five. The picture she'd painted hung on the wall. Folayan simply moved to live with a woman she already loved.

Adwoa's mother led them outside to the loom where Kofi sat weaving.

Kofi stood and, with anticipation, smiled at Folayan. "Son," his mother asked, "do you wish to take your wife to your new house or shall I?"

He led the women thirty yards through a cluster of trees. Suddenly, there it was, more long than square, the walls and cross beams were up. The thatch roof was partially completed.

⚷

"Oh, Kofi, this is good." In the adiho, Folayan looked around. She grabbed his hand and turned to her new maame. "Meda wase. Thank you. You have done such beautiful work."

Folayan stroked the smooth mud and straw walls. She loved the smell of the drying, still-fresh clay. She would have a house of her own soon.

Kofi nodded, appreciation in his eyes. "Yes, my maame and my sisters are the ones who deserve much praise. They did the most work. I just brought in the wood and other materials."

The women laughed. His eldest brother's wife said, "Kofi is too modest, he has worked on it every day since the last harvest. Even after fishing all night or working on the farm, he would come and do something each day. Sometimes, working here was the only time we ever saw him. We did our part and he did his."

Folayan looked at her husband with new understanding. *Could this have been why he had been so absent all that time she thought he was embarrassed at how he opened his heart to her?*

Kofi's maame guided them through the house. Her smile was broad with pride. "As you can see, we are not quite finished with the adiho walls, but with your help, Folayan, we should have it done soon."

Two weeks and three days later, Kofi and Folayan moved in. That evening Kofi and his brothers and father delivered all their belongings and set them in the center of the adiho. Then Kofi left to go fishing.

When she woke the next morning, Folayan separated the items into piles according to the rooms where they would go. She was entering the kitchen room with an armload of cooking pottery, the top one filled with sponges, when she heard Adwoa's voice from outside. "Hello! Me ma wo akye"

Followed by Adwoa's mother, eight people including Maame, Serwaa, and Folayan's brothers' wives had all come to help set her house in order. When the women entered the adiho, they voiced their astonishment at its length. Serwaa ran her hand over the loom's wooden frame. A one-third complete kente waited between the twines. Kwesi's wife asked about who was buying it.

"I think he is making it to have ready," Folayan said and tapped the back wall near the loom. "On these two sides, he will build out the other wall as our family grows and we need more room." She giggled. "He is very industrious."

"We shall be industrious, too," Kwamina's wife said while she ran her hand around the rim of one of the large brown clay jars. She counted one, two, three doors, plus the entrance. "Tell us where these things go."

Folayan and Adwoa worked in the kitchen room, putting items on the shelves. Her sisters-in-law worked in the roofed double room for sitting for rainy days when the family was not in the adiho. Finding places for every item, they all moved like ants—cleaning, polishing, and adorning the house.

Folayan had made paintings on woodcuts and cloth. Gifts brought to her during her Rite of Passage included cooking utensils made of iron, stone, pottery, and wood; as well as different sizes of coiled mats for the table, for sitting, and the floor.

The three elders organized the contents of her coming-of-age box. Maame and Serwaa had made six, knee-high, lidded, rectangular baskets for her. They folded her special garments and put them in the first basket, her daily wear in the second one, and her varied size and purposed fabrics in the third.

Kofi kept his clothes in one waist-high basket. Folayan waited until she could ask him for permission to touch his things, but she planned to make two or three baskets like hers for him.

Her friends stayed with her all day until time to prepare the evening meals.

Later, Kofi asked, "How did you do today?"

His mother said, "With all of those women's hands, we did six days' worth of work. Your wife needs another shelf in your sleeping room."

Kofi raised his eyebrows. "Is that so?"

Folayan nodded and smiled to herself at his man-of-the-house tone.

Five weeks later, in the evening of a hot, dry March day, Kofi rolled up all the coverings on the inside doors, allowing a welcome breeze to flow into the side rooms from the adiho. He sat mending a fishing net while Folayan plaited the rim of a nearly complete basket.

When that was done, she went to the kitchen room and reached under the waist-high food preparation shelf. She had cloistered the other baskets out of Kofi's sight. After setting them inside the adiho, she said, "I made something for you."

He looked up. "Something for me?"

She stood by the stack of long, flat baskets.

"I saw you making them, but I did not realize they were for me."

"I made them like mine, so all your personal things can be reached easily. Your big round basket does not fit everything you have. If you like, I will organize them in these."

"Meda wase, meda wase." He thanked her. "That is fine." He held up the first basket, examining the tight weave of the long grasses, pale and dusty green.

"These are well made." He thanked her again. Folayan sorted his belongings. He moved as if to join her, but she told him, "You finish your net. I will take care of this." He did not resist.

When she was done, she said, "Now, come see."

She stood by, watching him lift each lid with surprise, then pleasure growing in his face.

"You have made containers for everything, my fishing tools, my musical instruments, my clothing, and my weaving supplies!"

Basking in his appreciation, she envisioned that they would do well together, with their talents blended. It was already evident in this house: large clay water pots and cooking vessels; three wall hangings she painted, and two floor rugs coiled by Serwaa and Maame.

Brooms, cooking utensils, and cleaning tools were organized in containers made of clay and carved wood. She and Kofi were barely started, yet her house looked good, smelled good, felt good.

"I am blessed," she whispered.

"What did you say?"

"I am blessed to have you as my husband. We will accomplish great things together."

He nodded, thoughtfully, and went back to his mending. Before long, he watched her sort. When she caught his eye, he smiled and nodded again.

She was busy putting the cases away in the sleeping room and did not know when Kofi left the house. She took up her paint box and a medium-sized calabash. The pink and black adinkra strip across the neck of the yellow gourd would serve as her pattern for several pieces she was planning.

Since the Bakatue, her work had become much in demand. Other shopkeepers, including Kofi's mother, ordered items from her. And only a few days ago, a traveling merchant had bought all her calabash plates and two of her painted wall hangings. She was excited to build up her stock again. She selected the brushes she wanted to use: the feathers that she'd stripped down to the pointy ends and those with ox or horse hair ends for wider swaths.

When she settled onto her cushion with all her supplies, Kofi said, "Good, you are painting. Did the kwesi broni priest talk to you?"

"The priest?" Memory gave her a vision of several black-robes who lived at El Mina and sometimes came to Fort Kormantin. They all strolled self-importantly through the marketplaces. "Which one?"

"The old, white haired priest."

*Did he mean the one here at Fort Kormantin?* "The preacher?"

"Yes. He bought your last bowl my maame had on her mat."

"No. He did not speak to me." She thought back to Wednesday market. It had been so busy since her seclusion and the wedding. She didn't think she'd seen the preacher, as he liked to be called.

"My mother sent him to me at the boat. He told me he wanted to know where we got the calabashes. I told him my wife made them."

"He came to your fishing boat?" Now, Folayan could see the old man's face keenly in her mind. Three or four times since she had been selling, he stopped to buy from her. She always had the feeling that he wanted to talk longer with her.

Each time he left her wondering—*how well does he know my Maame?* She told Kofi, "He always asks about my maame."

"Is that so?" Kofi paused. "He only talks to a few people. He seems to like to talk to me."

Kofi knotted a rope and tied it off.

Remembering other discussions with Kofi's grandfather, Folayan put her feather down and stared at her husband. "What did you do?"

"I watched to see that no one else was with him when he came my way, and I walked and talked with him toward the market and stayed close. I knew I could overpower him, if need be, but I suspect anyone else from the fort. He asked me why I stayed away from him."

"That is the right thing to do. What did you tell him?"

"I asked him why he kept trying to get me to talk to him. He said he wanted to be my friend."

Kofi's glance cast up to the right of his forehead. "Do you remember when I told the group that at the Onyamedua?"

Folayan nodded. *How much time does he spend with this preacher?* Folayan watched her husband's serious face.

To the villagers and to Folayan, the black-robes were part of the intruder's castles and forts and the uneasiness which those structures raised in her heart. Except when the black-robes stopped at her stall, she avoided them. Still, Kofi was a wise man despite his youth. She would at least hear his words.

"That time," Kofi said, "the old preacher was in a stir about his holy day, Christmas. Apparently, this is a very special time for the Christians. He had much to say, but told me he had to be careful who he told it to.

"He spoke about the God that he worships, the great Fisher of men who lives in the sky. He wanted people to know that the Son of his God came to live on this earth, and they celebrated His birth on Christmas. But he was curious, too, about Onyankopon."

Folayan let her hands rest and listened.

"He told me that some of our Akan practices are like those his Great Fisherman has instructed his people to do. He wondered how that came to be, with no one to teach us those ways."

Folayan asked, "What practices did he mean?"

"One has to do with widows. If something happened to me and I died, one of my brothers would marry you."

She wrinkled her brow, but nodded it was true. She would not be left alone.

"And there are several that have to do with women's time of the moon and taboos against being around men and preparing our food."

Folayan nodded, she would have to go stay in their family's special women's house after she birthed a child, too, for forty days.

"He also said this Book of his gives instructions for circumcision on the eighth day."

"And we name our babies on the eighth day, too." Folayan said.

"He said he would show me some more similarities when he brings his Book."

"Oh." Folayan wondered if it was like the book Papa wanted, yet she felt uneasy and kept her mouth closed. He already told her he was careful with the preacher. She told herself to relax.

Kofi looked thoughtful. "I asked him why it was that his people often spoke in such a way. They act as if we have no history or knowledge, except that which they bring us. I told him that we have known the ways of Onyankopon for hundreds of generations. I told him how our people followed their herds to this place from our ancient empire of Ghana in Mali and before that, from the land of Kush."

Folayan felt like she was sitting with her family at her father's feet listening to him teach. Kofi also had much to teach and like her Papa he was a questioner, always trying to find out about the past and about people, why they do what they do, and think what they think.

"From what the priest said, their God is much like Onyankopon. He is Creator, the Most High, One who loves His creations. I wondered at this, for I have heard bits through the years about the kwesi broni God.

Folayan debated if she should share with Kofi the discussions her family had had about the kwesi broni God and Jesus. Now he was talking about a Fisherman. She decided to wait and let him say what weighed on his heart before adding her questions.

"And I have wondered about certain likenesses. Folayan, their god is not like the lesser gods or the fetishes. He is the Most High. There is only one Most High, Onyankopon!"

Folayan smiled to herself. Kofi's face told as much of the story as did his words. She decided she liked seeing him excited in discovery. Though she held her own opinions, it was clear he wanted to hear more about this God who became a man.

Kofi made the final knot in the net he mended. "I did not tell the priest what I thought, I only reasoned in my mind. And I did not take just his word. Before coming home that day, I went to my grandfather's house, to ask for his wisdom. I told him I was confused about two things. First, I saw similarities in the fetish priests and the kwesi broni priests. Both deal with demons that cause suffering. People ask both priests for help with desires, to be rid of spells and sickness. What most confuses me is the teaching about the gods—who are we supposed to worship and serve? Who is right the fetish or the kwesi broni priests?

"Grandfather Nana said, 'My heart tells me that the Most High is right. There is enough in that Book that shows the Most High wants to communicate with us directly, and we do not need a priest to tell us what God means. We do need the Book though and to be able to read it. When I told the kwesi broni that was a problem for people who did not have someone like him to teach them how to read it. He said he knew of people who learned to read the Book by themselves with help from the Holy Spirit.'

"As far as knowing whether the fetish priests or the kwesi broni are the ones to trust, Grandfather showed me two notes he had in his bowl of verses from the Book. One said: *By their fruits you will know them. So, by watching how they live, speak, and treat others—we know which people really serve the Most High and are kind and loving like Most High and obey His instructions.* The other note said: *If you love Me keep my commandments. They are not burdens. They show His love and guidance for us.'*

"Grandfather also told me to pray for all the priests-both kinds, because God wants to help them follow His way just like he helped him.

I asked again, '"How do we know who to worship? Then he told me other things he knew about the kwesi broni God. When we put what we know about Him and Onyankopon side by side--Folayan, they are too much the same not to be the same."

# CHAPTER 34

# *Kwesi Broni*

*When I look into the starry sky I know Someone greater than I, made it.*
*When I study a tree, I realize I have never seen two leaves exactly alike.*
*And what about the fish with all their designs and colors?*
*When I come upon a herd of zebra and not one of their*
*striped patterns is the same, I am amazed at the*
*Creator's carefulness and enjoyment of beauty.*

**October 1796, Kormantse Village**

Folayan followed Kofi's gaze to the adiho-framed night sky. Kofi's eyes held a faraway look of great thought.

"I would believe their God is who we also call Onyankopon Kwame except ... that they worship Him on Kwesi—the first day of the week. Since our beginnings, we have worshipped Onyankopon only on His day, Kwamemeneda—the day bears His name. Do you see?

*Onyankopon, God of the seventh day.* Folayan listed the seven day names. Kofi—a male born on the sixth day, the kwesi broni called it Friday. When she was a child, Papa often repeated that her day name was Ama, a girl born on the seventh day and how she must be ever mindful of that and her promise. If she were a boy, she would have been called Kwame.

Kofi continued, "Our names tell our history and our potential—they give us power, character. God's name should tell us about Him."

"It does," Folayan said. "The Creator. He has existed forever."

"If I were the Most High God, I would want all my people to know exactly who I am and what is important to me."

She glanced up. He was watching her. She wondered if her heart would always flip at his intense regard.

"Folayan, when we have children. I will select names to shape their characters and guide them."

Papa spent a week after her birth, choosing her name—her just-right name—*to remind me of who I am, to teach me how to live, to lead me through life's precarious journey.*

Kofi said, "What if our children change our teaching—stand in our faces and reject our instruction?"

Her already-straight back grew rigid. "That would not do. It would be like they did not want to be our children. We will only teach what is good and keep them safe.

She went to him and rested her head on his shoulder. "I know little children will test their parents, but why would that kind of defiance even come to their minds?"

"If somone else convinced them to—friends maybe. Like—"

"Afua making her own rules." Folayan crossed her arms.

"Exactly. I would be upset, very upset, angry."

"Hurt."

Kofi looked sharply at her. His eyebrow rose. "Yes. Much more than angry, I would be hurt."

He sat, his jaw working as he shaped his thoughts.

Kofi began softly, "If I were the Most High God, I would want everybody to know my commandments are my character—and that I will not change who I am … and I would be indignant with anyone who tries to change the commands I have given them."

Folayan patted his arm. "Understanding the mind of God is quite a goal; first, we must learn to be strong parents. Three times your mother asked me of any good news."

Kofi kissed her, then headed to their sleeping room, "I, too, am anxious, but before I have a child to teach, I need more wisdom about Onyankopon—and the Great Fisherman. Are they the same?"

She began painting the design on the next calabash.

Kofi came back out, and stopped next to her. "If they are the same, then we have much to think about." He took her gourd from her, pointing to the adinkra, "Gye Nyame. 'Except God … Nothing happens.' Do you believe this?"

"Yes, Kofi." She did not understand his agitation.

"God? Which God is this talking about?"

She said, "Kofi … you know it is talking about Onyankopon."

"With the pile of stones to ask: Where did all these  substitutes come from? They were not there at Creation."

She had no answer.

Several days later, at the market, as the sun rose, Serwaa and Folayan arranged their vegetables and fruits, stacking some in pyramids, placing others attractively on their mat.

Folayan surveyed the cove for Kofi on the sea. By mid-morning, fishermen pulled their canoes onto the sand.

Later, when they'd sold most of their catch, Kofi came to Folayan.

He greeted Serwaa, helped stack their empty baskets and rolled up the mat. "You finished early."

"Yes. Everything is gone. How about you?"

"All sold except for those fish that I am taking home, over there hanging from the boat."

"Serwaa, can you go up with other ladies today?"

She nodded.

"All right, you take the mat, we will carry these baskets."

Folayan followed him. Even from a child longing to sit in Papa's boat, Folayan was always surprised at how big they were. She would love to go out on the water with Kofi someday.

Kofi had started to climb into the boat, He scanned the shore and up the fortress hill. "Here he comes." Kofi pointed at the black-robed man hurrying toward them.

The preacher greeted them, and after Folayan answered his inquiry about her mother, he asked, "Are we going to sit up there?"

Kofi hesitated. "It would be more comfortable, but I think we better sit on the sand." Kofi climbed down and led them around the back nearest to the water. Folayan scooted closer to Kofi.

"Today, Folayan, we are going to talk about my questions." Kofi looked at the preacher. "Did you bring your Book?"

He pulled it from under the folds in his robe. It was twice as big as his hand-span.

A small paper slipped out of the Book. The preacher picked it up and read it. Folayan was intrigued at his face, his skin changed color; the pink faded, a tinge of gray remained. He looked at the fortress.

Watching his expression, Kofi asked, "Is something wrong?"

The preacher said, "Oh, it is just the soldiers, playing games." His hands shook as he tucked the paper back into the Book.

Kofi insisted, "Whatever it is, it is more than games."

The preacher looked far out to the ocean, speaking as if to himself, "There have been more like this telling me to stop troubling their money." He turned around finally, and looked at Kofi. "They want me to stop talking against the slave trade. I have told them the Bible speaks against stealing men."

Kofi sat up straight.

Folayan wasn't sure she heard him right. She asked, "What did you say?"

"That when I took part in the slave selling, I broke every one of the Ten Commandments.

"We repeat corporate lies about the slave trade and do not reveal the greed, lust, and  horrors inflicted on captives. We teach people to hate and believe you deserve the ill treatment of you, never knowing you.

"We paint false pictures to slave buyers around the world saying they are doing God's will by bringing God to the heathen. Numerous times, you've sent me to study Biblical customs that your ancestors practiced in Canaan land before migrating to the Gold Coast.

"We make up lies about Africans, and forget that we are and do the same things we condemn your people for. I reminded them that like others in the world, Europeans, Nordsmen, British, and Irishmen  do witch craft, magic, human sacrifice, and idol worship.

"I said study the Bible for themselves. God is not mocked.  He will hold us accountable for our deeds."

He turned back to the sea. Then after a long pause, he said, "Let me show you what I was explaining earlier. It is in the first book—"

"First book?" Folayan whispered to Kofi in Fante, "I only see one book." She forgot the elder knew the language well.

"This book is very special, and under its one cover are sixty-six books." The preacher glanced up at her. "We call this large part at the beginning, the Old Testament. It has thirty-nine books, all about what has happened in the world from the time of Creation. Adam and Eve were tempted into wanting to know good and evil—like God knows."

Folayan remembered the story about the first parents.

"It was the snake's trick" Kofi said. "They already knew good. The way God put things into place, they did not ever have to feel pain, sorrow, fear, or—Folayan, can you think of something else that they never would have had to suffer?"

"Tears? Death?" Folayan wondered, wide-eyed.

The preacher said, "Yes, our first parents began to know things they never would have known—evil things and results."

Kofi said, "Tell her how they knew their bodies had changed from the way they were created."

The preacher looked into her eyes, "As you said, death. Their perfect bodies—now began to decay. I imagine they felt a chill."

*And made clothes from fig leaves.* She was fascinated as he read the same story in his Book.

"God chose a tribe of people to serve Him and keep good care of His Word—this Book—to tell others about Him, how much He loves them."

She wanted to hold the Book herself. *Surely this is like the Book my brothers saw in Timbuktu, and Papa gave the bookmaker money to copy one for him?*

He turned pages and rested his hand past the middle. "This Old Testament tells what happened to God's people and the tribes they came into contact with, down to 400 years before Jesus's birth."

Scarcely realizing it, she held out her hands. He placed the Book in them. A prickling shivered on the back of her neck. In wonder she turned the thin pages of the smaller last section. The preacher said, "I came to tell your countrymen things in this Book."

*But we aleady knew some of what you said.*

"The last twenty-seven books are all about when the Great Fisherman, the Son of God, became a baby to save us. He grew to be a man who paid the price for us, so one day He will take us to live with Him—in heaven."

Folayan looked up at Kofi.

"Please, show my wife the rules you were telling me that God gave us so we will not be afraid of not pleasing Him."

Folayan realized Kofi had often repeated the preacher's words about not making or bowing or worshipping idols.

The preacher took the Book, found a page in the front part and read, "Make no images of anything in the heaven above, earth beneath, or in the water." She looked out at the ocean. *Fish? Animals? People? The setting sun glinted.*

She shadowed her eyebrow, and said, "I have seen images made of many of things, but not of the sky."

As if the preacher understood what she wanted to ask but did not, he said, "What about the sun?"

"The sun?" she squeaked.

"Yes. For thousands of years, men have worshipped the sun."

"How so?" asked Kofi.

"In temples designed so that they worship at times when the high noon sun penetrates the temple and leaves no shadows at certain parts of the day. Some pagan priests shave their heads bald on the top and leave hair combed down at the sides, the strands represent the rays of the sun and many people set aside one day each week to worship the sun."

Kofi hesitated. "What about you? Is that what you do, kwesi broni?"

*Pale skin Sunday man.* Folayan translated and studied the old man's craggy face. His troubled eyes. *Why did he bring the topic up?*

He spoke finally. His voice cracked. "Your people have gone astray from serving the Most High alone. They have made idols and bowed down to them. I am ashamed to say I have done my share of that, too … and in serving the sun deity."

"Why? Why do you come here and draw my people away to worship another idol?" Kofi was sincere.

"Kofi, I listen to questions you ask me. You have caused me to read this Word again and examine myself … I realize I cannot serve two masters. In my heart, I want to stop being kwesi broni; that is, I mean make a correction and stop teaching you people to disregard this Word … but, but this is my bread and butter."

*Bread and butter? What does he mean?*

Kofi opened his mouth, yet did not speak. He looked out to the sea, then began to pull in the rope that held his personal catch.

The preacher maneuvered to a stance. "Perhaps we will talk again," he said. Kofi shrugged and gazed at him.

Folayan picked up Serwaa's baskets. Kofi walked a few steps with him.

The old man said something to Kofi, and made his way up the hill to the garrison.

Then they turned in silence and headed for their own hill.

Midway up, when they passed the broken tree that had been struck by lightning, Kofi said, "Sometimes I think the fetish priests want to keep us in fear and in need of them. Because we do what the priests tell us to do without stopping to think for ourselves."

"What is the difference between them and your kwesi broni preacher?" Folayan retorted.

He did not answer until they reached the top of their hill. "The preacher does not do all his Book says, just like our priests; sometimes they tell us things of how they want it to be, not what God wants. How can I trust them?"

"Kofi, what is troubling you?"

"Why do we need lesser gods?"

*It seems that he has been chewing that idea much longer than the shrine incident.*

He continued, "They claim worship that belongs only to the One who created us. Then the priests make festivals honoring some stones that did not make us."

Now, he spoke like his grandfather, but he was confusing her. She did not like it. None of her friends talked like this, "Will you meet with the preacher again?"

"I want to know more of what is in the Book."

Folayan had mixed feelings. She wanted to know more, but knowing more, and not understanding what to do with the knowledge or not being allowed to use the knowledge made life complicated. They had reached the village gate. She thought he might stop talking, but he didn't.

"The villages have different gods they worship. But do you know what, Folayan? One thing is the same. In every village, they all know the Most High is the Creator who lives in the sky, beyond the sun."

"I wonder if my father found that true in his travels … but what about you, Kofi, not the preacher? Have you figured out who it is—Onyankopon or the kwesi broni God? What is His real name?"

They walked all the way up one row of houses before he spoke again. "When I look into the starry sky I know Someone greater than I, made it. When I study a tree, I realize I have never seen two leaves exactly alike. And what about the fish with all their designs and colors? When I come upon a herd of zebra and not one of their striped patterns is the same, I am amazed at the Creator's carefulness and enjoyment of beauty.

"That is who I want to worship." He touched her hand. "It does not matter to me the language. What matters is that He made and keeps this world. That is his name—Creator."

They reached their house, went in and chose not to sit in the adiho, but  under the roof in the long room. They sat still, both pondering. He caressed her back.

Kofi added, "It is not by chance that the preacher's Book and our wisdoms from thousands of generations teach the same customs from the Most High. It reveals Onyankopon's unmatched power and concern for us."

Kofi's head turned as if he heard something.

He looked back at her. "Folayan, when the old man left the market, he told me the Book says—before we knew the Creator, He loved us."

# CHAPTER 35

# Two Hills

*Beyond the fallen man, she spied the book, upside down*
*in the sand, its pages curled in the damp sea air.*
*She brushed sand off and shook it.*

**November 1796, Kormantse Village**

It was still dark the next morning when they awakened. As they dressed, they talked through the rooster's crowing. Then Kofi stopped. He listened. "Someone is outside."

Folayan wondered who would come at this early hour.

The person's footsteps sounded determined, not cautious.

Kofi went to the door. It was Jojo.

After he was settled and Folayan had offered him hot tea, he said "Kofi, I wish to speak to you about … I will just say it. I come with warning and with joy."

Kofi said, "Oh? Well, tell me the warning first."

Jojo asked, "Has Benaba spoken to you?"

"No. Why?"

"He has been complaining that you took the preacher into our boat. He is quite angry."

Kofi's brows furrowed, "That is not true. I alone was in the boat, then we all sat on the sand. If even that is a problem, I will find somewhere else to meet the preacher."

Jojo was silent.

Kofi said, "It is my business who I talk to, is it not?"

Jojo nodded. "Yes, but be careful. People are complaining and some of them are fetish priests. Be careful."

Before Kofi could glance at her, Folayan picked up work and went into the sleeping room. It was a courtesy, for she could hear their conversation through the curtained opening. To her relief they said nothing more about the priests.

She was most pleased to learn that Jojo intended to send a knocking to Fatima and wanted Kofi to be one of his emissaries. Kofi agreed.

"Also, I want to hire you to make a kente for me."

"Would you like it to be one piece fully woven, or to be blocked?"

"Well, I come to you, my friend, unguarded. I do not have as large a dowry as I would like. And since she does not have a father or uncle here, there is a question whether she will have a celebration. I know that Okwamu asked to buy her. When they told him, she had paid her father's debt, he then wanted to know if she had come of age."

Folayan fretted—*does Okwamu not have enough wives already?*

She detected agitation in Jojo's voice. "I do not have time to wait until I can save as much as I would like, and I cannot compete with Okwamu's wealth. My confidence is that we have spoken, and she has agreed to have me. So, I must move with speed."

"In that case, would you be interested in a kente I have already on hand? When I do not have a request for a certain kind, I try to complete at least one kente made with my pattern "

"Oh? Let me see them."

Kofi took him into the room next to theirs. Folayan knew there were three kentes hanging wide, each on a different wall. They draped full-length over horizontal poles secured on each end by ropes that Kofi had knotted outside and threaded through the wall just below the ceiling when the clay was still wet. The cloths were black and white, green and white, and striped white with blue.

"Are you wanting it for you or Fatima?"

"For her. I want it to be part of the bride price."

"These are all for men."

"I like the green one for me," Jojo said, then asked, "How long would it take for you to make a green and white kente for Fatima?"

"At least two months."

"I do not think I have that much time."

"Well, I could make new green strips to replace the blue strips in this one. That would save three or four weeks."

When they discussed price, Jojo said, "I have been saving money since my father gave me my machete, but I do not think I have enough for a kente for me and for the rest of Fatima's dowry."

He stood, staring at the kente on the wall. "I wish I had more time. I will figure something out for me to wear, but the whole village will see her beauty."

Jojo paid half the cost of the kente and made another offer. "If you do not mind, I will fish for the two of us so you can stay at your loom until the garment is complete."

Kofi agreed, then left shortly after Jojo, and returned to his loom before noon—without a word. She made hot hibiscus and ginger tea. "Meda wase," he said, taking three slow sips. Then he looked up into her worried eyes, and his wrinkled brow smoothed. "I went to three shrines to see if the priests were angry. Some grumbled that I was unwise, one asked, 'Should we be?'"

I said, "Remember sankofa. I asked my friends to fetch knowledge from their parents to know what and why we believe. I do not want to worship any god just because of tradition. Some priests said, 'Do not forget that there is power in tradition—Foundation. Wisdom. Guidance. Protection.'"

Her eyebrows raised, as Kofi said, "I told them the kwesi broni said similar words. I just want to know which traditions came first from the Most High God, and the ones that have been tampered with by men, and piled on top of Onyankopon's original plan."

"Kofi? You said that to the fetish priests? How did you even dare to go to them?"

"I have prayed for them. I still respect them. We all were respectful, but they warned me that many people who got too friendly with the kwesi broni have disappeared."

She gasped, "Oh Kofi!"

He stood, slipped one hand around her waist, and pulled her close, his chin rested on her forehead, "It is nothing I did not already know."

The next week, at Wednesday's market, about the time Folayan finished selling for the day, she saw that Kofi had left his loom and come down the hill to her.

"I want to talk to the preacher again" he said.

While Serwaa returned to the village, they waited beside the boat with plans to go somewhere else to talk. He did not show up. The sun dropped low, the breeze cooled her arms.

Folayan tapped Kofi, "Look." A predator loped in the sky.

"Let us go closer." Kofi said.

Her toes bumped his heels several times, while she watched long black wings lift and fall, sihouetted against the orange-striped, pink-hazed sun. Wings sailed higher on heat waves. Wings with eight-fingered feathers spread, gliding, choppy, looping low. A head of wrinkled pink, gray, and blue skin searched for prey, between two hills. Fort Kormantin perched on the left, Kormantse village atop the right.

"Something is dead," said Foyalan. The vulture soared, and dropped close, its shadow darkened their faces.

"That was strange," her husband said.

With her hand over her eyebrows, she peered up the hill to the Fort. Kofi told her the man had said to meet when the fort's shadow reached the top of the palm trees.

She followed Kofi toward the stand of palm trees. As he removed the fronds, dizzying questions and fright surged.

He lay, face down in the fronds. Yet, the black robe's collar was fastened at his neck. Only his pale hand showed past the wrist of his sleeve.

Dazed, she turned her head and walked away. Beyond the fallen man, she spied the Book, upside down in the sand, its pages curled in the damp sea air. She brushed sand off and shook it.

A note fell out and slipped under a reddened branch. She reached for the note. The palm thorns stabbed her hand. She did not soothe her two bleeding knuckles. Her fingers smoothed the yellowed page's jagged edge—yanked not from this one, but from his other book.

She shuddered, remembering.

She tucked the paper into the Book and held it at her heart. She forced herself to look back at the man. She saw a gash at the top of his head, and there was a fist of blood caked to the side of his skull. *When had it happened?* Kofi had last talked with him, seven days ago at the market, and decided to meet today. She walked several times in a widening circle around him looking for anything that would tell her what happened. Who? How many of them attacked him? Why? She stopped

It peeked up at her from between fronds. She bent and picked up the other book, the smaller one—black, flat, with strong words from his heart written by hand.

She blurted, "Maybe ... he is only wounded."

Kofi shook his head, but whispered the man's name and flipped the body over. They stared at locked, open eyes.

Her tears spilled. She turned away, then looked up, back and forth at both hills. "Who did this?"

Her husband took her hand, "Come. Let us go."

She protested. "Help me take him away from them."

"No, we will get help to bury him. It is not safe here now."

She heard feathers. The stench of death lodged oily, putrid in her throat. Four vultures circled, wobbling lower. Their strange fearlessness warned of danger. She wrenched from him and turned back.

He grabbed his wife. "Stop it!" he said. "The killer might be watching us."

She blinked, swallowed. He led her sprinting through the giant palms, their soles splashing across sucking sand.

She began to sob. "I do not want him to be alone."

Dry-mouthed, chests heaving, the pair stopped among fishing boats beached near the empty marketplace. The tide, sudsing cool around her feet, could not quell her heart's burning.

The wake of five vultures hopped onto the palm fronds, and hunkered in, first at the eyeballs. Tearing the cloth, sharp beaks ripped flesh. Others landed.

With her eyelids shut tight, trying to escape the birds' hissing, she clasped her hands to her ears, then stared at the sea, her cheek pressed hard against the boat's rough planks.

*How can I tell Maame that he is dead?*

Waves rose roaring. Resisting.

She held the books close, and she knew vultures could ravage him, but—never—never could they take his spirit.

Kofi turned. "We must go."

They grabbed up her empty baskets from the side of the boat and hurried home struggling against the harmattan wind.

After they were a third of the way up the hill, she asked, "Who will you tell?"

"No one."

"But Kofi, you said we will get help."

"We cannot. If it is soldiers, we will be blamed. Or what if it is somebody in Abandze or our village, maybe one of the fetish priests?" he said.

"Maybe one of your fishing mates?" she said.

Kofi stared at her, walked about ten paces and said, "His people will look for him."

# CHAPTER 36

# Weaving Dreams

*They stood like that, in the twilight, talking, then silent.*
*They listened to the present, looked out across the valley,*
*and beyond the sea, and scanned the expanse of the future.*

**May 1796, Kormantse**

Not a day passed that they did not tiptoe around the house, sometimes glancing at each other another time sighing, sorrowing. They read the anxiety in each other's eyes. Yet, they said nothing about him.

One week sped by.

Kofi had hidden the Bible. They dared not try to read it. They spoke in whispers about the preacher only when they were away fom the house.

Kofi said, "Everyone knows—walls have ears. Yet, I have heard not one person in the village mention his absence."

Near the middle of the second week, when Folayan returned from the farms, Kofi greeted her. "I have finished this kente. I want to take it to my customer at once. Then I will begin Jojo's."

Folayan admired his work, but shook her head when he tried to leave.

"You must eat first." She spread before him the food she had prepared with the other ladies of the family. While he ate, she went to put on one of her best garments, then twisted and tied a duku on her head. When he finished, she came out.

"Ooh. You look so pretty," he said.

"Meda wase." She smiled and asked, "May I walk with you? I would like to visit my parents."

They parted at the ofram tree, Kofi continued on while Folayan turned to go to her parents' house. She found neither her father, nor her mother, at home.

She hugged the children and her sisters-in-law who told her Serwaa was asleep in her room. Her niece and nephews had many things to tell her. Finally, she decided to go see if Serwaa had awakened. She had not. So Folayan sat down on the stool and waited. She looked around the room she'd shared for seventeen years. Without her box, Serwaa had much more space. On the wall shelf, stood the painting Folayan had made for her. Folayan took the memorial of that difficult day down and studied it. She was pleased with the work. It had certainly kept her mind off her troubles that day.

She wished also that Afua had forever been off her mind. She sighed, remembering the Wednesday Market, five days ago.

Which came first, hearing that name or feeling her presence, Folayan did not know, but when she looked up from straightening her tomatoes, Afua with her two young men were down at the end of the row. Too soon, she stood alone before Folayan wanting to buy pineapple.

The exchange was made, and Afua said, "You married Kofi?"

"Yes."

"He is mine you know."

Folayan told herself, *Remember, Ama Kwantunyi Folayan. Remember.*

Afua opened her mouth, "One day, I will have Ko--"

The two friends came up to her side. She looked up and smiled affectionately at one of them.

Folayan asked her, "Is there anything else that you would like to purchase?"

"I would ... if only you had not been so selfish and tried to destroy my life."

"If only you would think of helping and caring for others, instead of just what you want."

"Folayan you hurt me! That is the reason your lost your zebra."

Folayan winced. "I am sorry that you feel that way. In all of our years, I have done nothing to intentionally hurt you, Afua. My zebra is dead because of what you did."

Folayan wanted to say now please go away.

Afua snapped a carrot in half. "You should have let me ride him. You were selfish."

"I was trying to protect him. You did not listen to me. He became afraid easily."

"I am the chieftain's daughter."

"He was my zebra."

Afua glared at her. Folayan felt uneasy, but stood her full height and did not budge.

Serwaa came to Folayan's side. "Is there something you want to buy Afua?"

"No." Afua said, "I have all I came for." She walked away.

Folayan helped two more customers. Feeling the pressure of a gaze, she glanced up.

Afua stood near the palm trees staring at her, then she turned and walked with the men toward Anomabou.

Folayan shivered.

Serwaa turned on her pallet and cleared her throat.

Folayan waited for her aunt to awaken.

When Serwaa smiled at her, they talked for a good while about the painting. "I look at it every day." Serwaa said, "It brings me joy."

"I am happy it does. I think it is my best painting."

"And I am thankful for you and your talent."

Folayan said, "I am surprised to see you in bed in the afternoon."

"Of late, I seem to get tired more easily."

"Are you feeling sick? Is something troubling you?"

"No. The bed just calls me more often."

Folayan studied her. "Is there anything I can get you. Some water?"

"Yes. I would like that."

When Folayan returned with the water. Serwaa took three slow sips. "There is one thing that keeps coming to my mind."

"What is it Serwaa?"

"You are not the only one who has dreams. I, too, have been having one over the last few moons."

Folayan's eyebows raised.

"In it I am running, running and I cannot get away. I think it is about the end of the world. I want … to know more about the king's dream and the big Rock your brothers told us about … I want to know how to be safe."

"Oh Serwaa. They will tell you. Just ask them."

"No. I … do not want anyone else to know about my dream." She drank the rest of the cup and motioned for Folayan to fill it again.

She watched Folayan pour.

"Folayan. I want you to ask them for me."

Surprised, Folayan put the gourd down on the nearby table. "Yes. Serwaa. I will find out as much as I can. It will not be today, but I will talk to them soon."

Serwaa lay back down. Folayan rubbed her forehead.

Serwaa, smiled and patted Folayan's hand.

Footsteps approached. Maame called, "Folayan?"

"I am here Maame, with Serwaa!"

Maame pulled the curtain open. "Oh Serwaa. In bed again?"

Serwaa chuckled, "Yes. Again. See how pretty our daughter is? She says she has some questions to ask you." Serwaa nodded to Folayan. "I think I will rest a while longer here."

"Uh yes. Maame, can we talk in your room?"

"Of course."

Folayan followed her into the adiho.

Her mother pointed toward her sleeping room. They spoke in whispers. Folayan told her, "Something is happening in my body."

Folayan explained.

Her mother nodded, crinkles curled at the corners of her eyes. Maame looked up in praise. "Thank you, Onyankopon! Thank you. Thank you!"

She wrapped her arms around her daughter. Then Maame bent toward the box and reached down, into Papa's little compartment in the front corner.

"I found it." She spoke softly.

She pulled out a small patch of folded cloth. Then she peeked inside, pinched something up and closed it in her hand. She looked at Folayan. Her eyes sparkled. Her cheek revealed the dimple Folayan seldom saw.

Maame said, "Something happended on the day you were born. A few days earlier, I had been at the market selling fish and other items. The kwesi broni preacher came to my space to buy vegetables."

Folayan had heard the story before when Papa became angry about the gift being in the box, but she listened eagerly now to let Maame tell it without anxiety.

After relating the conversation she had with the preacher, Maame told Folayan, "Three days later, I woke up very early and went out to the cliff to throw away the thing he had given me. But then I could not. I had a strong feeling that I should keep it."

Folayan looked at her mother's serious eyes. This part was new.

"As I made my way back to our house, the harmattan wind whipped up, and it snatched my etam from me. As it flew like a large bird toward the fortress, I heard sounds I had never heard before. Women were screaming, trying to get out."

A chill raced up Folayan's arms. So often, Maame had told her and her brothers, and anyone who would hear her, to beware of the fortress.

She had tried to get her people here in her village and her relatives at Edina to take measures to protect themselves, and go with her to warn other villages to stop selling slaves and to imprison the nsafo who connived with the kwesi broni slave merchants. She had said many times that the Most High did not approve of His creations being treated cruelly.

"Folayan, my daughter, my only girl child. Do you remember your promise?"

*My name—To know the Most High God, to return from every journey, to always walk in dignity and help others along the way.* "Yes Maame—I remember."

"I want you to take up your part and help me in this quest. This selling slaves away from us is wrong. Selling to these people who take them away from our land is wicked—as wicked as the ones who buy them."

She pointed toward the Fort Kormantin.

"The difference begins in the fortress and castles. It is not good. And we must do anything, everything we can to stop it. One day maybe enough people will hear us and think, and stop."

"But Maame, how will that stop the kwesi broni? They have posts with the cannons every three miles along the shore."

"If we do not sell them to—these kwesi broni, if we stand up and have nothing to do with the greedy nsafo, we can stop it. We can take away their profits. One village at a time, we can help them stop and think about other things to do besides selling our people away to some strange island."

Folayan looked at her mother. She wanted to help, but her belly trembled at the same time. And this was not why she had come today, not for this worry.

"I know we can," Maame said. "There are more of us than them. And the nsafo! Why should we let a few spoil our right to live free of fear? There is no place safe from them. So, Folayan our only hope is to try to change the thinking."

The dead preacher loomed in Folayan's head. Serwaa had whispered the news of his death to Folayan several days ago, surely her mother knew how he died. If not, Folayan was still uneasy to reveal it.

"Maame, why do you tell me this now?"

"One, for a short time, mothers can shape the thoughts of their children. Two, children influence other children and therefore the village, and then the nation. Lose not one precious moment. Do not let yourself become so caught with demands of being a Fanti woman, caring for your family, and the traditions of the village. Do not neglect the most important things—teach your children to fetch our history, to know how God has led us through it all, and how to think for themselves."

Her mother turned around. Folayan could fully see her fingers moving. Then she turned back and eased something—small, cold and odd-shaped—into her daughter's hand. She pressed Folayan's fingertips around it. Without looking, Folayan recognized it, knew its message, and knew the weight of the charge her mother had just entrusted to her.

Folayan looked her in the eyes and nodded.

When Kofi came for her and they were walking home, Kofi sighed and said, "I feel so relieved that that kente is done." He stretched his neck, rotating his head right to left trying to release tightness in his shoulders. "I did not realize how tense I have been."

Folayan said, "The breeze will help you relax. I know a good place where we can go sit and I can help you feel better. Let us go this way." She led him to the place on the hilltop where the side dropped straight down to the sand and sea, but to the left, the hills her Papa journeyed past could be seen until it dipped into the valley below.

When Kofi was seated, she massaged his neck and shoulders. "It is beautiful out there?"

"Yes, it is. How do you know this place?"

"My papa first brought me here when I was a little girl, so I could watch for him to return from his journeys. Then as I grew older, I came here to think."

"I like this place," Kofi said.

"Yes." She stopped massaging when she noticed a narrow wooden box, about the length of Kofi's forearm. "Where did you get that Oware game?"

"My customer was so happy with the kente, he wanted me to have this special gift. He carved the lid himself."

"Is that a whole village?"

"Yes, our village."

"Look, there is the Onyamedua." She studied the complicated detail. "He does fine work."

"He does. Want to play?"

"Oware? Are you not fearful that I will win? I am a fierce competitor."

"Not fearful at all." He opened the box and divided out the forty-eight seeds, four in each of the hollows along the two rows. "I will even give you the first move."

They played, circling the board, sowing one seed at a time in each hollow cup until their hands were empty of seeds, capturing others.

"Augh!" Folayan exclaimed, "You took my man!"

"You should not have let him stay out of the village so long by himself."

"Well, I was on my way to get him."

"Tsk, tsk. Be more careful. Always keep your men safe in the company of at least four—more eyes, more ears, more strength. You never know who may lurk about to steal your stragglers."

Just a few minutes later, Folayan took revenge. "How about this?"

She picked the twelve seeds out of one of her hollows, and pillaged Kofi's territory, emptying four hollows and leaving him with only one man in his last and forcing him to move that last man into her first cup, leaving his entire side empty. Though she was bursting to rejoice in her victory, she did not.

"You do not have to gloat." He cautioned her with a twinkle in his eye.

"Gloat? I did not say a word."

"You did not have to. Your smile is eating half your face. But you know you cannot leave me helpless. You must leave me at least one seed so I may survive. Those are the rules."

"I think we should change the rules."

"Not today. If that is not just like a woman—change the rules. Wife, put some seeds back in my cups." He pointed to her fourth hollow with five seeds. "Move these and fill my cups. The game is not over."

She laughed. "Just like a … ooh!"

She glared at him in mock indignation, looked away, at Fort Kormantin that marred her view. She looked again at her husband. "And how is it you think you can tell me which seeds to choose?"

The move he wanted would put a seed in his first two cups. She took up the fourteen from the space behind the one he had chosen. She knew they would count out to put a man in each of his cups and bring her back to her own side, but she also planned to start to recapture those solitary men.

Kofi smirked. "I knew you would defy me, Wife. With the move I gave, you could have won the game in a few turns, but now ..." He shrugged and dropped the seed from his fourth hollow into the third.

Folayan captured his first two cups, removing four seeds from the board. But there was no triumph in it, for she saw at once how she spaced her men. From that turn forward, she was on the run, moving only in defense of the most men she could protect.

Kofi came from behind, capturing her men a little at a time, as a snake would rob eggs from a bird's nest. She knew she won the next game because Kofi deliberately misplayed several moves. They continued, teasing each other, until Kofi had won seven games to Folayan's four.

"I am not ready to quit. I need another chance." She pouted as he declared an end to their seed war.

"It will not make a difference." He stuck his tongue out at her, snapped the box shut, and stood. He put his hand out to help her up. She complied. The harmattan wind whipped at their clothes.

While he helped her brush the back of her garment off, she smirked. "I just have one question."

"What about?"

"About the game. Is that how you will teach your daughter to play Oware?" She wrapped the ntama tight around her shoulders.

"Yes. My daughter will be a champion."

"Did you hear that?" Folayan looked down at her stomach. "Your Papa will teach you to be ruthless."

He stared at her.

She watched him sideways, a soft, slow smile growing bright.

"Folayan, what are you saying?" His eyes were wide, his face filled with hope.

"I am saying you are going to be a papa."

He cupped her face in his hands with joy, then embraced her.

"Do your parents know?"

"I told Maame what has been happening in my body. She said, by all signs, I am with child. She was excited." Folayan reached under her head wrap. "Look at what she gave me. She said the old kwesi broni preacher gave it to her before I was born."

Kofi took the small gold nugget between his fingertips and examined it. "The old preacher?"

Folayan nodded, her mood dropping. "She told me some things the preacher had said to her many years ago."

Kofi saw her conflict and took her hand. "What is it?" There was a protective look on his face. If anything was a threat to her, he would defend her, she knew.

She shook her head. "Just something to make me think. I wish … I wish I had asked him more questions."

"Yes. I do too. We must to learn to read the Book."

Folayan thought about her father and brothers, and Serwaa. When could they begin reading it, too? Not now. Not this soon. Maybe after the baby … She thought about the little one growing inside her.

She smiled up at her husband, "We are going to have a child."

"Yes, a girl child." His eyes twinkled.

"But what if it is not. Remember my parents. Six boys—"

He stopped her words with kisses—nibbles at the corners, one soft and full, and one more long determined confirmation.

When she was breathless, he tilted his head back and laughed.

She laughed with him.

And he repeated, "A girl child."

Kofi tightened his arms around her. She rested her head on his chest.

They stood like that, in the twilight, talking, then silent. They listened to the present, looked out across the valley, and beyond the sea, and scanned the expanse of the future.

# Discussion Questions

1. What are some instances when Folayan had to examine her self-control?

2. When Folayan says "They won't let me hate her," what do her elders tell her? Find out what hatred does to the hater—physically, emotionally, spiritually, socially. Does her elders' advice help Folayan or hinder her? Why do you think so?

3. Where did Folayan find her strength?

4. What sustained Folayan's faith?

5. What does the word part—YA—mean in the Twi name Onyanko-pon? In its different forms, the name is present in most African languages. Beyond Africa do you know any other language the YA part of? If so, what does it mean?

6. What is the difference between self-control and dignity? Can you name a person in the world who demonstrates both?

7. In Chapter 11, Folayan's age mates are involved in "rituals that kept the village strong, each one doing their part. Maintaining togetherness in marriage. Showing that men and women need each other. Children needing parents. Women teaching girls how to spin the cords that flow throughout the home. Men teaching boys how to weave and bind the house and family together." How important is the Sankofa (Go Back and fetch it) and other rituals? What happens when roles change?

8. How does the knocking tradition differ from today's courtship?

9. If marriage age young adults in your society played the game "Kings and Queens," how might it benefit you? What if you played it again changing partners—before real marriage. What differences might it make in your life?

10. What are some positives and negatives about allowing your parents to choose your spouse? Do you think it was easier for boys and that they had more ability to choose their wives than young women had to choose their husbands? How does having shared beliefs enhance a marriage?

11. Can you think of a scene in the Bible/history/politics that is like what happened in this book?

12. Why does Kofi want to help the girls after their experience at the shrine? What does he want them to think about? Why does he use stones to help them think about it?

13. The preacher says he has learned that the Akan people do traditions that the Book teaches. What are some customs that you observed from the story?

14. Why did Adwoa refuse to go in the shrine? Was she afraid? Why did the other girls go in? Why is Afua so forceful about it? Who was stronger?

15. Folayan had to spend forty days away from her family, proving she had learned the skills she needed to be a wife. What do you think about that time of honest instruction for young women? How do young women today learn how to be a wife?

16. Is there any part of Folayan's instructional period you wish young women today still had to do? What about for young men?

17. Have you had any rite of passage experiences that helped you in becoming and making or recognizing that you have attained the skills an adult needs to thrive? Would you be willing to share your experience? We'd love to hear from you at *www.TheGoldBandedBox.com*

18. Every Akan baby begins life hearing the proverb about the relationship between water … life … truth. What did the water stand for? The wine? How did Folayan's parents and the village reinforce that proverb in the lives of the people?

19. Folayan's mother asks *How is it that I have never heard the cries from the fortress before?* What have you not paid attention to? What conditions? Pain? Discrimination have you ignored? What accomplishments? What thanksgiving for others who are in your life? How can you begin to live the proverb?

    Please share on the website your thoughts and results? *www.TheGoldBandedBox.com.*

20. What is the gold in you?

## GOLD BANDED BOX BOOK GROUP

GBB Book Group members participate in special activities, and have opportunities to converse with the author during some of your meetings. I sincerely hope you enjoy all the books in the Gold Banded Box series. I'd love to hear from you.

To sign up to begin a GBB Book Group, go to my website:
*www.TheGoldBandedBox.com*

Thank you so much,
Phyllis Jane Brown

# *Glossary*

It is common that many Africans throughout the continent are multi-lingual with the ability to speak a variety of languages and dialectcts. The Akan languages such as Twi, Fante, Bono, Wasa, Nzema, Baule, and Anyi are accounted in the Kwa branch of the great family of Niger-Congo languages, some form of which 85% of 600 mmillion Africans speak. Akan dialects extend over several West African countries: mainly in the Gold Coast central regions equaling much of the southern half of Ghana, and flanked by eastern Ivory Coast above, with central Togo and Benin below. All Akan speakers understand each other rather easily.

The Akan languages were transported across the Atlantic Ocean with the captives who came together in the slave dungeons such as El Mina castle on which construction began in 1471. It is said that two decades before his famous voyage to sail to the "New World," Christopher Columbus was a young sailor on a ship that brought stone blocks used in building El Mina which was completed in 1482.

By 1598 the Dutch arrived in the Gold Coast territory and took control of the slave trade including Forts Komenda and Kormantin. They associated with the Fante people in business, military alliance, education, and inter-marriage, but during that time, the language spoken by Dutch and Africans in Edina (El Mina) was mainly Dutch.

Danish, German, and British missionaries (Roman Catholic and Protestants) started writing down the Akan languages in the 1600's and 1700's. The Bible was first translated into Akuapem Twi dielect. Then in 1871, an Akan Twi translation of the Bible was first published, by the diligence of the German Johann Gottlieb Christaller with African scholars and Akan linguists David Asante, Theophilius Opoku, Johnathan Palmer Berkoe, and Paul Keteku.

Currently, in Africa 22 million people speak Akan as their first language. It is also spoken in Surinam, Jamaica, and other parts of the Americas. Some universities in the United States of America offer courses in Akan.

To help your understanding of this book and for your enjoyment in learning some of the Akan language, here are a few words or phrases used in the Legacy of the Gold Banded Box series.

# SANKOFA – Go Back and Fetch
## Akan Words and Phrases

| Term | Pronunciation | Definition |
|------|---------------|------------|
| Abena | Ah- bee- koo | Girl born on the third day of the week, Tuesday |
| Abeeku | Ah-beh-nah | Boy born on the fourth day of the week, Wednesday |
| Adiho | Ah-dee-oh | West African home made in square with an open square atrium/center sitting area. All the rooms open into it. |
| Adamfo | Ah-dahm-fo | Friend |
| M'adamfo | M-ah-dahm-fo | My friend |
| Adomfo | Ah-dom-fo | Traitor |
| Adwoa | Ad-ju-wah | Girl born on the second day of the week, Monday |
| Adzenkye | a-jee-ehn-cheh | Good bye |
| Maachi | maa-chee | Good morning |
| Afenhyia | Ah-feh-she-yah | Year |
| bosome | Bos om | Month |
| nnanson | n-nahn-son | Week |
| adaduanan | ah-dahd-u-nahn | 40 days |
| Afua | Ah-fwee-ah | Girl born on the sixth day of the week, Friday |
| Agoo | Ah-goo | Knock, knock (call to attention) |
| Amee | Ah-meheh | Come in (response to a call) |
| Akan | Ah-kahn | Ashanti (northern egion), Akuapim (south east, north of Accra), Akyem (eastern region) Fanti (coastal, south central region) Kwahu (Ghana and Cote-de voire) |
| Akonor | Ah-koh-nor | A surname |
| Akosua | Ah-koh-shu-ah | Girl born on the first day of the week, Sunday |
| Akua | Ah-kwee-ah | Girl born on the fourth day of the week, Wednesday |
| Akura | Ah-koor-ah | Village |
| Akyire | Ah-chee-reh | Later |

| Term | Pronunciation | Definition |
|---|---|---|
| Akwaaba<br>Responses :<br><br>Yaa nana<br>Yaa agya<br>Yaa Ena<br>Yaa nua<br>Yaa oba | Ah-kwa-aba | Welcome!<br>After being told "Welcome."<br>Responses:<br>to elder<br>to father<br>to mother<br>to sibling<br>to child |
| Alkebulan | Ahl-kee-boo-lahn | African name forAncient Africa |
| Ama | Ah-mah | Girl born on the seventh day of the week,<br>Saturday |
| Amoasa | Ah-moh-ah-sah | Pad or dressing for menstruation |
| Anne<br>dabbi<br>ebi a | Ahn nee<br>Deh Be<br>Eh be ah | Yes<br>No<br>Maybe |
| Ananse | Ah-nahn-see | Spider |
| Anansesem | Ah-nahn-seh-sem | Ananse story |
| Andinkra | Ahn-deenk-krah | Symbol saying goodbye.<br>The last time this name or characteristic will<br>be mentioned in a gathering, but after that<br>the name may be mentioned only between<br>individuals speaking of him/her. |
| Asafo | Ah-sah'-foh | Warrior doing the king's bidding |
| Ashanti | Ah-shan-tee | ethnic group in the middle belt |
| Ayefro | Ah-yeh-fro | Wedding |
| Bakatue | Bah-kah-twee | Festival in the first Tuesday in July celebrating<br>the beginning of the fishing season, and<br>honoring the sea and river gods worshipped<br>by the people. The estuary embankment is<br>opened so fish can swim into the holding<br>area and then a dam is made to keep them<br>inside for the fishing activities. |
| Broni (obroni) | Bro-nee | Pale, very light skinned person |
| Bukyia | Boo-chee-ah | A 3 piece fire pit to place of molded earth<br>stands upright cooking pots on 3 piece cook-<br>ing; others cook on ground pit with stones in<br>three to put pots on and cook. |
| Da yie | Dah- yeh | Good night/ sleep well |

| Term | Pronunciation | Definition |
|------|--------------|-----------|
| Daniel | English | A teenage prince of Jerusalem captured by King Nebuchadnezzar. Daniel became the wisest of all the kings men. God gave Daniel the interpretation of the Kings dream recorded in Daniel chapter 2. In chapter 6, Daniel survived being thrown into the Kings Lion's Den. In chapter s 7-12 Daniel records important prophecies that reach to the Time of the End and connect with the Book of Revelation. |
| Djembe | Jem-bay | Goblet shaped drum, used for peaceful gatherings |
| Donno | D-no | Musical instrument. Hourglass shaped talking drum: sounds like human voice drummers send messages to villages 4-5 miles away. |
| Dua | D-wah | Tree |
| Duku | Doo-koo | Woman's beautiful headwrap elaborately twisted and knotted with several yards of fabric. |
| Edina | Eh-dee-nah | Local name for the town near El Mina |
| Ekom de me | Eeh-kom-deh-me | I am hungry, or We will go to market, or Let us eat |
| Ekow | Eh-koh | Male name |
| EkyerE sEn? | Eh-chee-her-eh seng? | What does that mean? |
| Eye fe | Eh-yeh-feh | It is beautiful |
| Emissah | Eh-mee-sah | Male surname |
| Etam (Fante) Ntama (Twi) | Eh-tahm or n-tah-ma | Long fabric to wrap around a woman or man's body; mothers secure babies tight to her body in a second etam. |
| Eto | Eh-to | Mashed yam, plaintain, cocoyam offering, might have mashed egg also. |
| Ezekiel | | A major prophet of Israel who gave God's method of interpreting prophecy that says a literal day stands for a year in the prophetic time period. Ezekiel chapter 4:6 |
| Fanti | Fahn-tee | Ethnic group living in the south central region |

| Term | Pronunciation | Definition |
|---|---|---|
| Fatima | Fah-tee-mah | Arabic name meaning Beautiful |
| Fetish | Fe-tish | A non living object worshipped for supposed magical powers from a supposed spirit dwelling inside it; idol worship |
| Folayan | Foh-lah-yahn | One who walks in dignity", Nigerian name from group that speaks Yoruba. |
| Fort Kormantin | | Built by the Portuguese; renamed Fort Amsterdam by the Dutch |
| Fufu | Foo-foo | staple of Ghana, casava (yucca) peeled and sliced with plaintains or flour pounded and mashed into a doughy ball, Boil. Eaten with light soup. |
| Garden eggs | | Europeans brought eggplant to Africa. |
| Gua do | Gwah-doh | At the market; Let us go to the market to buy food |
| Gunsa | Gwoo-nsah | Libation; offering drink to ancestors by pouring it out on the ground. |
| Gye Nyame | Jee-nyah-meh | But God... Except. God... God alone Two spellings: Gye Nyame, Gye'ame |
| Hwaani hwaani | wha-ah-nee | "Who is that?" light when black and light slightly begin to break; barely can see shadowy forms |
| Kenkey | Kehn-keh | Cornmeal made from pounded corn |
| Kente | Kehn-tay | Cloth woven in an intricate design especially worn by royalty or distinction. Made of silk, it is one of the most expensive fabrics. |

| Term | Pronunciation | Definition |
|------|---------------|------------|
| Kormantse | Kor-mahn-tsee | Village on top of a hill not far from El Mina and Cape Coast Castles. The Gold Banded Box is an historical novel set in this village. But fictional Folayan never really lived there. |
| Kormantin Kromantin | Kor-mahn-teen | Two common spellings of the The fort in Ghana built for trade in valuable goods, including slaves. |
| Coromantee | Kor-oh-mahn-tee | Comes from Fort Kormantin. The enslaved Ashantis were called Cormantins, Coromanti, or Kormantine by the English captors in Jamaica. Eventually, all Akan groups from the Gold Coast or modern day Ghana. Slaves who became the Maroons were the most dangerous and rebellious. They were different. They were freedom fighters. Haughty, fierce and resistant. |
| Kose | Ku-she | Sorry |
| Kofi | Koh-fee | Boy born on the sixth day of the week, Friday. |
| Kora | Ko-rahah | 1. A serving/food dish/bowl 2. A musical instrument. The full round bowl made into a musical instrument with 21 strings. (Like a guitar or violin with a drum belly) |
| Kwadwo | Kwah-djoh | Also , Kojo, Jojo Boy born on the second day of the week, Monday. |
| Kwabena | Kwa-bena | Boy born on the third day of the week, Tuesday |
| Kwasi | Kwa-see | Boy born on the first day of the week, Sunday. |
| Kwame | Kwah-meh | Boy born on the seventh day of the week, Saturday, also  Kwamina. |
| Kwesi broni Kwesi (Fante) Kwasi (Twi) | Kweh-see bro-nee | Pale (fair) skin, Sunday man; man who worships  on the first day of the week (Kwesi); European missionary |
| KyErE me | Cher eh may | Show me/ teach me |
| Kyen-kyen | Chin-chin | Bark of this tree is pounded into cloth. |
| M'a men | Mah-men | I have eaten enough, I am satisfied |

| Term | Pronunciation | Definition |
|---|---|---|
| Mali | Mah-lee | Mali is a country in West Africa; one of the three great Sudanic empires-ancient Ghana, Mali, and Songhay with important cities: Mopti, Djenne, Walata, and Timbuktu —knowledge and bookmaking and trade centers—rich in gold. Famed for knowledge and universities |
| Marones (Spanish) | Mah-roh-nehs | Maroon, coromantee, Africans who formed villages after escaping from slavery in the Americas. |
| Meda Wase | Meh-dah-ah-say | Thank you |
| Memma w'kye Response: Maakye | Mi-Maa-waa-chi Maa-chi | Good morning |
| Mema wo aha Response: Maaha | Mi-Maa-Waa-ha Maa-chi | Good afternoon |
| Me ma wo adwo Ma-jo | Mi-Maa- jo | Good evening |
| Mepa wo kyEw | Me-pah wo chi | Excuse me/I am sorry |
| Memeneda (Twi)<br><br>Memenda (Fante) | Meh-meh-neh-dah<br><br>Meh-men-dah | Day of the ancient Supreme Sky God; when He loves to visit with His created beings. |
| Mensa | Men-sah | Third born son |
| MenteasE | Men-teh-ah-she | I do not understand |
| Mo | Moh | Compliment/congratulation |
| Nana Nanabarima nana-ba Asa Nanabesia | Nah-nah Na-na-bah-ri-mah Na-na-bah Ah-sah nah-o-beh-see-ah | Grandparent, elderly person, griot, respect-able fellow, chief, Queen Mother, male/female grandchild |
| Nante yie | Nan – ti- yeh | Safe journey |
| Niger | Nee-zjair | Country in sub Sahara |

| Term | Pronunciation | Definition |
|------|---------------|------------|
| Numbers | | A book written by the prophet Moses who led the Hebrew slaves from Egypt to Canaan. When ten spies who were sent in to search out the land came back  AFTER 40 DAYS with a fearful report, the people lost trust in God who had fed and protected them for two years in the wilderness. They ignored Joshua and Caleb, the other two spies who said they should obey God and go forward. The people balked at going into Canaan. Then God said the rebellious people could go back into the wilderness, and He promised to bring their children back for a second chance to go into Canaan, but He prophecied  that it would be a total of 40 years (2+38 more = 40) 40 DAYS TO SPY = 40  years total in wilderness  A DAY FOR  YEAR. Numbers 14:34. This is a standard for understanding times in Biblical prophecy, such as in Daniel and Revelation. |
| Nsafo | Nn-sah-foh | Warriors for kings or chieftains involved in slave trade; others who became cohorts with slave dealers  from other continents; also compared to vultures. |
| Obarima<br>Agya , Ose<br>Kunu (okunu)<br>Wofa<br>Agya | Oh ba ri ma<br>Ah-je-yah, Oh-she<br>Ku-nu<br>Wo-fah,<br>ah-je-yah | Boy, male<br>Father<br>Husband<br>Uncle (mother's brother, father's  brother) |
| Obouroni | oh-boh-uro-nee | foreigner |
| Obosom | oh-boh-som | idols, gods |
| Odikoro<br>Omahene<br>Asantehene | Oh-di-ko-ro<br>Oh-mah-heh-nay<br>Ah-sahn-the-<br>heh-ne | Village chief<br>Divisional seat<br>The king |
| Onua | O-nu-ah | Sister or brother |
| Onyankopon | On-yahn-koh-pohn | God Almighty, the Creator |
| Onyame | Ohn-yah-meh | One that is worshiped, the sky deity, Akan diety of the spirits. Nyame can sometimes refer to a lesser god. |

| Term | Pronunciation | Definition |
|------|---------------|------------|
| Onyamedua | Ohn-yah-meh-d-wa | A wide spreading tree in a village courtyard where villagers congregate, worship, visit, deal with public issues. |
| Osew | o-serw | Father-in-law, Mother-in-law |
| Oware | Oh-wah-reh | Game in which players capture the pebbles in the wooden holes of their opponents; also called mancala in other countries. |
| Patuo | Pah-too | Owl |
| Rio Amazonas (Portuguese, Spanish) | Ree-oh Ah-mah-zoh-nahs | Amazon Fiver in South America; longest river in the world. |
| Sankofa | Sahn-koh-fah | Symbol meaning: Go back and fetch it: keep and retrieve wisdom of the past, teach it it to the children so they will know their heritage. |
| Serwaa | Say-wah | Father's sister |
| Sukum deme | soo-kuum deh meh | I am thirsty |
| Takyiman | Tah-chi-mahn | A village to where the Ashanti migrated after leaving Timbuktu. |
| Tekua | Tek-oo-wah | Elaborate hairstyle interlayed with gold |
| Timbuktu | Tim-buck-too | Famous trade center in the great Sahara Desert |
| Tweaduampon | Tweh-doo-ahm-pohn Twere-doo-ahm-pohn | Name meaning: God is a cut tree you can lean upon but it will not break. Creator metaphor |
| Wei yE sEn | Way yeh seng | How much is this? |
| Woho tesen Answer: Mehoye Na wu su e | Woh hoh teh sen Meh-hoy- yeh Nah-woo-su-eh | How are you? Your family? I am well And you? |
| Wo din de sEn? Me din de | Wo deen day seng May deen day | What is your name? My name is ____ |
| Wo firri he mefiri | Who-fri-heh Mi fri | Where do you come from? I come |
| Yaa | Yah-ah | Girl born on the fifth day of the week, Thursday. |

| Term | Pronunciation | Definition |
|------|---------------|------------|
| Responses:<br>  Ya ason<br>  Ya-nua<br>  Ya Ena<br>  Ya agya | <br>Yah-sahn<br>Yah-nia<br>Yah-enna<br>Yah-eh-je-ah | Responses to persons of different age groups:<br>Good Morning/afternoon/evening<br>To a younger person<br>Same age range as you<br>To a woman much older than you.<br>To a man much older than you |
| YEbEhyia | Yah-abay-she-yah | We will meet again. |
| Yenna ase | Yen-nah ahsay | You are welcome. |
| Ye woo wo he | Yeh-wooh-wo-heh | Where were you born? |
| Ye woo me<br>wo ta | YE woo me wo | I was born in |
| Yoruba | Yur-oo-bah | Nigerian group that speaks Yoruba . |

# Acknowledgments

*Meda wase.* Thank you, my dear husband, William, and my children, Damian and Ayanna. You have run the gauntlet. Thank you. Thank you. I could not have done it without your patience, support, patience, prayers—and patience! If I could scoop up my appreciation for you, it would fill the Gold Coast seashore.

*Meda wase.* Thanks to Kwasi Opoku-Boateng, who suggested that I use Ghana for the setting of the book, proved to me why, inspired me, and answered so graciously my hundreds of questions and many thanks to his wife: Esther, her cousin Comfort, Lily and his brother, Joe Opoku-Boakye who brought me my first Akan-English language book from Ghana, Kofi Opoku-Agyemang with his special focus on the traditions, Samuel Brown for Fante background, and—Ghanaian historians Dr. Matthew Bediako, and especially, Dr. Kofi Owuso-Mensa for being one of the editors for Book I, and for his book, *Saturday God and Adventism in Ghana*, a significant source for me.

*Meda wase.* Thank you to the members of Elnora King's writing classes. Elnora coached and modeled for serious writers how to be courteous, caring, yet mediocrity-crushing, and we became an increasingly award-winning published village. For all their scrutiny and encouragement, I am thankful and extremely grateful to Karin Robinson, Debbie Martinez, Vicki Caine, Barbara Capell, June Koligian, Twyla Smith, Carrie Padgett, Susie Bessinger, C. J. Sharpe, Sherri Humphreys, Cyndi Trippel, Penelope Childers, Scott Becker, Toni Weymouth, Howard Hurt, Judith Dickey, Bethany Goble, Terrell Bryd, Martha Tessmer, Ralaine Fagone, Nancy Wright, Karon Ruiz, Tully Michailides, Elizabeth Hiett.

*Meda wase.* Also, to the Mass Communications professor at Pacific Union College, who called me to her desk the last day of the semester of my senior year, and told me that I had a gift for writing, and that if she was not moving to the East coast, she would like to coach me to become the writer she envisioned I could become. To Steve Yarborough at California State University at Fresno; and to one fellow student with me in Professor Yarborough's writing class who encouraged me by such confidence in the book that she asked me to autograph a chapter, back then.

*Meda wase.* Thanks to my prime encouragers and beta-readers, Katherin Doyle and Catherine Brown who both stuck by me through the whole time. It was Catherine who started it all by "harassing" me until I made that first call to Elnora.

*Meda wase.* To all of you—words cannot express how much I appreciate all of your support throughout this journey.

*Meda wase. Meda wase. Meda wase.*

Read on for a sneak peek of

# *Emily's Lament*

The Second Book in
The **Legacy of the Gold Banded Box** series
by Phyllis Jane Brown

# CHAPTER ONE

*If Only*

*Adye akye asa! Survive we must and survive we will!*

**December 1796, Gold Coast Sea**

Fishing near the opening of the cove in the dark hours before dawn, Fanti men worked out on the calm sea. As the sky grayed, gusts rocked the boats.

Kofi turned to see how rough the ocean played, churned by the harmattan. "Abeeku, look." He pointed at a large dot on the horizon.

Their friends started pulling in the net. Scanning the catch, Abeeku stopped them and glanced at Kofi.

Kofi agreed. "Let us wait a little longer."

After a while, they hauled up the net, mackerel and herring wriggling. When everything was packed in, Kofi turned to see the dot again—as large as their own boat now, and growing. All gazed, watching it bow, dip, and swell, moving swiftly in the wind.

Kofi shook off a chill. Without a word, the men took up their paddles and rowed to shore. Muscles straining, as they fought the whirring harmattan that determined to push them out into the deep.

The market crowd was small. The kwesi broni rested today. Few of them would come to market on Kwesida, the first day of the week.

More and more Fanti had stopped selling on Sunday, following the customs of the intruders.

Kofi had told his fishing mates that no matter how many people liked the kwesi broni ways and changed, he would never forsake the day of rest that bore the Creator's name. Kofi vowed to resist the idea of Africans forgetting their own traditions for those of people who took too much away.

He and his companions sold a small amount of their catch and carried the rest home. Their wives would fry the fish and send it or bring it with them to the big midweek market. Before heading up the hill, Kofi glanced back at the wide ocean.

Giant, white-winged and black bellied, the ship sailed silently past the cove's entrance—on its way to Cape Coast Castle or to El Mina.

⊙⸺⚍

Kofi usually woke before her.

Folayan breathed in deeply, opened her eyes, and smiled back at her husband, who greeted her with tender kisses. "Good morning," he whispered.

"Ummm, good morning." She loved waking beside his strong body, cuddling next to him, resting her head on his chest. In these few moments before light, she loved how he would tell her about his yesterday, but this morning he had few words.

"Our catch was small. I am sure we will do better on market day."

She waited. When he said no more, she raised up on her elbow to study his face.

He stared at something on the wall. She saw nothing.

"Kofi? Is something wrong?"

He turned back to her and sighed. "I saw a ship yesterday."

"A ship?"

"Yes, a kwesi broni ship."

"We have seen their ships many times before."

He remained silent.

Pushing back anxiety, she caressed his forehead, "Kofi?"

"Yes, many times, but this is the first one I have seen since I have a wife … since I have you and our baby." He drew her to him and traced his finger across her belly.

Footsteps approached outside. "Kofi!" someone called.

Kofi got up and dressed.

Folayan crawled out from under the covers and spread the pallet flat and taut.

From the large terra cotta pot that sat on the floor beside her kwantunyi box, she dipped water out to wash herself. Then she reached for her garments that lay folded on top of her box.

After pulling on her bright pink kaba from neck to waist, she wrapped her ankle-length of tie-dyed yellow and green skirt around herself, then knotted and tucked in its top corners just above her breasts. She spread out, then refolded another long etam.

"Mema wo akye." Speaking soft morning greetings to the child hidden inside her, she smoothed her hand over her small—but growing—middle, and smiled. How proudly she'd wear her colorful etam, in the turn of five full moons, with her firstborn tucked in securely on her back.

Every night before bed, she hung her necklace on the wooden carved giraffe that sat next to the bronze fertility mask on the small table near the door. Over her head, she pulled the cord of the kente pouch her Maame gave her. One side was black with the sankofa bird symbol in gold coiled cord, and on the blue kente side, she had painted the Gye Nyame adinkra.

It held the peanut sized gold nugget and the key to her gold-banded box. She wore it daily. It helped her remember to talk to people. When they asked about it, she told them the preacher's words, "We need to figure out ways to protect ourselves, and to live in peace."

Folayan combed her hair, concluding that most of the time she felt peace. She opened the door and joined Kofi and their visitor in the adiho courtyard. She surveyed the room. Morning light shone on the items in that interior room.

Everything was tidy. Since she moved into her house, she and two nieces, who had been sent to help her, had worked every day to get the floors to harden like clay. The floor was beginning to gleam through daily hand polishing with red ntwuma dust. It looked nice beneath the coiled floor mats.

She was proud of the carved stools and three small tables; one for eating meals, one for doing handwork, another for displaying her pretty calabashes and terra cotta plates and pots that people not only bought at the market, but also came to the house to purchase, like they did for Kofi's kente cloths.

This morning's first customer, Jojo, had returned and stood watching Kofi near the loom.

"It is not a good way to begin a marriage," Jojo said. "But my father came to me. He told me he understands my situation and that I would have had time to earn all the money I need for her dowry, if the old man was not so determined."

*For a much younger wife to add to his four.* Folayan shuddered, remembering how insistent Okwamu had been toward her after the Bakatue.

Jojo continued, "So, since I did not ask, my father has loaned me part of the money and I have also earned enough for one more kente. Is the green one still for sale?"

"It is." Kofi smiled.

"How much will you charge me for it?"

Kofi told him.

Jojo said, "I will bring the money for it tomorrow. The chief has already accepted my knocking!"

"Oh, I am so happy, Jojo!" said Folayan. "Fatima is such a good person and had a difficult life living under Afua's bad attitude all those years."

"Thank you, Folayan," said Jojo. "Life is good."

"Yes, it is." She smiled and took Kofi's hand. "Yes. It is."

# CHAPTER TWO

# *Afua's Strangers*

*From out of the shadows came men with fire-spitters,*
*white slave hunters and black slave merchants.*

**December 1796, Kormantse hillside**

Two days later, weary from her night of fitful sleep, Ama Kwantunyi Folayan woke early. Kofi had gone fishing. A short while later, she slipped out of the house with her market basket filled with vegetables and fish. Just outside her door, she sat down in the warm, dark stillness to wait and to think.

Folayan told herself the twinge gnawing in her was just baby sickness, but her uneasiness was due to more than that.

A cock crowed.

Her ears strained for other sounds of morning, but only breezes whispered through trees and scrub brush surrounding her slumbering Fanti village. She wished she could hurry the people awake, especially her aunt and the other market women. Be patient, she told herself.

She sat peering through the dim hwaani hwaani light for their shadowy forms. She thought about the fears wavering inside her. Kofi's fears … her fears.

Last night, Folayan had sat in the adiho, watching Kofi get ready to join his fishing companions. He put his net, mending hook, knife, and other tools in a woven bag by the entry door, then turned and stood there in the hallway looking at her. Her eyes tried to drink in all of him, so tall, broad-shouldered, handsome and—troubled. An apprehension stirred in her.

She wanted to hold him, to feel his arms strong around her. She got up from the seat. "The worry in your eyes makes me afraid," she said nestling her head on his chest.

He embraced her. "Do not be afraid," he whispered.

She looked up at his face, and considered his brow, betrayed by a line of concern. *Is he afraid to go fishing? Is he thinking something will happen to him? Will he come home to me?* "Kofi." She wanted to say something to stop the tumbling inside her. "Kofi, I love you."

"How much do you love me?" He smiled at her, warming her.

She wanted to tease him to laugh, but something in his eyes told her this was not the time. Her worry hobbled toward anxiety imagining perilous possibilities each wider, deeper, thicker, more frightening, until she shook her head and stopped the thoughts.

She squeezed him as tight as she could. "I love you this much. Oh!" She felt movement above her navel.

"What was that?" exclaimed Kofi. "Was that the baby? Did the baby thump you?"

"Yes." She giggled. "It did! It also bubbled up two days ago when I was working at my family gardens. I asked the women, and they told me I was right. This time I know for sure what it feels like."

"I felt it, too!"

"You did!"

"I felt my baby! It kicked me right here." He pointed to a spot below his navel. He threw his head back and laughed a pleasure from deep within.

Smiling, she laid her head again on his chest. The stirring stomach before was just the baby causing sour *abofono* to bubble. "Surely, we both felt it, Kofi. Together." A lump rose in her throat.

"See those stars up there?" he said. Clasping her so close, they were one body looking up at the watching sky. His voice was husky. "That is how much I love you."

She wanted him to kiss her … to never let her go … to stay there with her. The fishing could wait until another day.

She wanted to ask him to stay home today. "Kofi …"

He covered her mouth with his, full and soft, seeking. He held her like he was in charge of holding fast the world, like he could not get enough of her. Like he could take her unease and cast it into the sea. He held her close to him for a long time, their hearts beating against each other like two drummers.

His hands finally relaxed. He cupped her face like he often did, bestowing small, succulent kisses. He finished tenderly. "Folayan, do not go."

"What?" She looked at him, surprised.

"Do not go to market tomorrow."

Her heart sped up. "But Kofi, I need to be there." She caressed his face.

"I think you should stay home." His eyes beseeched her.

She did not respond.

"We need to take some time to think," he said. "Remember, '*Woto wobo ase dwa ntetea a, wohunu ne nsono.*'"

She winced at the proverb: "When you carefully and patiently cut an ant open, you see all its guts." An ant's guts? What did he mean? Her brow wrinkled. "Are you teasing me?"

"No, Folayan. I am very serious. This fear we have is a problem." He added, "We will find a solution when I get back. In the meantime, think about the vulture's nest."

"It does not actually look like a nest?" she said.

"No, and they make them in hard-to-reach places." He picked up his bag. "Where one can watch and wait." He kissed her once again and left.

Now, sitting outside in the shadows thinking, Folayan turned to stare at the fort. *Did Kofi mean those soldiers were vultures? Or ...*

Startled by a tap on her shoulder, Folayan gasped and whirled to see her old aunt standing there. Relieved, she said, "It is you, Serwaa."

"Why do you look surprised?"

"It is just that I have been upset. I did not sleep well, thinking about Kofi. Lately, he's been more and more troubled."

"Troubled?"

"About slave hunters. He says a few days ago, they burned and raided a village to the north of us."

Serwaa's hand gripped Folayan's shoulder. "What is it you say?" She looked off in the distance, shaking her head.

"Besides that ..." Folayan cleared her throat. "Kofi says a new ship sailed past the harbor three days ago. He does not want me to work at the marketplace today. But I have a strange fear. I am worried. I must know if he is safe."

Folayan felt her aunt's comforting arm around her. "You were wise to marry Kofi, who loves you so much. But remember, our people have lived through slave hunters and slave ships for more than 300 years, since the Portuguese first came and built El Mina."

"Humph! The Portuguese—and the Dutch, and others they tempt to come. Are they not our enemies? They bring the slave ships. This island where they say they take our people to work is bad." Thoughts of her mother's gold nugget and Kofi's indignation sprang out in her voice.

"Your mistrust will cause you fear and unhappiness. You sound like our Ashanti kin up in the hills who seldom have to come into contact with them. Fanti live on the coast. The kwesi broni will not go away and neither will we."

*So we trade with them, work for them, tolerate their presence, and sell only certain types of people to be slaves.* Folayan rehearsed the statement in her mind. *Debtors, warriors, war captives, and criminals.* Serwaa said it each time she tried to get Maame to return to the market.

This time Folayan tried, in Maame's place, to reason with her aunt. "But Serwaa, it is not like it used to be. Kofi says they hire wicked men—some Fantis who, in their greed, have lost their honor—they steal people and make them slaves for none of the reasons you say! The reports are getting so much worse and the kidnapping is causing tribal battles."

Folayan glanced down, rubbed her forehead, and then looked back at her aunt. "Have you thought about how that provides them with hundreds, even thousands, of warriors instead of the handful they usually get—warriors who are trying to protect their families and villages because these thieves have set tribe against tribe?"

Aunt Serwaa pursed her lips, "We may as well sit down and die right now if we cannot go on, in spite of rumors we hear from time to time. I do not let them hinder me. I just tell myself what the old men say and keep on going."

Folayan puzzled. "What do the old men say?"

"You have heard it all your life." Serwaa's words were determined and deliberate. "Adye akye asa! Survive we must and survive we will!" She paused, cupping her hand to her ear.

Folayan turned to see the group of women come around a corner.

Serwaa raised her basket to her head, walked a few steps, then turned back. Her eyes and voice softened. "Come, Folayan. If you do not, you will lose courage and be too afraid to go the next time. You know how long that good place has belonged to our family. Besides,

Kofi will be there selling his fish. You can talk to him and you will feel better."

Folayan debated with herself. She remembered the day her Maame stopped going.

Folayan touched the kente pouch hanging at her neck, and breathed a deep sigh. She rubbed her hand over her face. She had to make a choice—her husband or her elder—defy one to obey the other? If only she knew the best thing to do. If only ….

She drew in a deep breath. Maame was wrong to stop going. Serwaa was right then. She must be right now.

Lifting her basket to her head, she hurried along with Serwaa to catch up to the other six ladies. They chatted in whispers as they moved through the neat rows of square houses. Several minutes later, they approached the gate, turned out of the akura, onto the path that led down to the beach and the rolling waves they could hear, but not yet see.

They had not reached the halfway point when it opened.

At the first crack of a branch, Folayan turned. Chills traced up her spine, to her neck, to her shoulders. From out of the shadows came men with fire-spitters, white slave hunters and black slave merchants.

The women dropped their baskets every which way, cassavas, garden eggs, melons and plantains, and pineapples bouncing, rolling, causing some men to trip and fall and dodge the slippery produce, giving the women distance.

They scattered. Folayan ran to the tall trees. No time. They would see her up there before she could get high enough to disappear. To her left, she saw patches of bush. Breathing heavy now, she pushed herself. Footsteps pounded hard on the ground, she could not tell how far and dared not look back.

"Get away! Get away!" One woman hollered in the clump of trees that Folayan had turned from.

Folayan's feet touched the first blades of grass. Sweating and sucking in breaths, she hoped the weakening darkness prevented her assailant from seeing where she entered. Dropping to her knees, she lay down. Women's voices, then three loud, strange sounds in the air: women cried out in pain.

For the first time she wondered about Serwaa. *She is too old to run as fast as the other women. Where is Serwaa?*

Now men's voices, coming together, came near to her. Her body soaked, she wiped sweat dripping from her forehead, cheeks, and neck and she felt the cord. *Maame! Oh! Maame you stopped going to market!* She pinched the pouch. How could she keep it safe? She could not hide it in her clothes.

Where would men not think to check? She wished her hair had not been shaved during her Rite of Passage. But wait, she still had the hair at the top of her head which had not been shaved. It was thick enough. She wound the cord tight around the pouch, and lock-knotted it. The voices drew closer, calling to each other. Her chest heaved. Quickly, she finger-combed the hair over the pouch, re-braided, tucked half of the braid into itself, and patted it, hoping the kente blended in.

Footsteps raced, pounding the dirt, a man yelled, a woman screamed just a short distance from her. A woman was fighting back. Two men— kwesi broni, a high voice, another low—yelled at the woman, hitting her again and again until she whimpered submission. Folayan's heart beat so hard she knew it thumped the ground. Could they hear it? She turned slightly; her belly felt better in that position, too.

*Where are the men from our village? Is there no one to come to help us?*

The men.

They were fishing or clearing bush. Kofi and all his age mates were fishing … and Papa, with her eldest and youngest brothers had gone on a journey. She wanted to cry out! She wanted to cry out.

The nsafo, in Fanti, yelled, "There are three more. I saw one go this way, she cannot be far." Folayan held her breath so long she became dizzy; she began to see things.

She blinked and strained to see clearly the snake that slithered past her a body length away.

"Here she is!" Folayan startled, gasping for breath as he jerked her up. "I have got one! Hah!"

Folayan tried to fight. She too, screamed, kicking, trying to get away. But he grabbed her by the neck, and locked her in his elbow, cutting off her air passage. He pushed her head back and dragged her, coughing, choking to the place downhill toward the other captives. She struggled twice more as he pulled her.

The nsafo guarding the coffle asked, "Did you get all the women?"

The traitor dragging her, said, "Two escaped. There are three over there in those trees, dead. I am surprised at how long that old one hung on."

Folayan's mind tried to summon strength to go to her aunt, but exhausted, her eyes blurred, heart throbbing, she could barely make a step. The nsafo kept yanking her up with a rope, trying to get her close to the coffle of other captives. Just before the bamboo collar was placed around her neck, Folayan jerked her head to look back.

Serwaa lay slumped sideways on the ground, blood bubbling from her mouth.

Faint, Folayan's knees buckled.

Helpless, she sank, crying out one long, anguished, echoing, "Kofi-i-i!"

# Phyllis Brown

As an author, educator, and speaker, Phyllis Jane Brown loves to journey to places she includes in her books. In pursuit of historical authenticity in preparation for *Folayan's Promise* and in a quest for her own genealogy on three continents, Phyllis visited 39 countries, including 14 in Africa.

Coupled with her love of travel and heritage, she spent 40 years researching histories, slave narratives, cultural traditions, triumphs and African contributions to the world. She also used these studies for her Master's Degree thesis entitled *Narratives of Enslaved People: Lifting the Veil, Resisting the Peculiar Institution.*

From her research, she garnered factual information and Negro spirituals which inspired scenes in The Legacy of the Gold-Banded Box series. In which the characters represent those who survived the shark-stalked, bloodied, bone-marked trail at the bottom of the Middle Passage, encountered perils of enslavement, made daring attempts to escape on the Underground Railroad in the Americas, and endeavor to cope in the current times.

Phyllis is speaker, founder of Village Folayan: a mentoring program, and an educational consultant who accomplished over 31 successful years as an elementary and high school English teacher. She was honored to be a finalist for the local Public Education Fund Teacher of Excellence. The Gold Banded Box received the Outstanding Fiction award at the Southern California Writers' Conference.

PhyllisJBrownAuthor@gmail.com

Phone: 559-601-0434

To schedule Phyllis Jane Brown
**For Your Event, Contact**
Phone: 559-601-0434
Mon.-Fri.   8:00 A.M.-4:00 P.M.  PST

Lasan Press
3644 Mission Ave., Carmichael, CA 95608

PhyllisJBrownAuthor@gmail.com  |  www.PhyllisJBrown.com

Go to *www.TheGoldBandedBox.com* to learn about these speaking topics and more:

- **Danger, Dungeons, and Determination** 400th Anniversary of the Beginnings of the Trans-Atlantic Slave Trade 1619–2019

- **Go Back and Fetch It** Mentoring Program

- **I Will  N̶E̶V̶E̶R̶  Return** Author's Reflections about Travels to Fourteen African Nations.